AF571781

painting your *favorite* animals

in pen, ink and watercolor

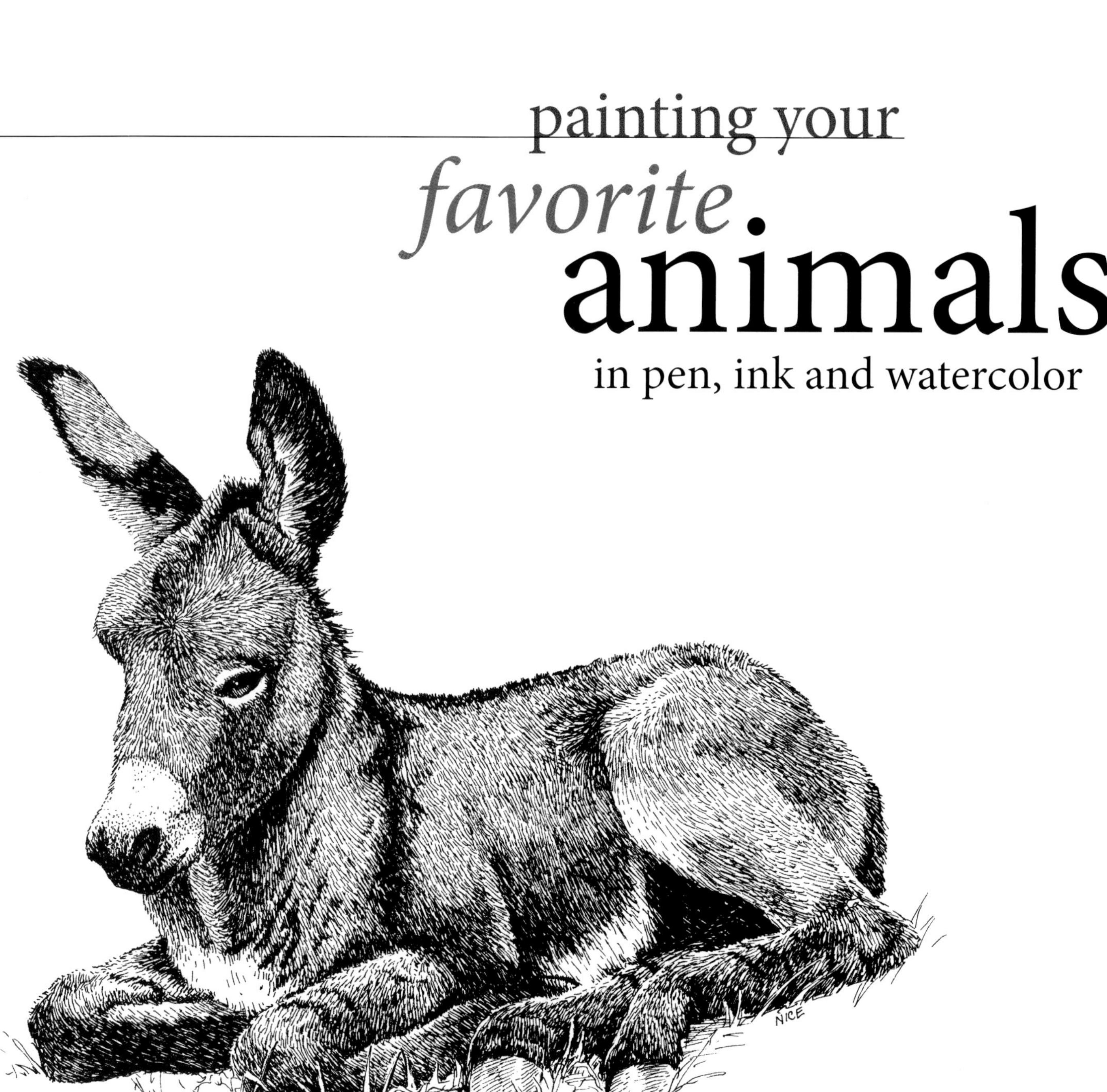

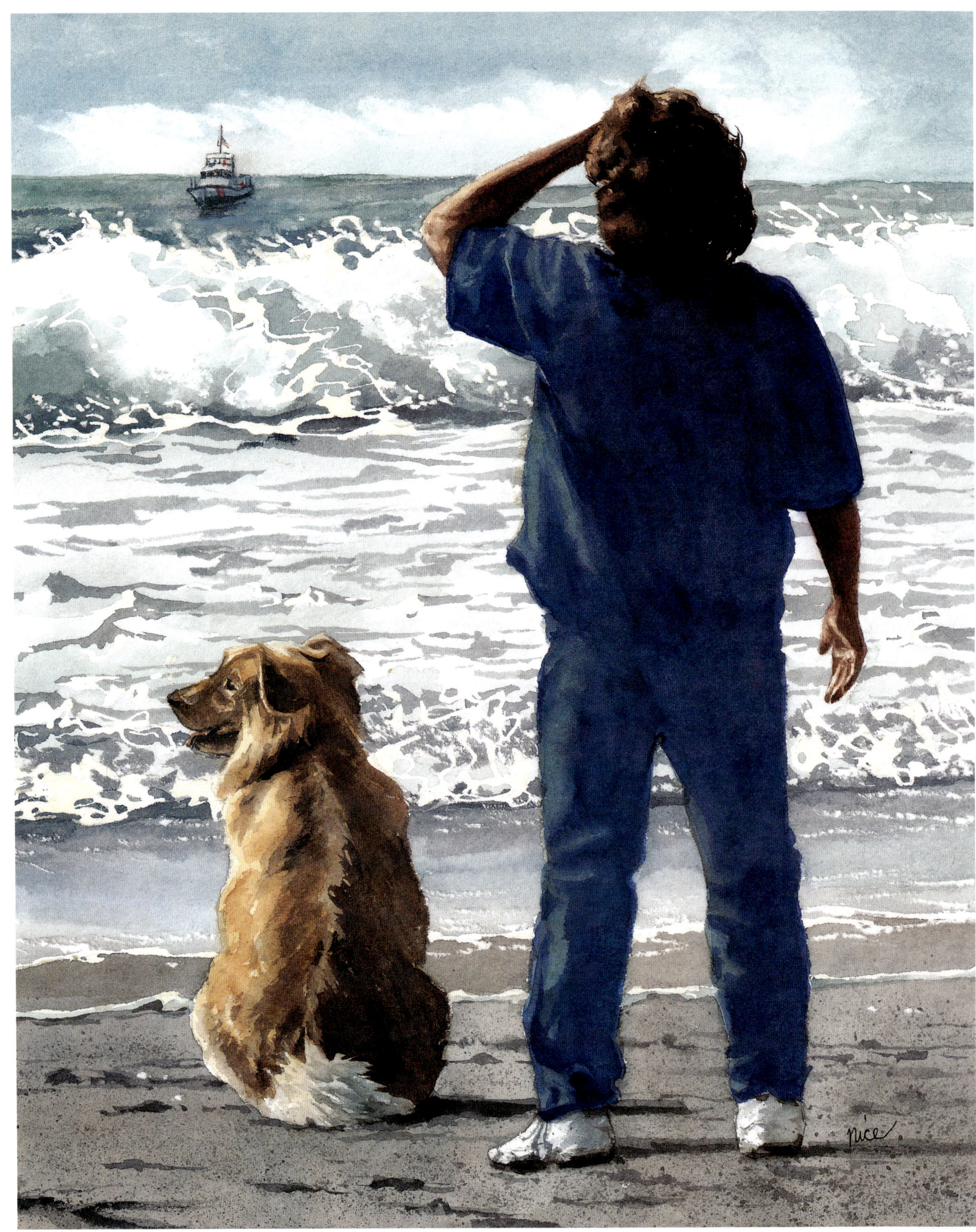

ON WATCH 8" x 10" (20.5cm x 25.5cm) Watercolor

painting your *favorite* animals

in pen, ink and watercolor

Claudia Nice

NORTH LIGHT BOOKS
CINCINNATI, OHIO
www.artistsnetwork.com

about the author

CLAUDIA NICE is a native of the Pacific Northwest and a self-taught artist who developed her realistic art style by sketching from nature. She is a multi-media artist, but prefers pen, ink and watercolor when working in the field. Claudia has been an art consultant and instructor for Koh-I-Noor/Rapidograph and Grumbacher. She is also a certified teacher in the Winsor & Newton Col Art organization and represents the United States as a member of the Advisory Panel for the Society Of All Artists in Great Britain.

She travels internationally conducting workshops, seminars and demonstrations at schools, clubs, shops and trade shows. Claudia also has her own teaching studio, Brightwood Studio (www.brightwoodstudio.com), in the beautiful Cascade wilderness near Mt. Hood, Oregon. Her oils, watercolors and ink drawings can be found in private collections across the continent and internationally.

Claudia has authored nineteen successful art instruction books. Her books for North Light include *Sketching Your Favorite Subjects in Pen & Ink*; *Creating Textures in Pen & Ink With Watercolor*; *Painting Nature in Pen & Ink With Watercolor*; *Painting Weathered Buildings in Pen, Ink & Watercolor*; *How to Keep a Sketchbook Journal*; *Painting Country Gardens in Watercolor, Pen & Ink*; *Watercolor Made Simple*; and her latest book, *Creating Creatures of Fantasy and Imagination*, published in 2005.

When not involved with her art career, Claudia enjoys gardening, hiking, and horseback riding in the wilderness behind her home on Mt. Hood. She passes on her love of art and nature by acting as an advisor to several youth groups.

 Published by North Light Books, an imprint of F+W Publications, Inc., 4700 East Galbraith Road, Cincinnati, Ohio, 45236. (800) 289-0963. First edition.

fw
F+W PUBLICATIONS, INC.

Other fine North Light Books are available from your local bookstore, art supply store or direct from the publisher.

10 09 08 07 06 5 4 3 2 1

Distributed in Canada by Fraser Direct
100 Armstrong Avenue
Georgetown, ON, Canada L7G 5S4
Tel: (905) 877-4411

Distributed in the U.K. and Europe by David & Charles
Brunel House, Newton Abbot, Devon, TQ12 4PU, England
Tel: (+44) 1626 323200, Fax: (+44) 1626 323319
Email: mail@davidandcharles.co.uk

Distributed in Australia by Capricorn Link
P.O. Box 704, S. Windsor NSW, 2756 Australia
Tel: (02) 4577-3555

Library of Congress Cataloging in Publication Data

Nice, Claudia.
Painting your favorite animals in pen, ink and watercolor / Claudia Nice.
p. cm
Includes index.
ISBN-13: 978-1-58180-776-9 (hc : alk. paper)
ISBN-10: 1-58180-776-7 (hc : alk. paper)
1. Pen drawing--Technique. 2. Watercolor painting--Technique. 3. Animals in art. I. Title.

NC905.N5294 2006
743.6--dc22

2006042516

Edited by Kathy Kipp
Designed by Clare Finney
Production artist: Sandy Conopeotis Kent
Production coordinated by Greg Nock

METRIC CONVERSION CHART

TO CONVERT	TO	MULTIPLY BY
Inches	Centimeters	2.54
Centimeters	Inches	0.4
Feet	Centimeters	30.5
Centimeters	Feet	0.03
Yards	Meters	0.9
Meters	Yards	1.1
Sq. Inches	Sq. Centimeters	6.45
Sq. Centimeters	Sq. Inches	0.16
Sq. Feet	Sq. Meters	0.09
Sq. Meters	Sq. Feet	10.8
Sq. Yards	Sq. Meters	0.8
Sq. Meters	Sq. Yards	1.2
Pounds	Kilograms	0.45
Kilograms	Pounds	2.2
Ounces	Grams	28.3
Grams	Ounces	0.035

dedication

"And God said, 'Let the earth bring the living creature after his own kind, cattle, and creeping thing, and beast of the earth after his kind': and it was so."

— GENESIS 1:24

The animals came and mankind was fed and clothed, his burdens were carried and his travels were made easier. The animals that entered his home became his companions, keeping watch by his hearth and sharing his joys and trials. To the many animals that have blessed my life, and to their Creator, I dedicate this book.

I also wish to thank my parents who taught me to love and respect animals; my husband who enabled me to keep so many of them; and the editors and managers at North Light Books who encouraged me.

Claudia Nice

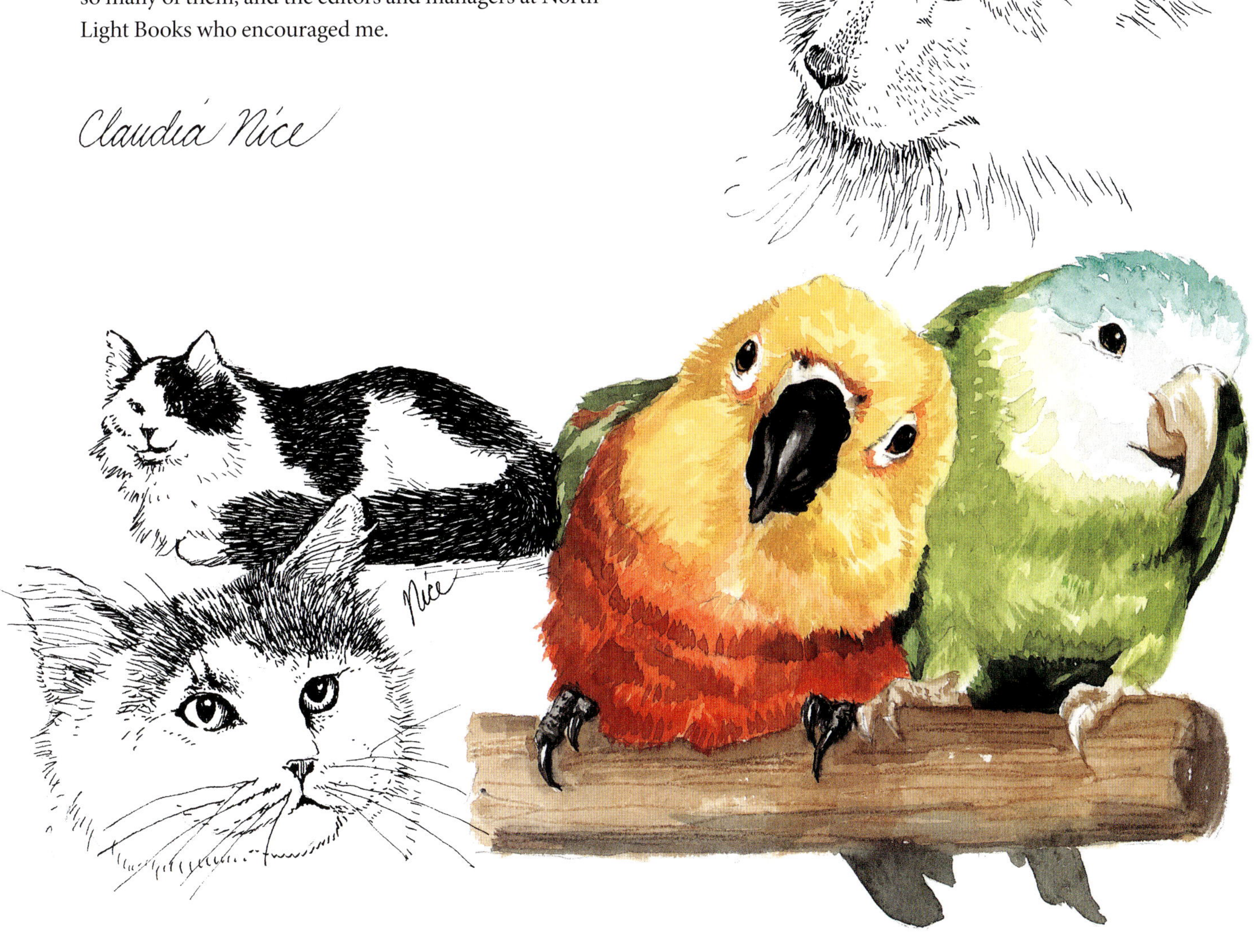

table of CONTENTS

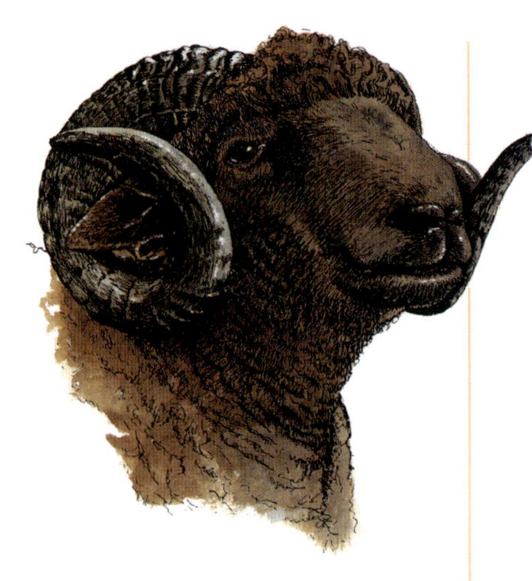

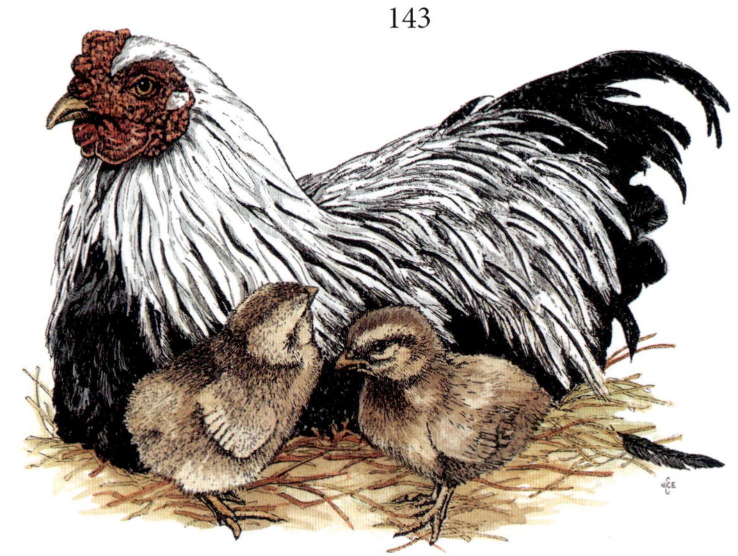

introduction

ANIMALS ARE A FAVORITE drawing and painting subject of mine, especially those that are pleasantly familiar. As the animal begins to take shape, line by line, stroke by stroke, my mind is flooded with memories that help the image on the paper spring to life. If the animal is a passing acquaintance, perhaps a deer I encountered on a camping trip, I might remember how the sun danced along the edges of her face and bounced off the shiny black surface of her hoof. As I add the bits of life experience into my work, I am transported, and with a smile on my face I revisit a nostalgic moment from my past.

If the animal I am capturing on paper is a beloved companion, love is added to the mix. The creative process then becomes a delightful experience full of passion, each stroke a tribute to the times we've shared.

On the other hand, a truly delightful art experience can quickly vanish if frustration enters the picture. Inexperience, self-doubt and frustration are the spoilers of creativity. Inexperience says "You don't know how." Self-doubt whispers "You will fail" and frustration mocks every less-than-perfect effort. It is my desire that this book will encourage you and help you overcome these "spoilers," that you may find joy and satisfaction in your creative efforts. And should the final result be less than you had hoped, keep in mind that art is a learning process. If you had a pleasant experience and learned from your mistakes, then the time you spent was not wasted.

I would also like to comment on a couple of favorite tools and products I used in the creation of this book. I enjoy the Faber Castell Pitt Artist Pens (brush nib), and the Masquepen by Cruddas Innovations Ltd. (U.K.), which applies masking fluid for watercolor with no mess. I do not represent these companies, but highly recommend their products.

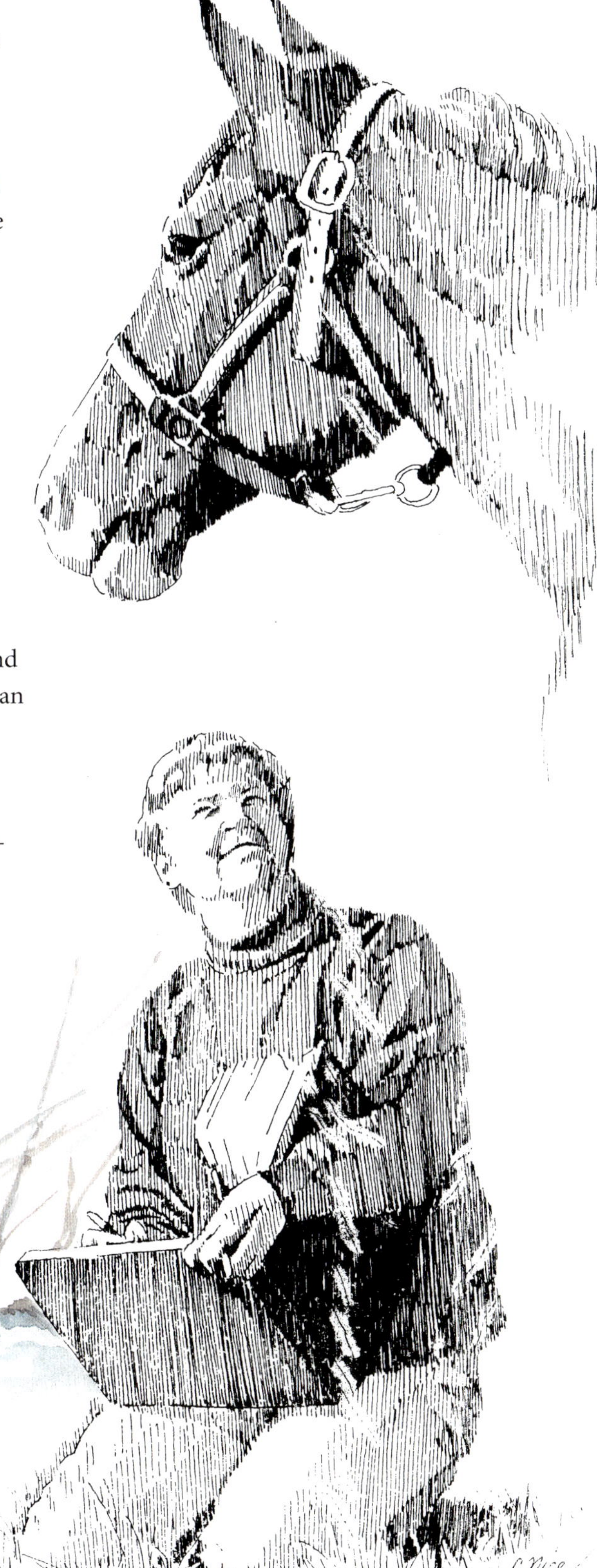

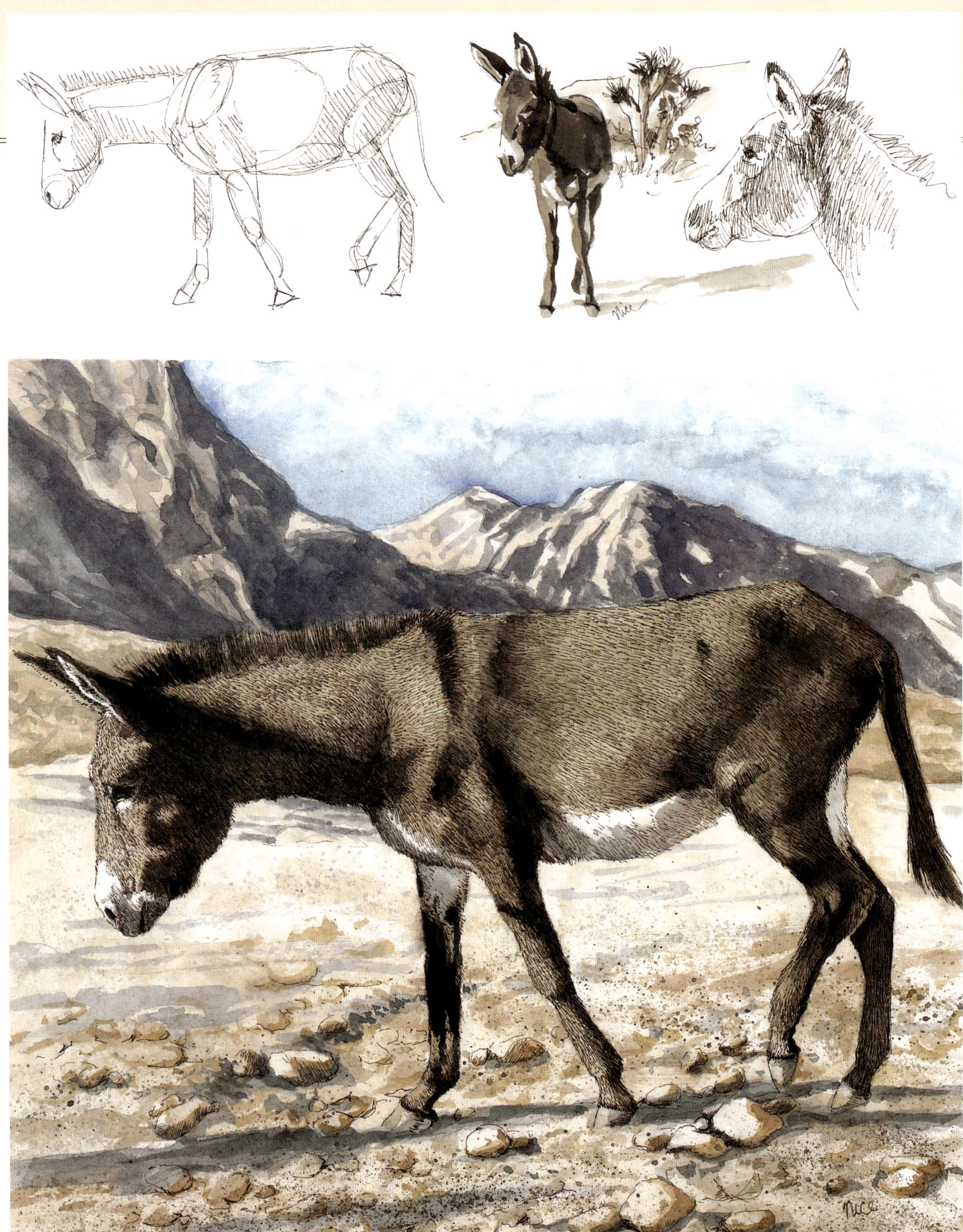

DESERT BURRO 9" x 8¼" (22cm x 21cm) Watercolor overlaid with sepia ink work.
The preliminary field sketches were made on location in Red Rock Canyon, Nevada.

simple BEGINNINGS

1

I BELIEVE that if a person can see, has passable hand-eye coordination and has the desire, he or she can learn to draw. Desire is the driving factor, but seeing is the key to the process. I am referring to a special kind of sight, not merely the eye recognizing an object, but the eye also discerning shapes, angles, comparative sizes, textures, values, and color as it gazes at a subject. This type of observation is seeing with an "artist's eye." It is the objective of this chapter to show you how to see with the eye of an artist. It takes practice, but once you have mastered it, your drawing skills will improve, and the mistress of mistakes will no longer be an overwhelming entity. In addition, the world about you will take on a new vibrance and vitality as you see it again with eyes that are primed for discovery.

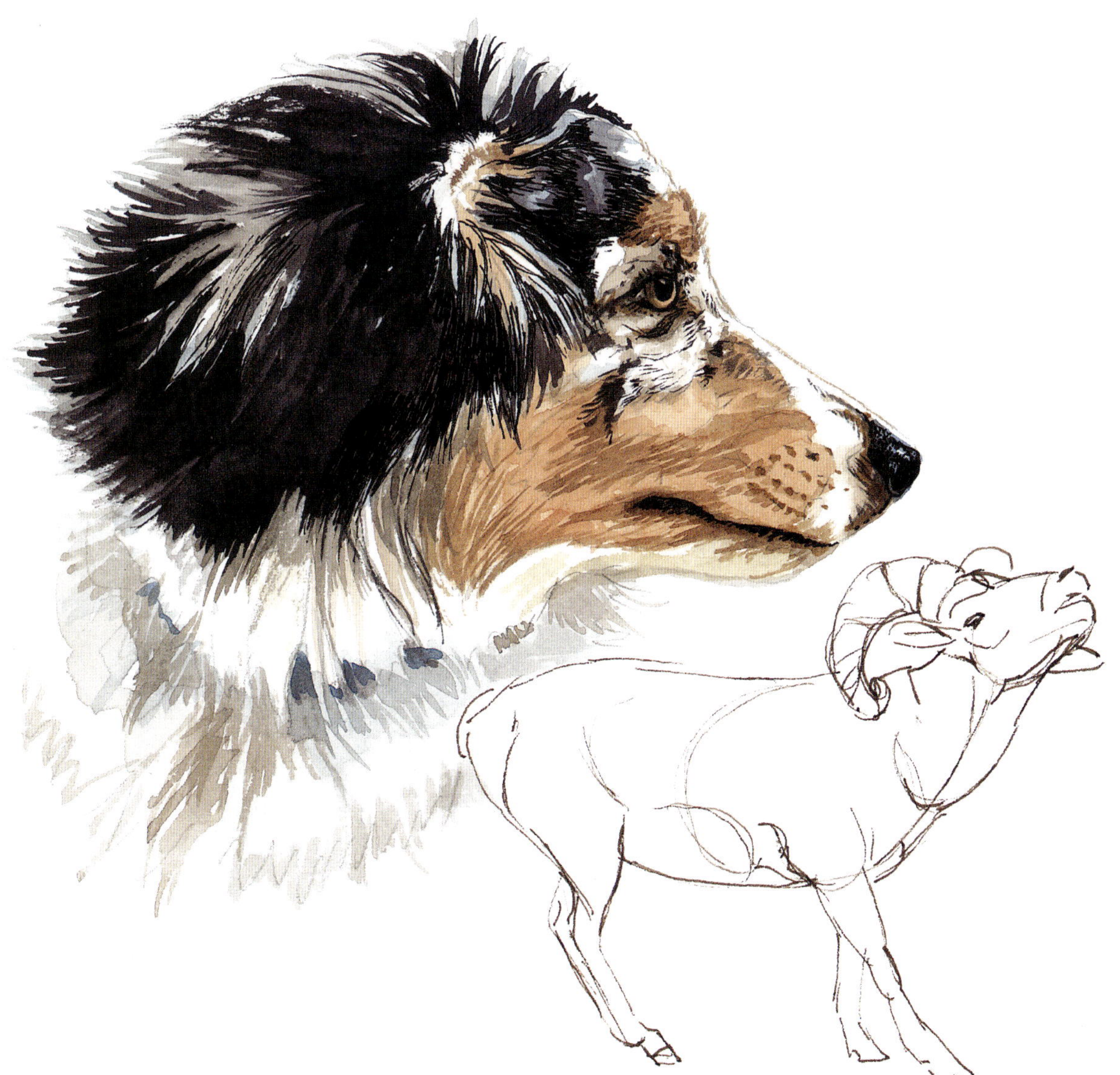

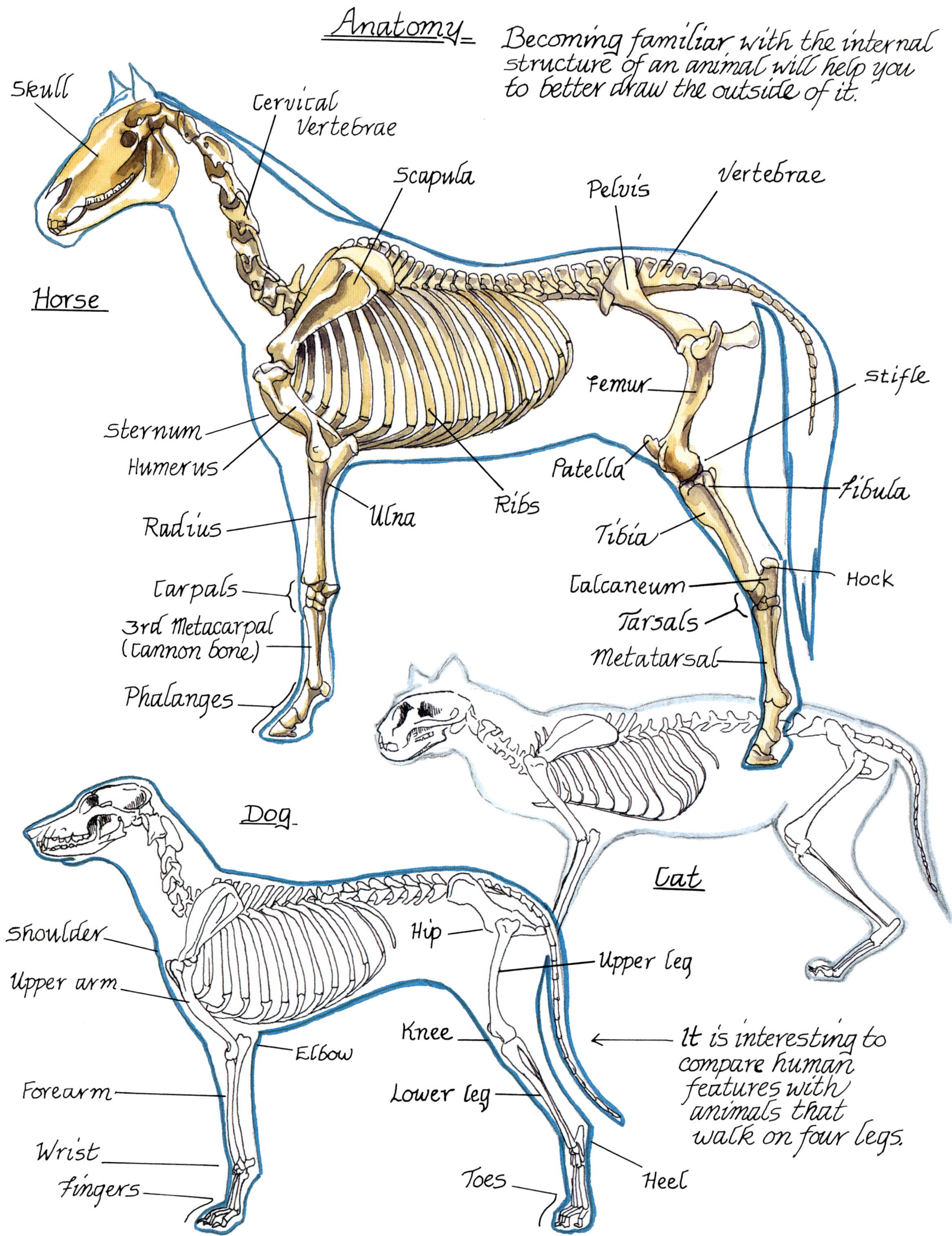
Anatomy
Becoming familiar with the internal structure of an animal will help you to better draw the outside of it.
Horse
Skull
Cervical Vertebrae
Scapula
Pelvis
Vertebrae
Femur
Stifle
Sternum
Humerus
Ribs
Patella
Fibula
Radius
Ulna
Tibia
Carpals
Calcaneum
Hock
3rd Metacarpal (cannon bone)
Tarsals
Metatarsal
Phalanges
Dog
Cat
Shoulder
Hip
Upper leg
Upper arm
Knee
Elbow
It is interesting to compare human features with animals that walk on four legs.
Forearm
Lower leg
Wrist
Heel
Fingers
Toes

Geometric shapes can be used to represent the bones and the muscles that lie over them.

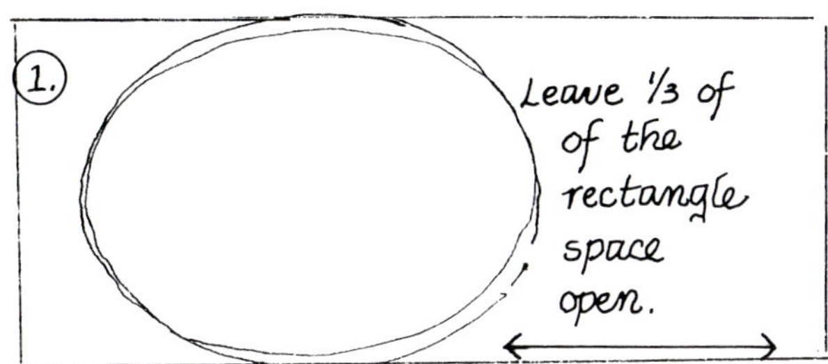

① Use a rectangle to represent the general shape of the trunk. Add an ellipse to the left area of the rectangle to define the ribs.

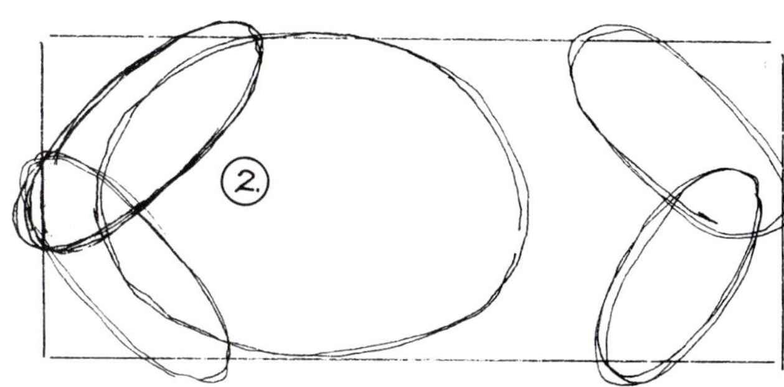

② Chevrons formed from narrow ovals depict the shoulder and hip bones.

③ Long, narrow ovals can be used to represent the leg bones. Pay attention to the angles and length. On this horse the length of the front leg from the elbow to the wrist is approximately the same as the height of the rib cage ellipse (a).

A slight "S" curved line represents the neck. A cone can define the skull with small ellipses added to round out the cheek and muzzle. To keep it in proportion, compare the length of the skull to the length of the scapula plus the point of the shoulder (b). They should be similar.

Note how the geometric shapes can still be seen on the rounded outer contours of the body, forming shadows.

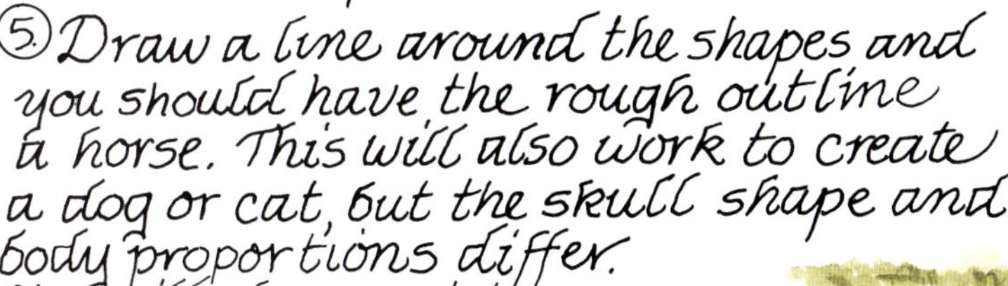
⑤ Draw a line around the shapes and you should have the rough outline a horse. This will also work to create a dog or cat, but the skull shape and body proportions differ. You will also want to construct paws instead of hooves.

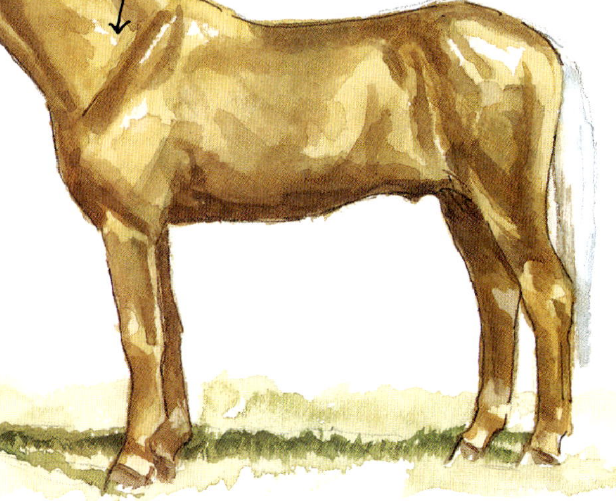

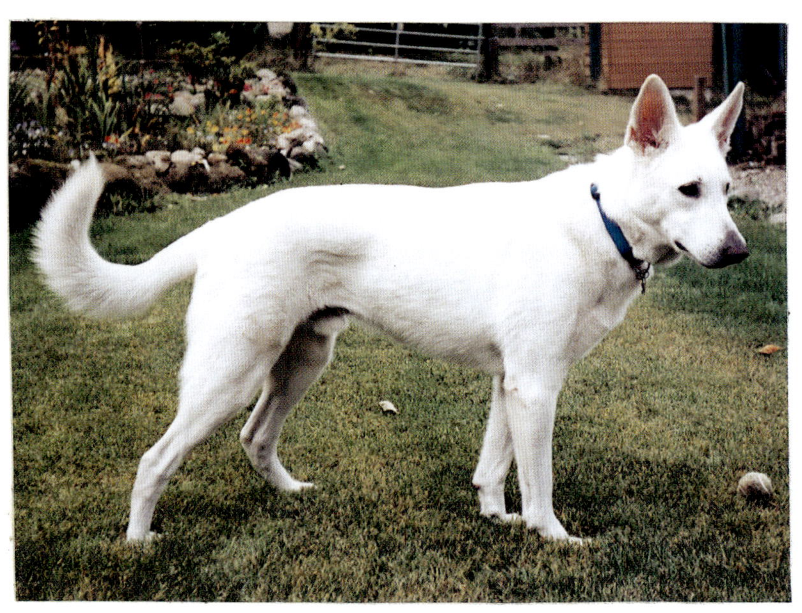

This is a side view of my White German Shepherd, Dakota Snow. Side poses are the easiest to draw because the features are in familiar positions and apparent.

Study the photo and see if you can locate the contours of the hip and shoulder (marked in red in the preliminary pencil drawing below.) Before I start drawing any animal, I study its form to locate skeletal contours and areas that suggest geometric shapes. It is easier to build simple shapes into an animal than to pick a spot and proceed to outline a horse, dog or cat in perfect proportion.

I begin sketching the trunk area first. This determines the size of the rest of the animal. I pay special attention to the curve of the back.

Next the neck, head and legs are added. I make several comparisons as the work progresses to see how the appendages line up with the rest of the body.

Negative spaces also form shapes.

Ink detail work can be placed over the light pencil drawing. Pencil marks can be erased as soon as the ink is dry.

Did you notice that the point of the shoulder and the lower jaw are even? If they didn't line up in the drawing it would mean that the head was too big or small.

Using Geometrical Shapes as Building Blocks

Sometimes the anatomical structure of an animal is unclear due to long hair, pudginess, flat lighting or the way the animal is posed. In such cases the artist must rely heavily on the geometric shapes his mind's eye reveals to him. Each artist viewing the animal may see the shapes within the animal's form differently. As long as the artist sets down the shapes the way his eye sees them and doesn't substitute preconceived ideas, the drawing should turn out reasonably well.

This line indicates the slant of the head.

Study the photo (left) of the cute cross-eyed cat. What geometric shapes do you see? I have depicted the shapes I see and how I used them to draw the likeness of the cat.

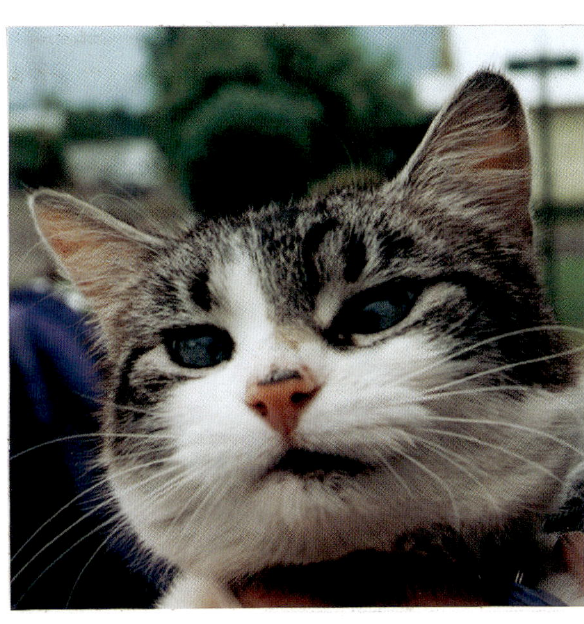

(1.) An ellipse defines the shape of the head, with curved, crossed lines to help line up the facial features.

(2.) Triangles and oval shapes helped me rough in the face and ears.

(3.) Corrections were made and details were penciled in.

(4.) Pen and ink texturing was begun.

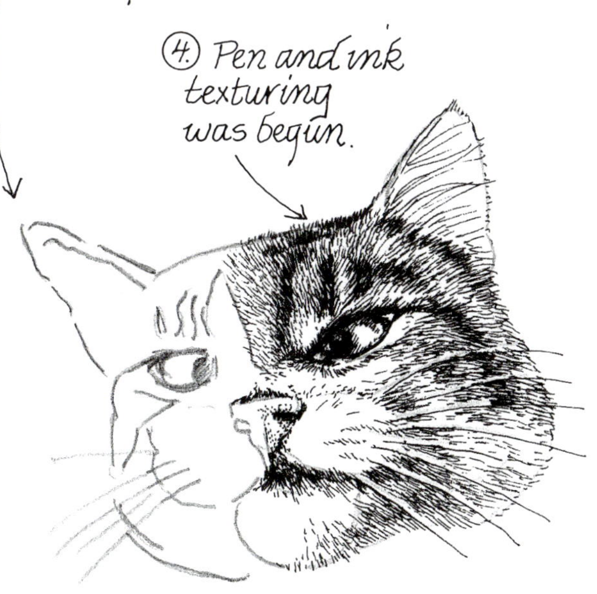

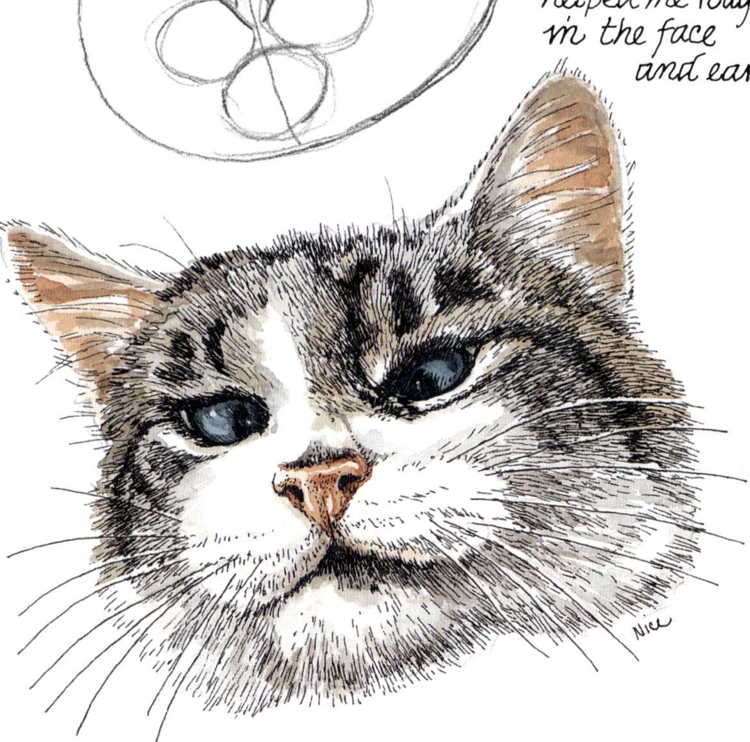

(5.) Watercolor washes were added over the ink.

When I studied the photo of this fluffy fowl I saw these basic shapes

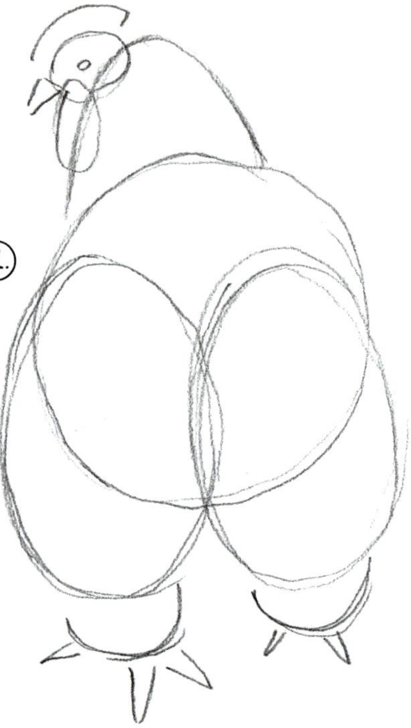

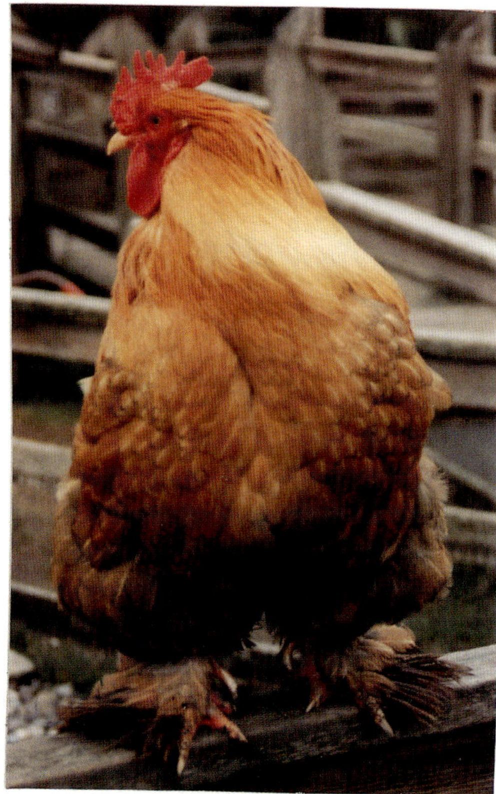

(1.)

Rough preliminary sketch based on the simple shapes in figure 1.

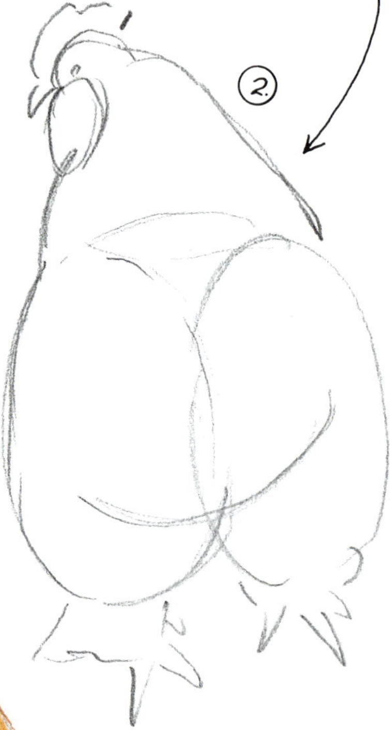

(2.)

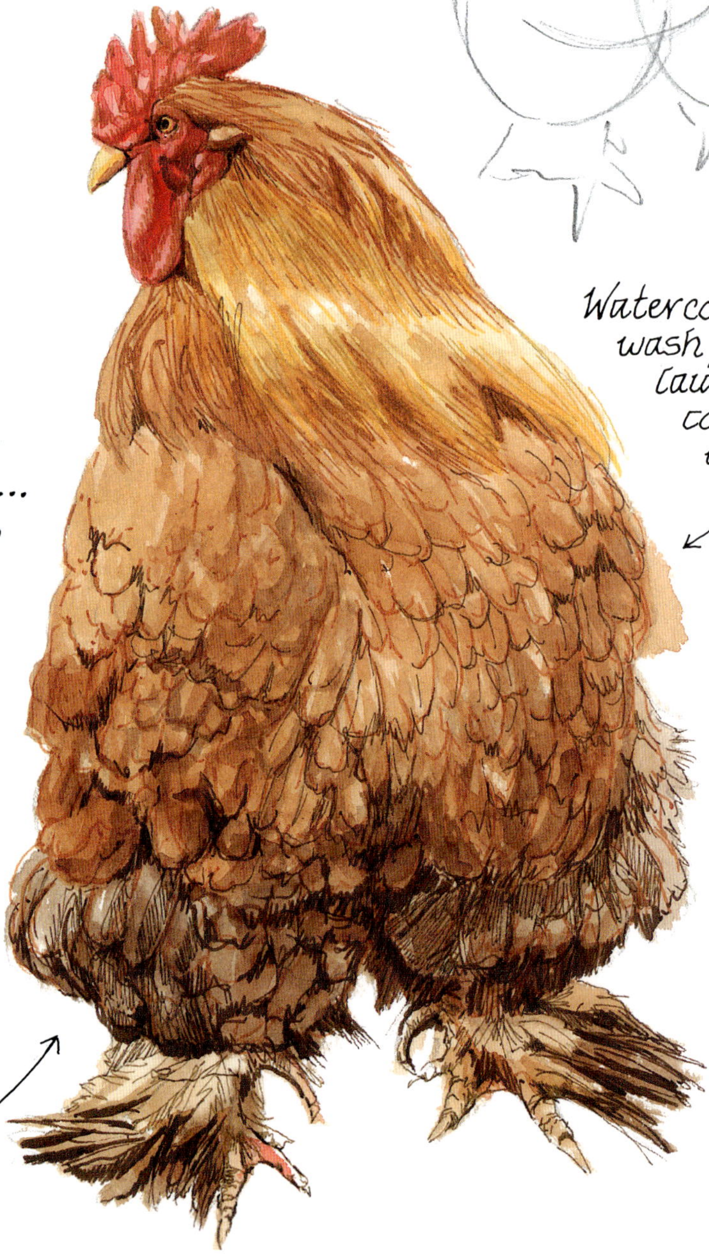

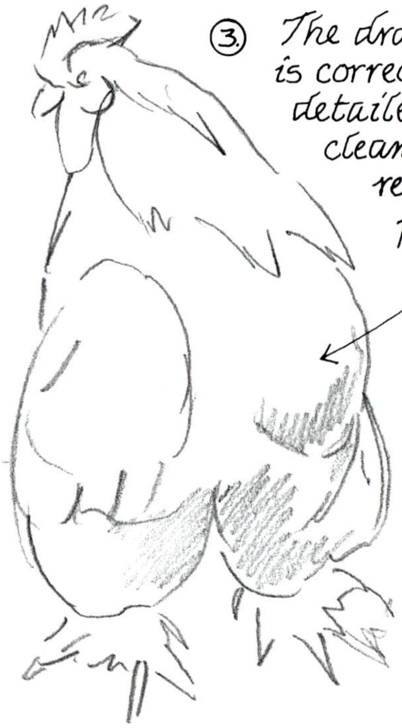

(3.) The drawing is corrected, detailed and cleaned up… ready to paint.

Watercolor wash over-laid with colored ink.

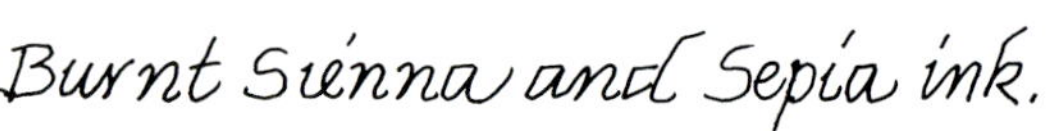

Burnt Sienna and Sepia ink.

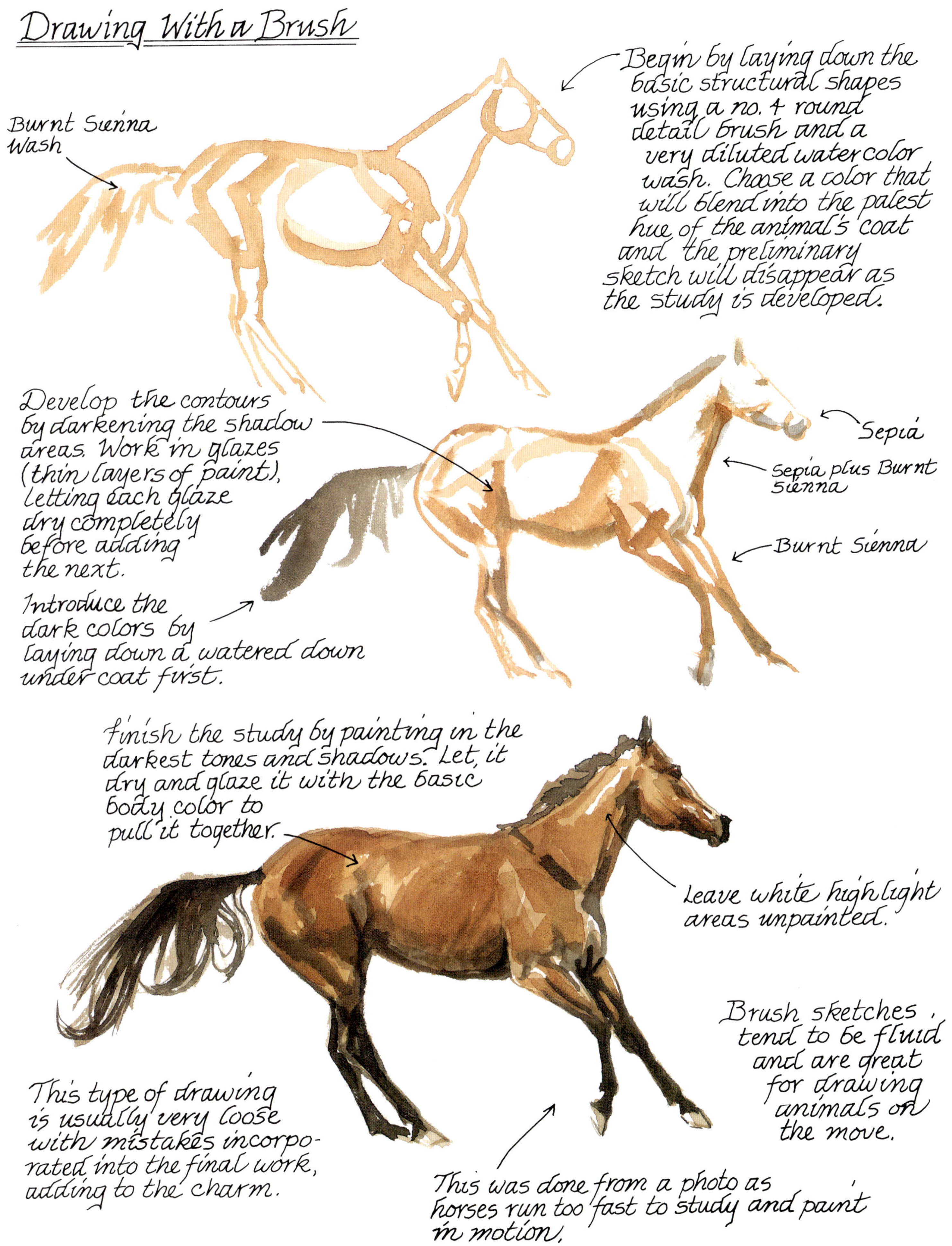
Drawing With a Brush
Begin by laying down the basic structural shapes using a no. 4 round detail brush and a very diluted watercolor wash. Choose a color that will blend into the palest hue of the animal's coat and the preliminary sketch will disappear as the study is developed.
Burnt Sienna Wash
Develop the contours by darkening the shadow areas. Work in glazes (thin layers of paint), letting each glaze dry completely before adding the next.
Sepia
Sepia plus Burnt Sienna
Burnt Sienna
Introduce the dark colors by laying down a watered down under coat first.
Finish the study by painting in the darkest tones and shadows. Let it dry and glaze it with the basic body color to pull it together.
Leave white highlight areas unpainted.
Brush sketches tend to be fluid and are great for drawing animals on the move.
This type of drawing is usually very loose with mistakes incorporated into the final work, adding to the charm.
This was done from a photo as horses run too fast to study and paint in motion.

Using a Straight Edge to See the Subject Better

The mind often plays tricks on the viewer, presenting what the eye sees in whatever manner the viewer can best relate to it. Such preconceived ideas can greatly hinder the artist from seeing the true form of the subject.

B.

C.

A.

Two handy straight edges.

no. 2 pencil

Clear plastic ruler

Several straight lines drawn across the photo of the subject, both vertically and horizontally, can be used to make the comparisons that will help the mind define the contours more accurately. See the photo above.

If you are working from a live subject, hold the straight edge of a pencil or ruler up in front of you in a vertical or horizontal position and sight in the subject behind it to make comparisons.

Study the photo of the deer and the sketch to the right with the lettered lines. With the help of the lines it's easier to see that the bottom of the inside eye lines up with the highest point of the back and that the tip of the ear corresponds to the dew claw on the left front leg. Did you also notice that the hind leg rests at a slight angle and is lower than the fore leg? No matter what size sketch is made from the deer photo, the body parts need to line up in the same manner or it's out of proportion.

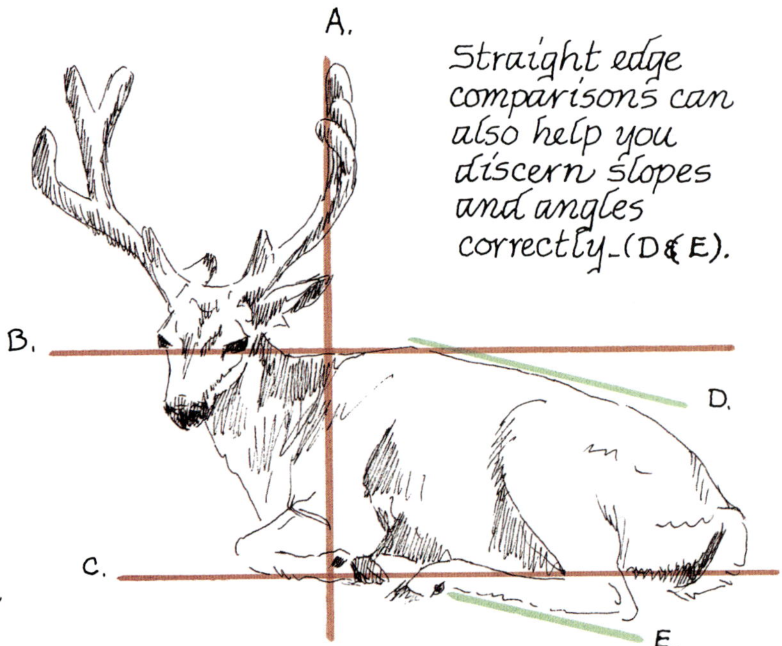

Straight edge comparisons can also help you discern slopes and angles correctly-(D & E).

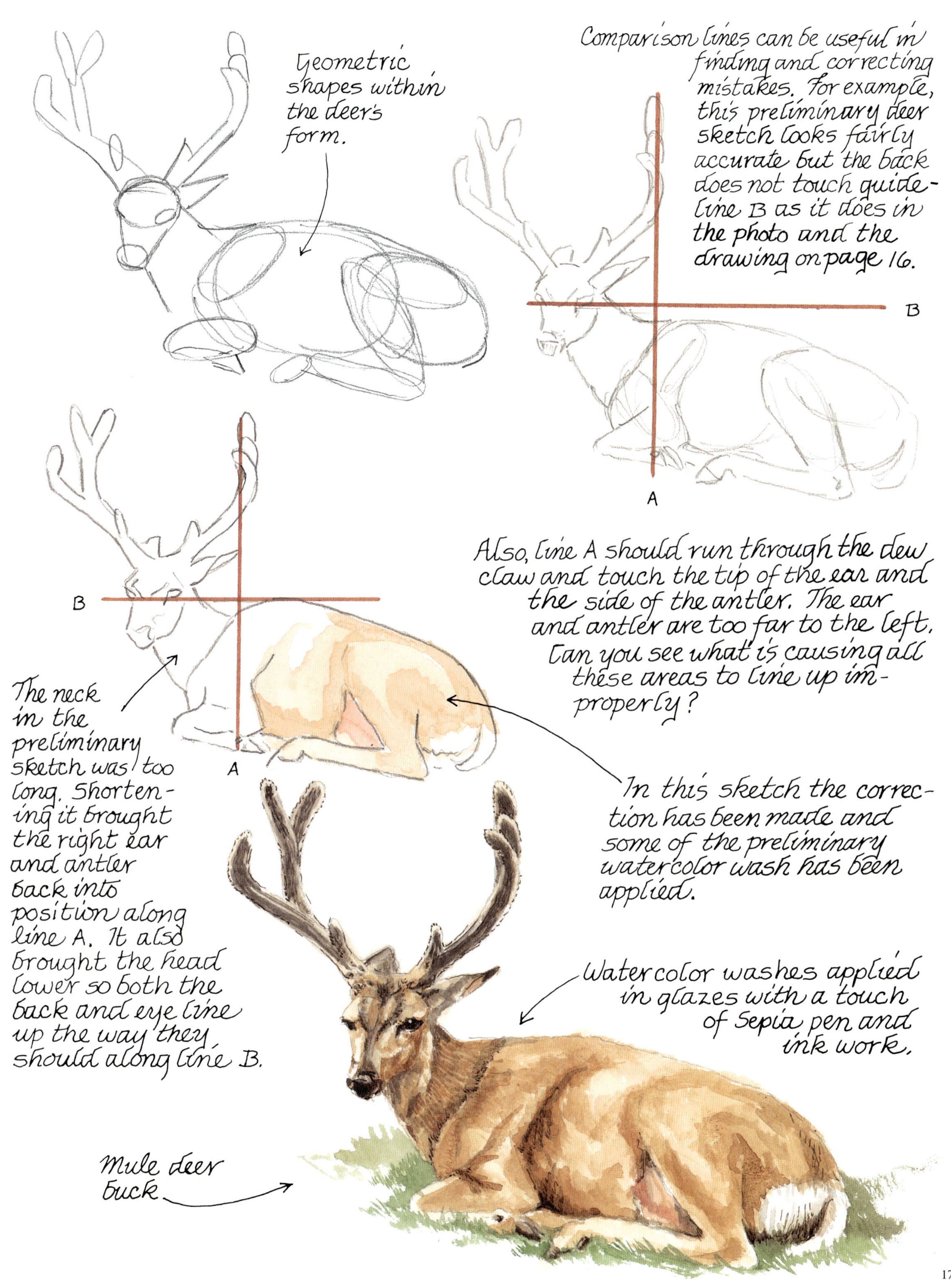
Geometric shapes within the deer's form.
Comparison lines can be useful in finding and correcting mistakes. For example, this preliminary deer sketch looks fairly accurate but the back does not touch guide-line B as it does in the photo and the drawing on page 16.
B
A
B
A
Also, line A should run through the dew claw and touch the tip of the ear and the side of the antler. The ear and antler are too far to the left. Can you see what is causing all these areas to line up improperly?
The neck in the preliminary sketch was too long. Shortening it brought the right ear and antler back into position along line A. It also brought the head lower so both the back and eye line up the way they should along line B.
In this sketch the correction has been made and some of the preliminary watercolor wash has been applied.
Watercolor washes applied in glazes with a touch of Sepia pen and ink work.
Mule deer buck

Making Size Comparisons

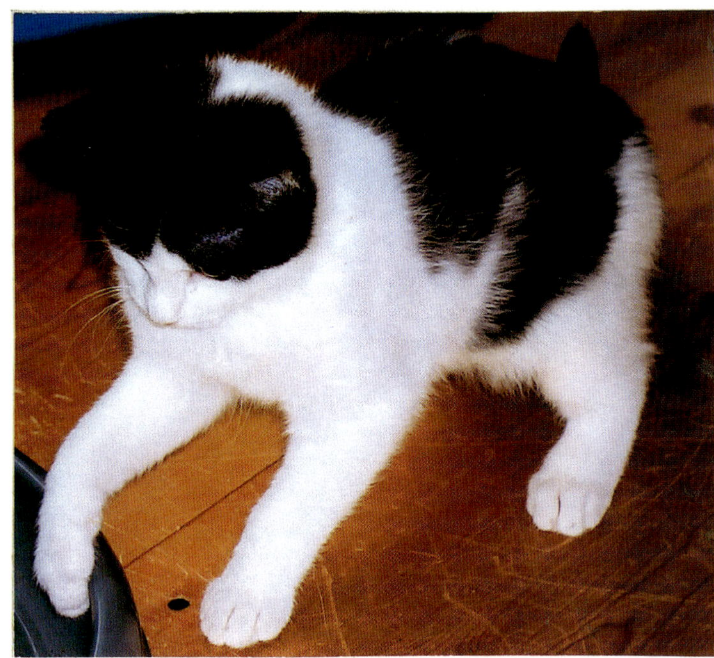

Catzilla as a kitten

Drawing the head too large or small for the body is a common mistake. It can be avoided by laying a straight edge across the width of the head and marking the width with your thumbnail. Then, with your thumbnail still in place, slide the straight edge across the body to see how many "head widths" it contains. No matter what size drawing you make of the animal in that particular pose, the width of the head compared to the body should remain the same.

This drawing is out of proportion. There is only one "head width" across the body (marked with red dots.) It's too narrow!

In the drawing above, the width of the head has been marked with a red dot on the pencil. The second red dot shows the width of the head compared to the body. In this pose there are just under 1½ head lengths across the kitten's body. Use a straight edge to compare it to the photo.

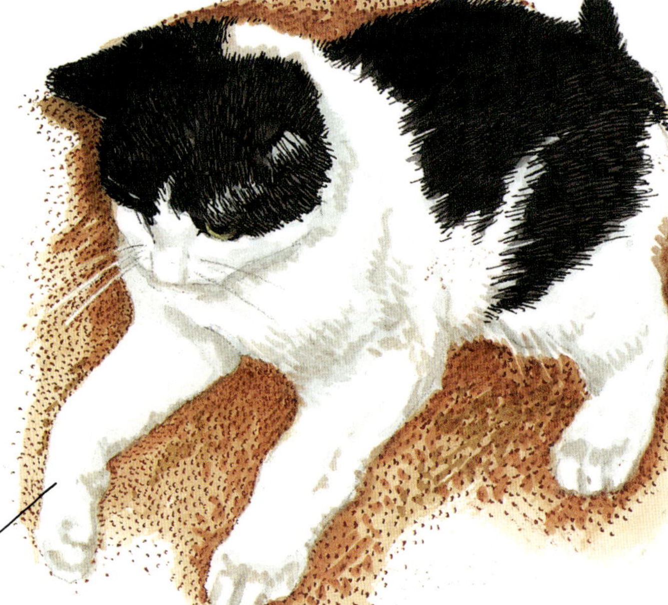

Watercolor glazes and colored ink.

Project Page No. 1

Use a straight edge and find the main mistakes in each of the sketches below.

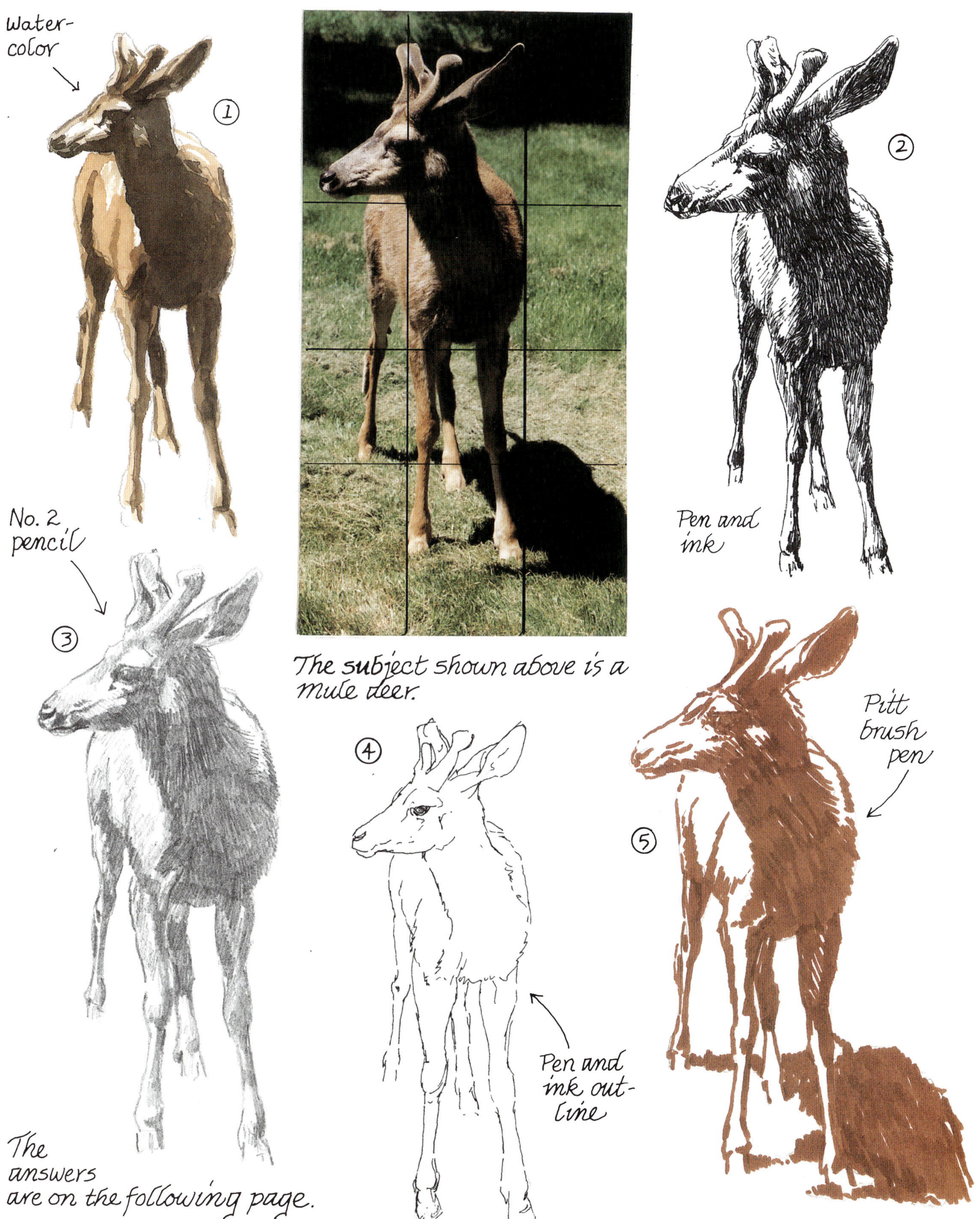

Drawing Foreshortened Subjects

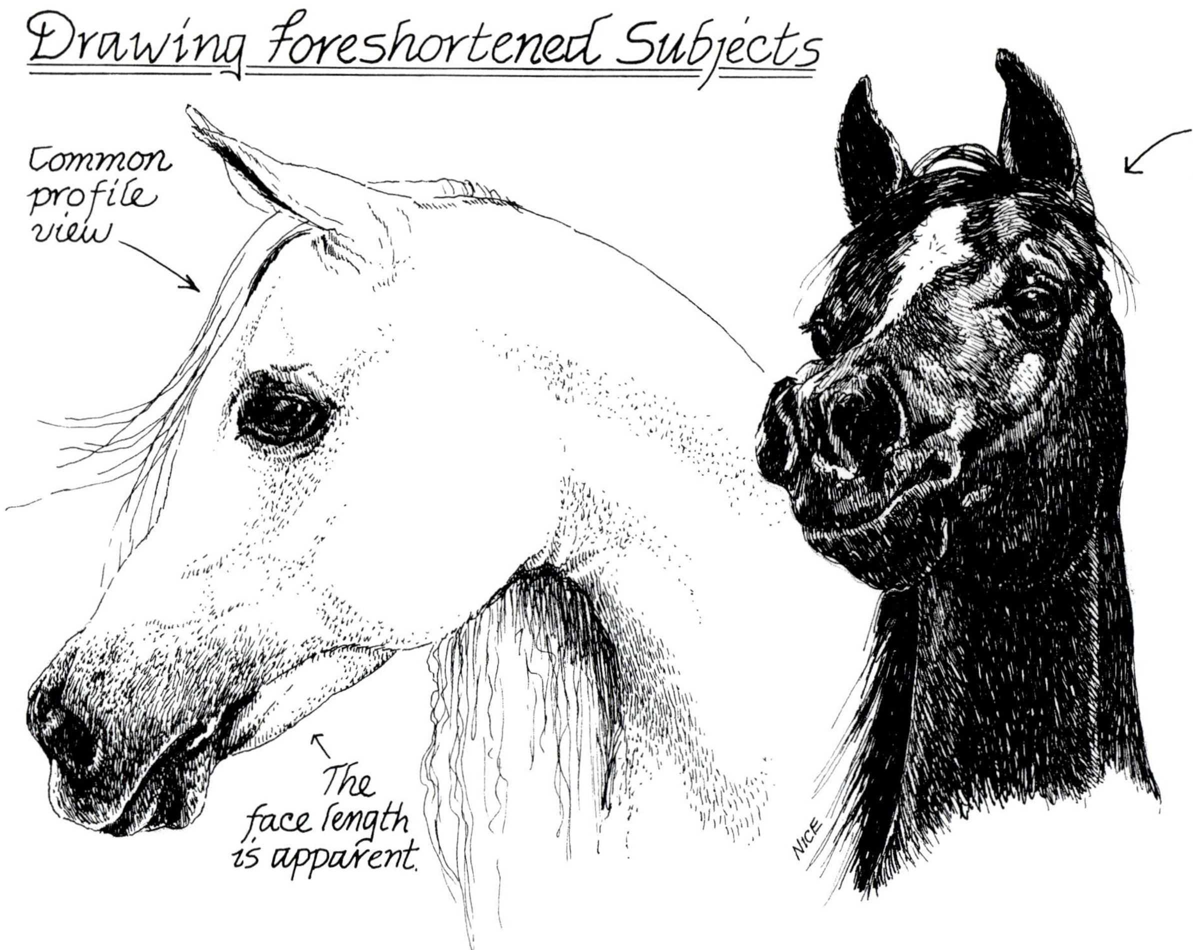

In this foreshortened view of an Arabian horse's head, the nostrils and lips appear very large because they are the closest point to the viewer. The actual length of the face is hidden from view. The effect is dramatic but more difficult to draw.

Foreshortening occurs when a familiar object is viewed at an unusual angle, making it appear distorted. This most commonly happens when a long, narrow object is viewed from the end and the length of the object is no longer apparent to the eye. Drawing foreshortened subjects can be tricky, because the mind wants to set the proportions in recognizable order, prompting the artist to add "length" where none appears. Therefore it is vital to put aside pre-existing knowledge of the subject and draw it exactly as the eye sees it.

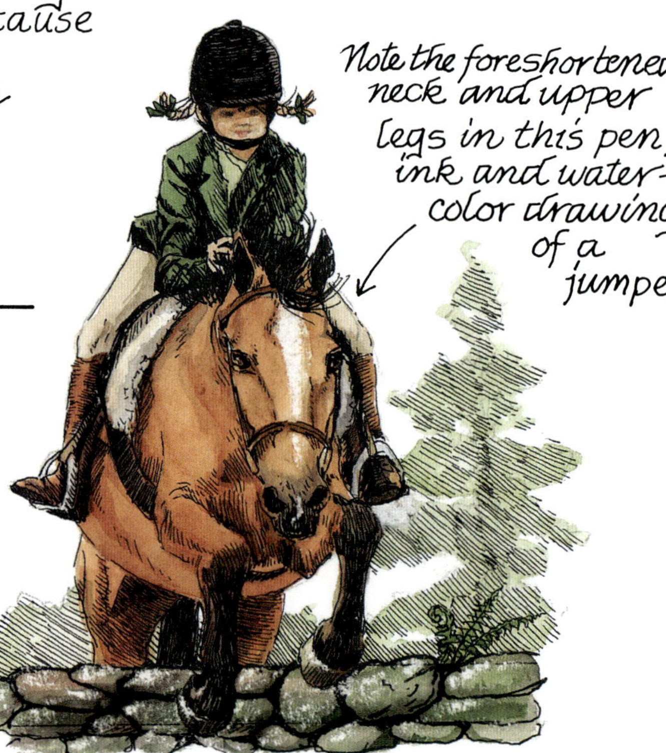

Note the foreshortened neck and upper legs in this pen, ink and watercolor drawing of a jumper.

Answers to Project Page No. 1 (page 19)

① The head is too small for the body.

② The head is too large for the body.

③ The deer's right hind leg is too short.

④ The forelegs are too long.

⑤ This drawing is in proportion but incomplete. Part of the right antler was not drawn in. With this antler section deleted, part of the right ear would be showing.

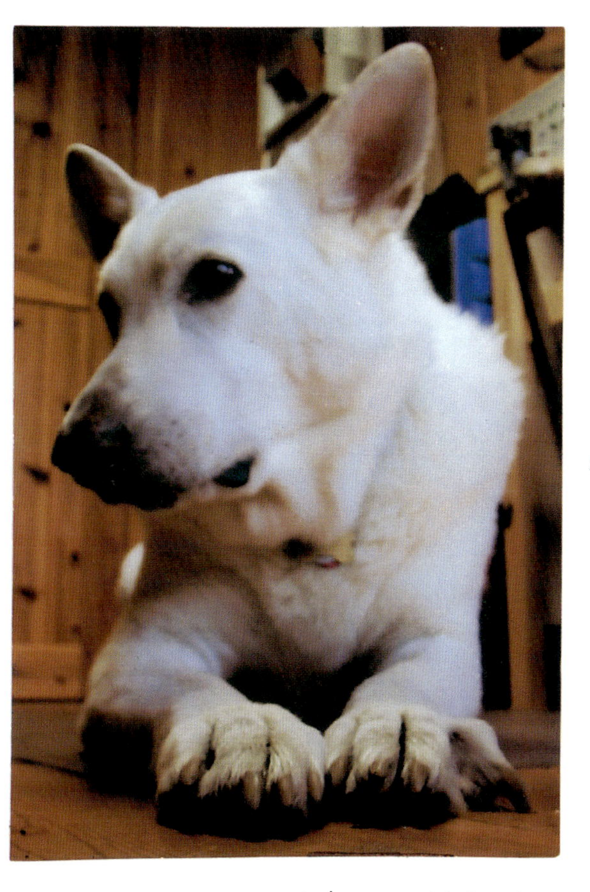

Side view showing the full length of the forelegs.

foreshortened view of the front paws and legs.

Some things to remember when drawing foreshortened views —

1. The subject will look distorted. Rely heavily on the shapes your eye discerns.

2. The body parts closest to the viewer will appear abnormally large.

3. Cameras sometimes distort the subject beyond what is acceptable to the mind.

Pencil study of basic shapes.

Pencil drawing of foreshortened paws and legs.

Watercolor and Pitt brush pen painting. This view is distorted, but still within the realm of "believable."

Working from Photographs

Although sketching from a live subject gives you a better feel for the animal, they don't hold still unless they're asleep. Therefore I make quick action sketches from live animals and rely on good photos for details.

A good reference photo for portrait work, like the Weimaraner on the left, should be clearly in focus and close enough to see individual hairs. Good shadow contrast is also important to define the contours of the face.

Jaeger-Weimaraner

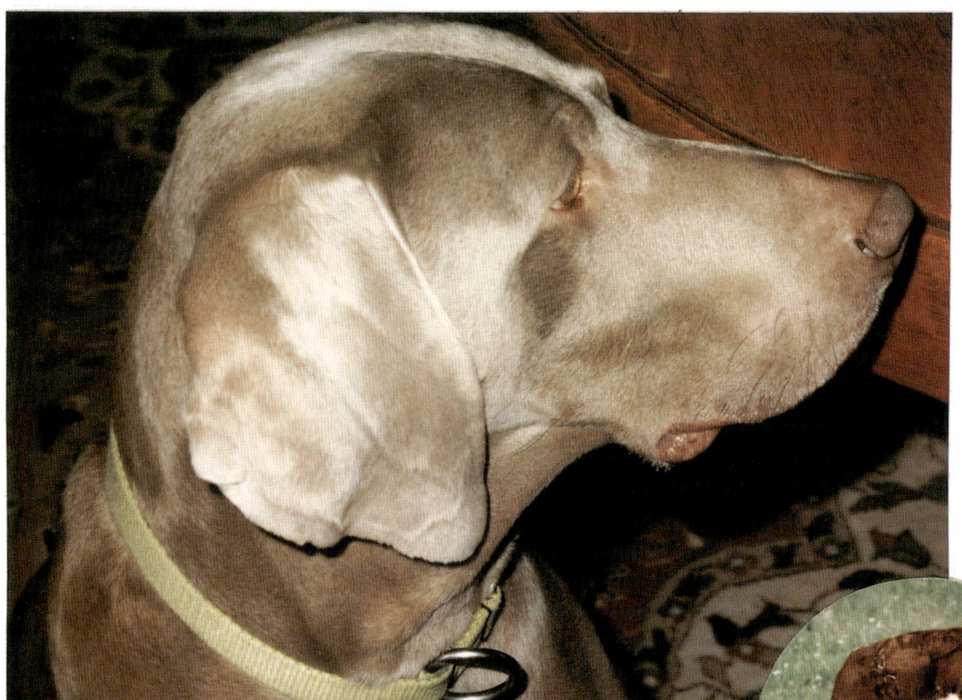

This calf is too far away to see details. It would make a good background subject for a landscape.

Oops! The dog moved in too close to the camera, creating an extremely foreshortened view that isn't flattering. I wouldn't paint this pose.

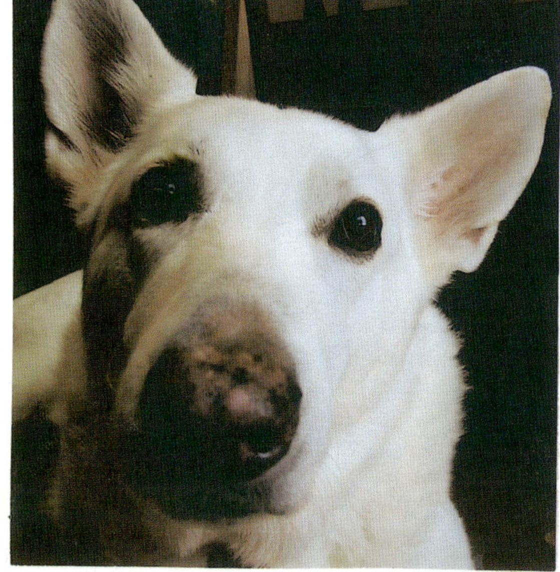

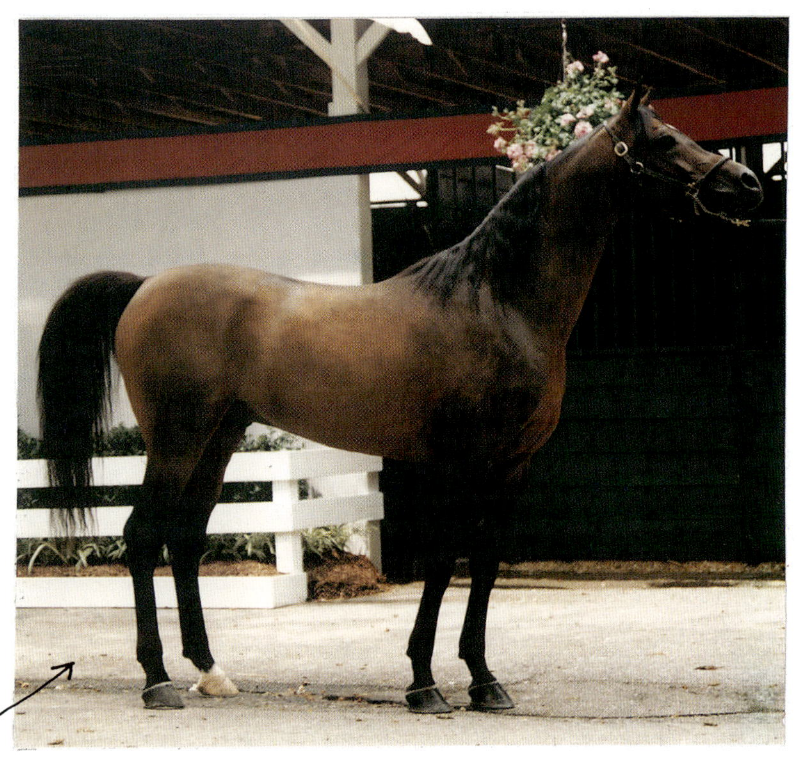

This is a good horse photo, but the background is distracting. In a painting, I would create a light, non cluttered background that sets off the horse.

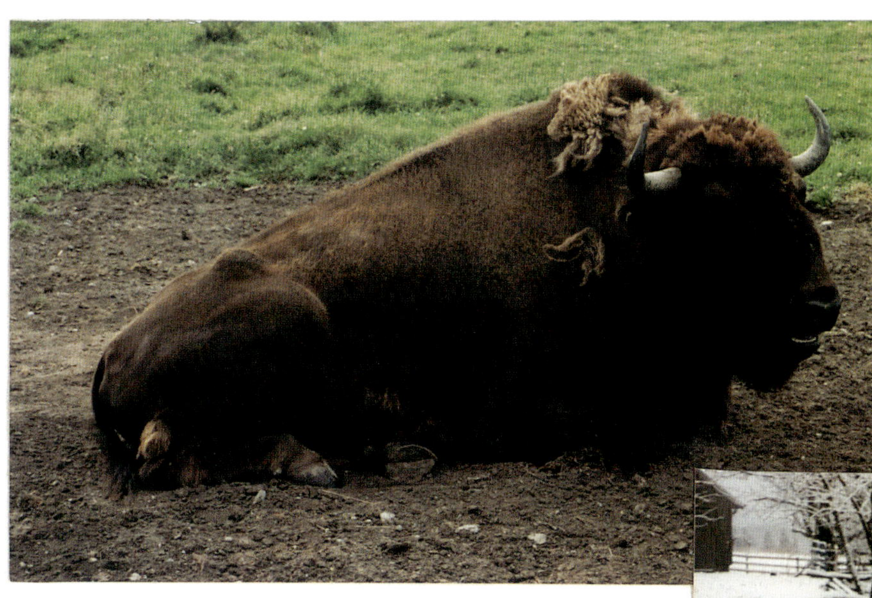

Clarity and good lighting are essential in a reference photo. The photo of the bison on the left is clear, but the back lighting obscures the important features of the face.

This is a great action shot of my mare Lady Tawi. Too bad the flat winter lighting provided no value contrast.

Beware of the woes of flash photography. The flash provides frontal lighting which can flatten out the features. There is also the danger of the pupils of the eyes reflecting back red or green.

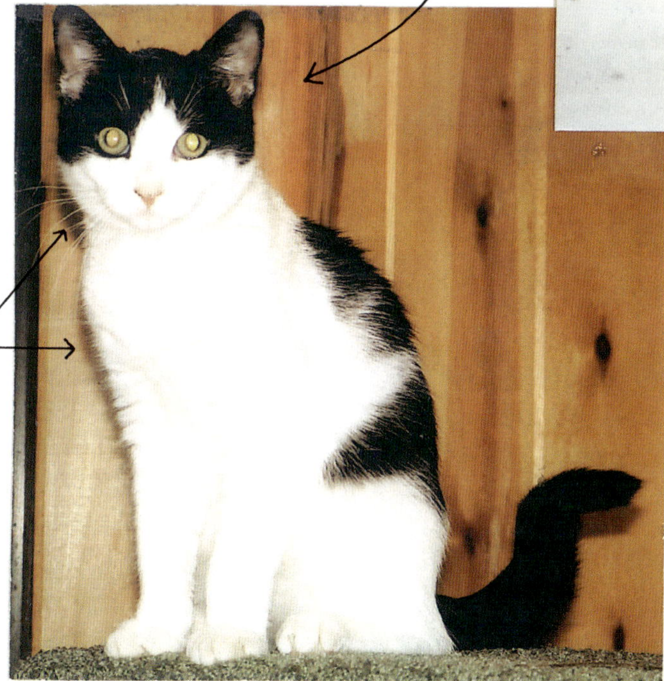

Outline shadow caused by flash bulb.

Reflective pupils can be corrected in the drawing or painting by filling them in with a dark color. Don't forget the highlight dots; they will be in the middle of the pupils.

When absolute accuracy of form is required, photos can be placed in copy machines, overhead projectors or enlargers, and the results traced. However, I would encourage you not to skip the drawing step entirely. It provides a feel for the contours of the animal that can't be duplicated by tracing.

Creating Hair Textures

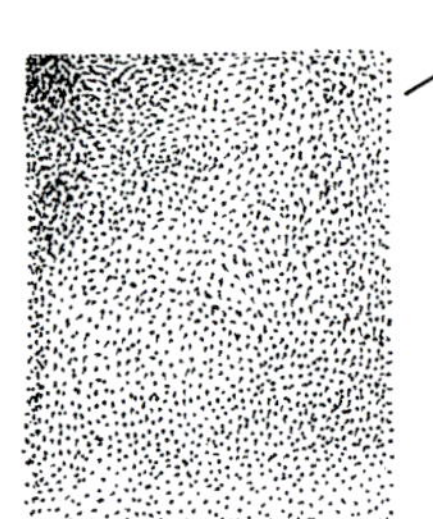

Stippling is a series of dots produced by touching the pen nib to the paper surface while the pen is held in a vertical position. Use stippling to depict short, velvety hair.

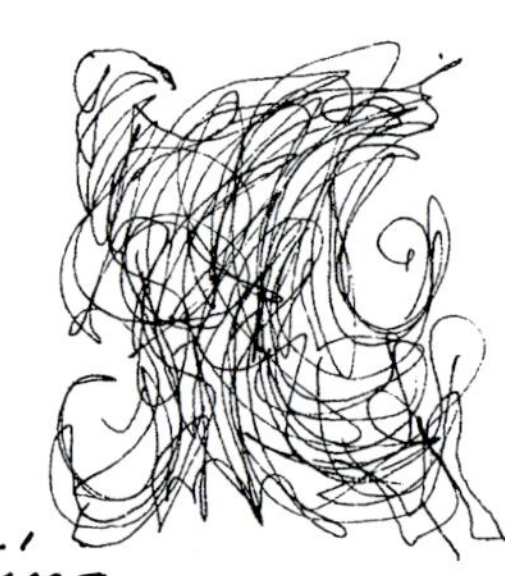

Scribble lines are continuous looping lines that are drawn quickly and loosely. Use scribble lines for curly or thick, tangled hair. They also make good "quick sketches" where lines are restated to make corrections.

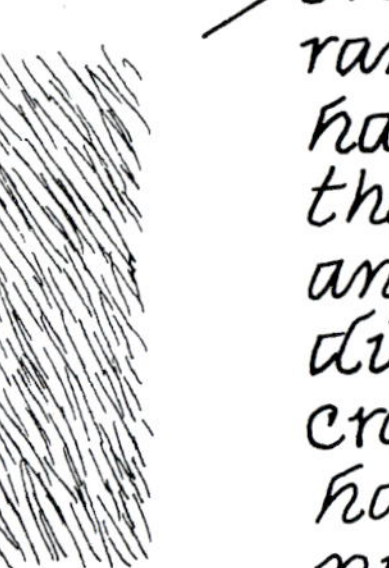

Crisscross lines are randomly crossing, hair-like strokes that are semi-straight and flow in one direction. Use crisscross lines for short hair. A .25 mm pen nib works well.

When stroking crisscross lines, avoid working across the animal in rows. It will result in a furrowed pattern.

This hair looks fried because the ends of the lines are curved.

To create the watercolor hair coat on the right I used crisscross lines applied with a no. 2 round detail brush. The paint was stroked on in layers. Each layer was allowed to dry before the next was applied.

① Base wash of Burnt Sienna and Yellow Ochre.

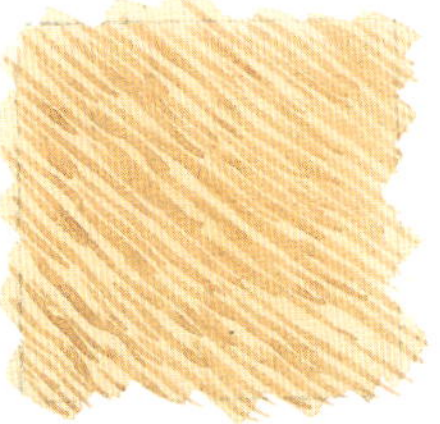

② Hair strokes in Burnt Sienna plus Yellow Ochre.

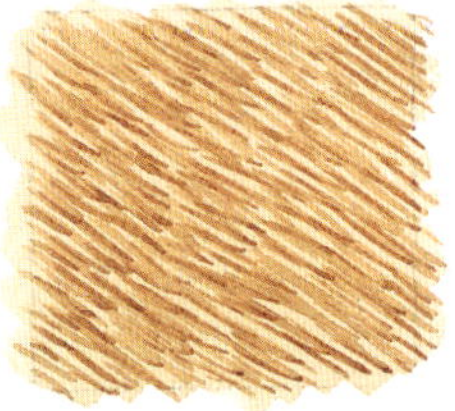

③ Hair strokes in Burnt Sienna

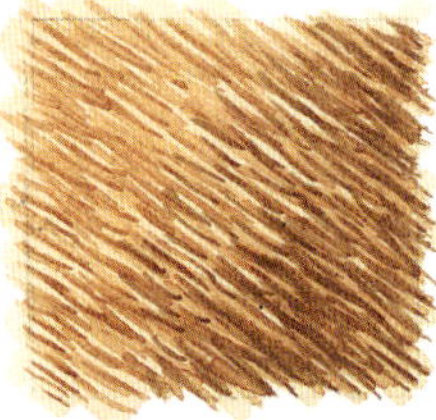

④ A shadow area is created by adding hair strokes of Burnt Sienna plus green.

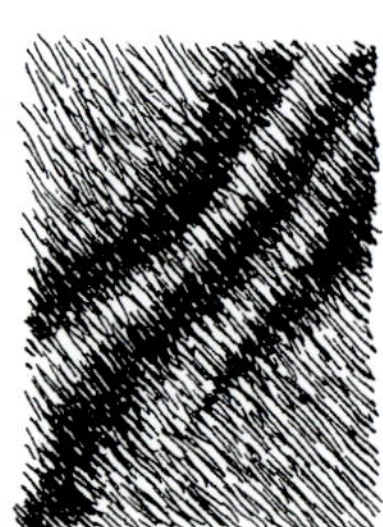

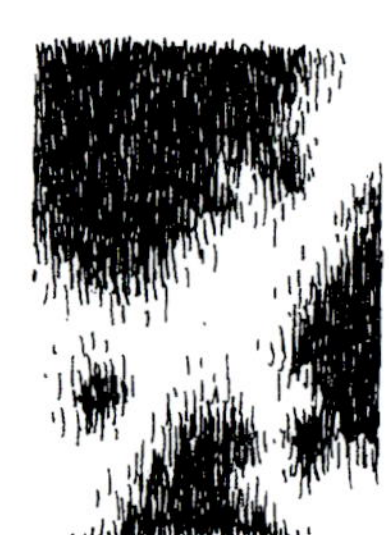

Varying the number of strokes in an area creates stripes, spots and dappled patterns.

Long, wavy lines are perfect for defining horse tails, manes and shaggy dogs.

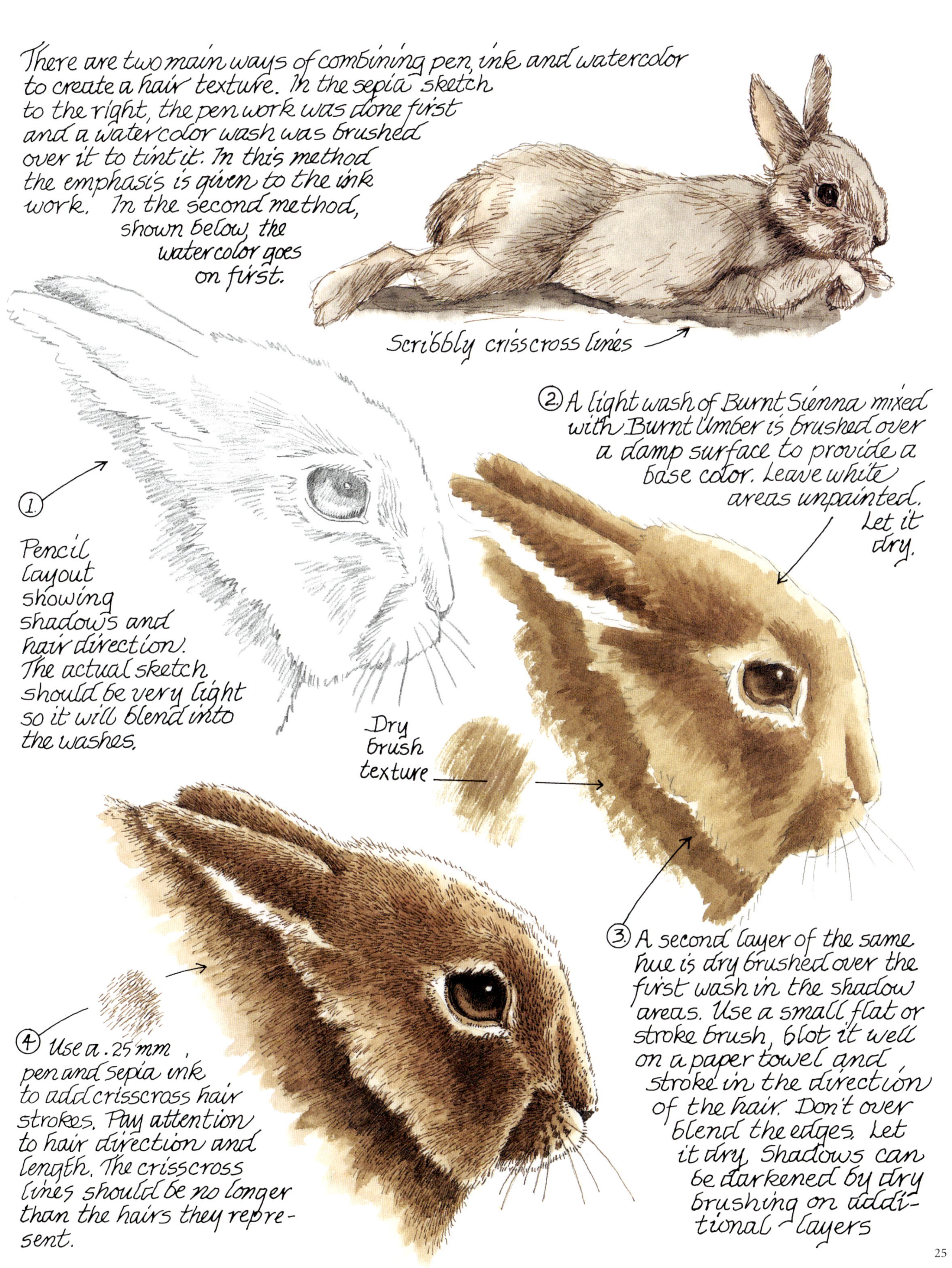
There are two main ways of combining pen, ink and watercolor to create a hair texture. In the sepia sketch to the right, the pen work was done first and a watercolor wash was brushed over it to tint it. In this method the emphasis is given to the ink work. In the second method, shown below, the watercolor goes on first.
Scribbly crisscross lines
② A light wash of Burnt Sienna mixed with Burnt Umber is brushed over a damp surface to provide a base color. Leave white areas unpainted. Let it dry.
① Pencil layout showing shadows and hair direction. The actual sketch should be very light so it will blend into the washes.
Dry brush texture
③ A second layer of the same hue is dry brushed over the first wash in the shadow areas. Use a small flat or stroke brush, blot it well on a paper towel and stroke in the direction of the hair. Don't over blend the edges. Let it dry. Shadows can be darkened by dry brushing on additional layers
④ Use a .25 mm pen and sepia ink to add crisscross hair strokes. Pay attention to hair direction and length. The crisscross lines should be no longer than the hairs they represent.

Making Quick Sketches

Quick sketches are useful for outdoor drawing, where time is limited because the subject is apt to be on the move. Although some quick sketches are more complete than others, they are *meant* to capture the essence of the animal rather than a complete likeness. They are perfect for entries in sketchbook journals.

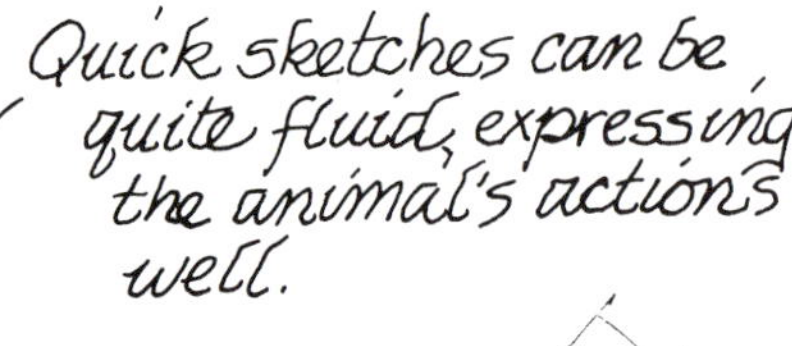

Quick sketches can be quite fluid, expressing the animal's actions well.

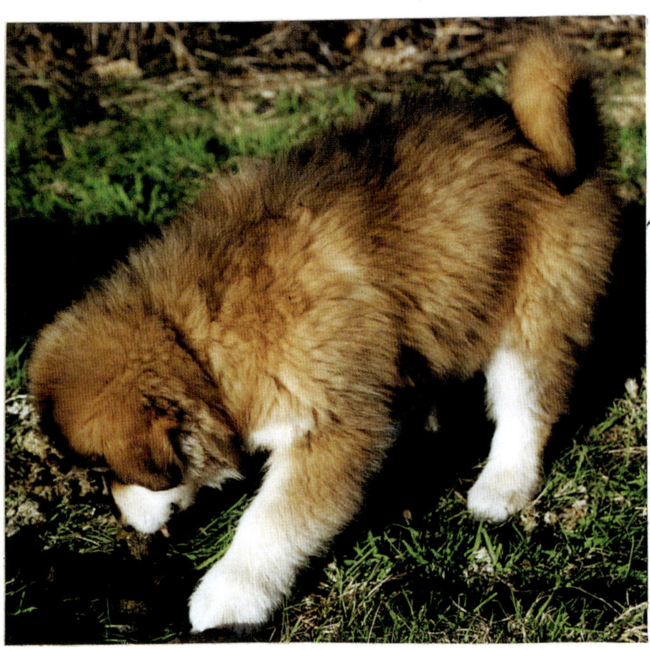

The subject – Malamute mix puppy

① Study the subject. Set the basic form in your mind before the animal moves.

② Start with the trunk. Set down the angle of the back and the rib cage.

③ Quickly add the shoulder and hip shapes. Make corrections by restating lines, but don't get too fussy.

Sepia ink

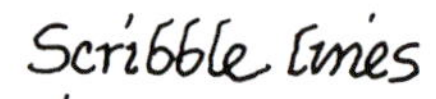

Scribble lines

④ Add the neck and head shapes. A quick visual comparison will help keep the head in proportion to the body.

⑤ Sketch in the legs and whatever features you remember. Don't add preconceived details, they are apt to look out of place. The sketch is meant to look loose, simple and sketchy. Don't overwork it.

The two line drawings below are examples of <u>Contour drawings</u>. In this type of exercise, the pen or pencil remains on the paper and the eyes remain on the subject. The results are quite loose, often disconnected and sometimes down-right comical. However, contour drawings are a great way to loosen up for a day of sketching. They will help train your eye to see and your hand to express freely.

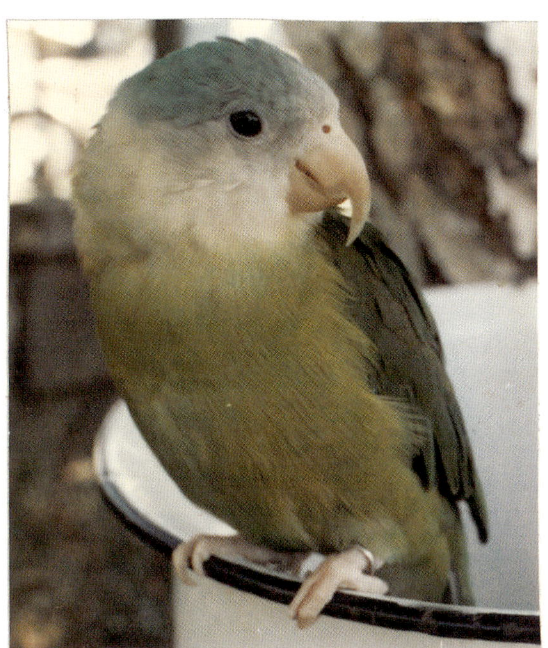

The subject - a Gray Cheek Parakeet.

Pitt brush pen

.25 Rapidograph

When this chipmunk was finished with his caramel corn, he stampered away. Here are the quick drawings I made in my sketch book.

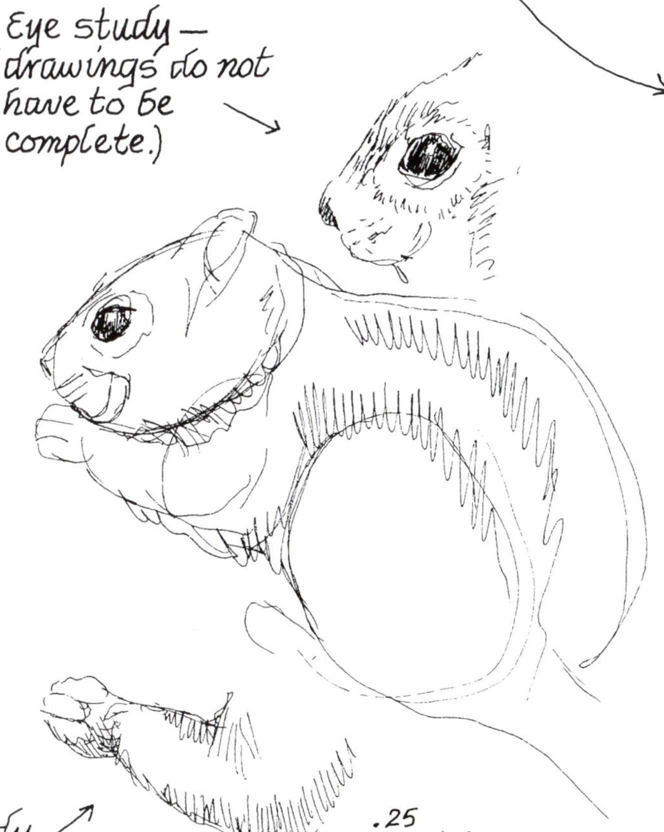

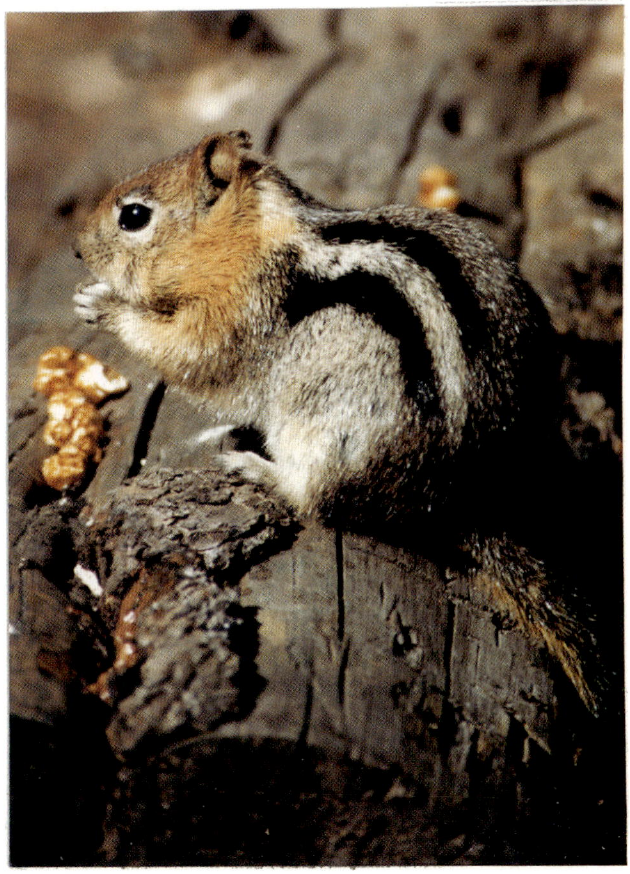

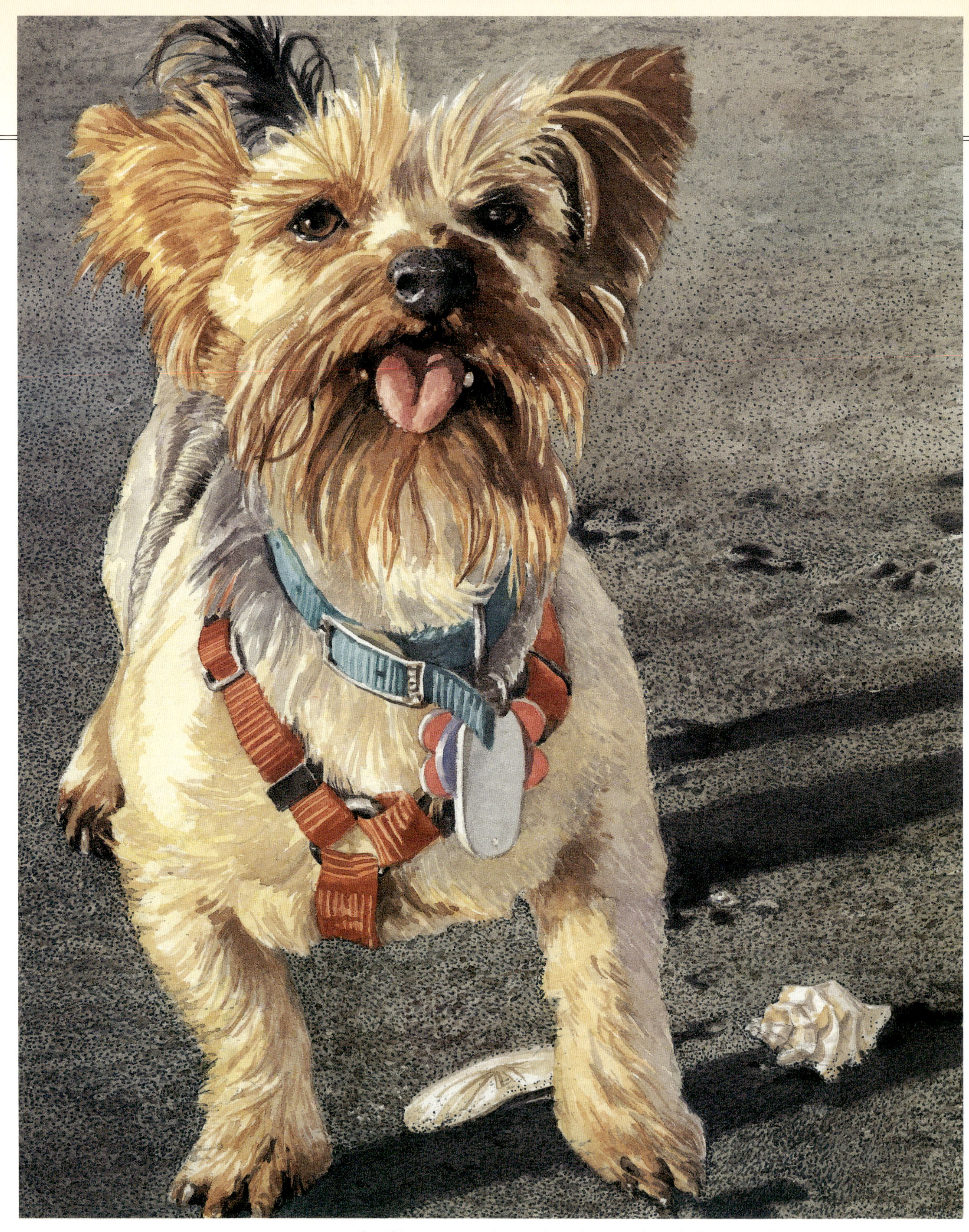

YORKIE AT THE BEACH 8" x 10" (20.5cm x 25.5cm) Watercolor with pen stippling in background sand.

DRAWING DOGS *of all descriptions*

2

EVER SINCE THE CHILD OF THE WOLF made himself at home by man's hearth, artists have tried to depict him. At first it was his hunting prowess that captured man's interest, his likeness rendered in charcoal, chasing deer across cave walls. Since those primeval times, the dog has evolved into multiple types with bodies, abilities, and personalities to meet all the modern needs of their human companions. Whether your favorite canine is a svelte athlete, a burly protector, an ambitious hunter, or simply a cuddly lap warmer, let the dog you love inspire your artistic endeavors. This chapter is designed to help you depict the tricky parts of the dog—his feet, nose, and eyes. Although there are many more breeds than drawing space allows on these pages, I've tried to include a good variety of canine examples. It's up to you to grab a dog biscuit and entice your furry friend into a suitable pose for painting. Snap lots of photos, but don't forget that spontaneous quick sketches might be just the thing to capture the essence of his personality.

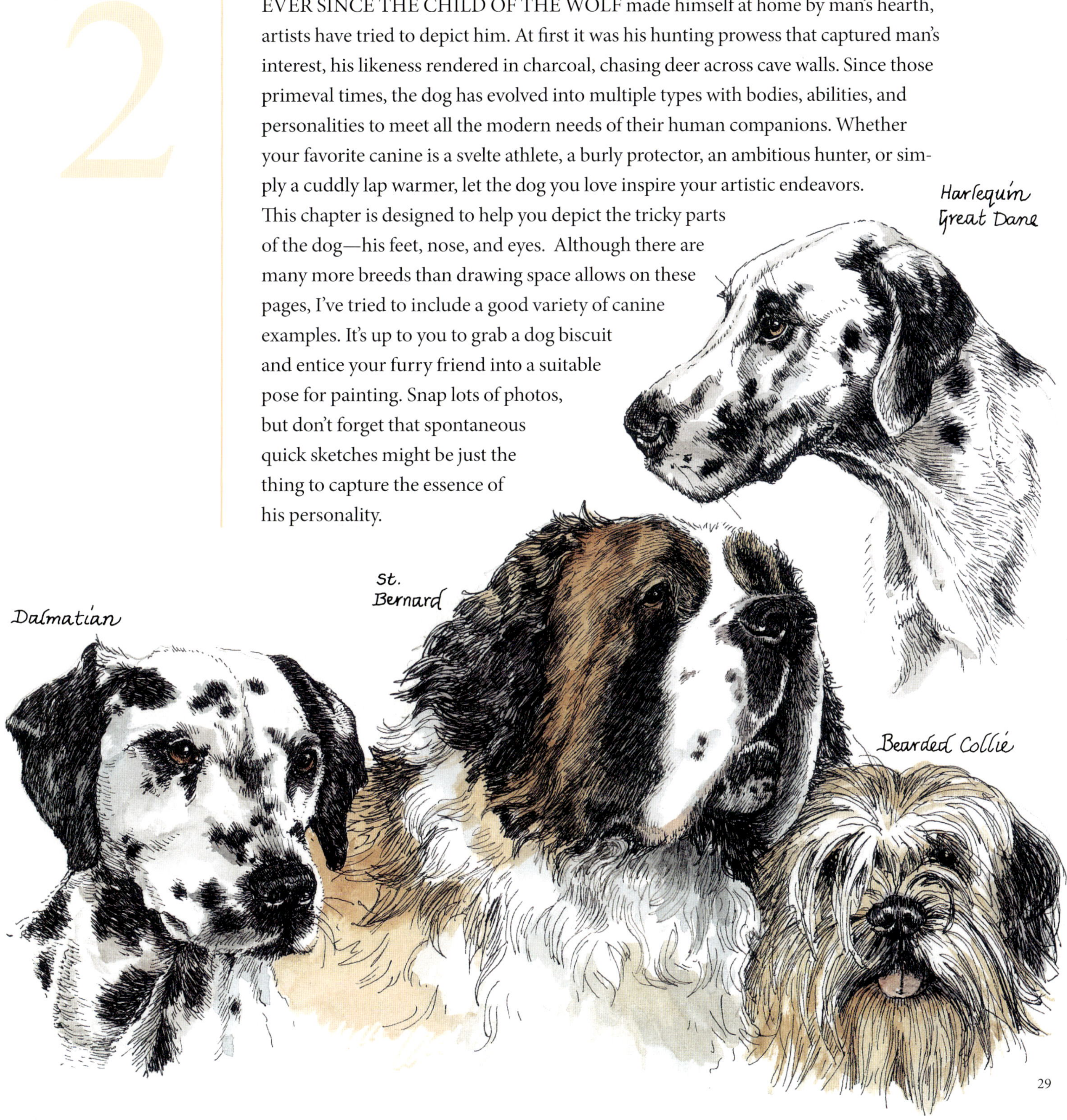

The Basic Dog Shape

Even though these two hounds vary greatly in looks, especially in the length of their legs, they share the same basic structure.

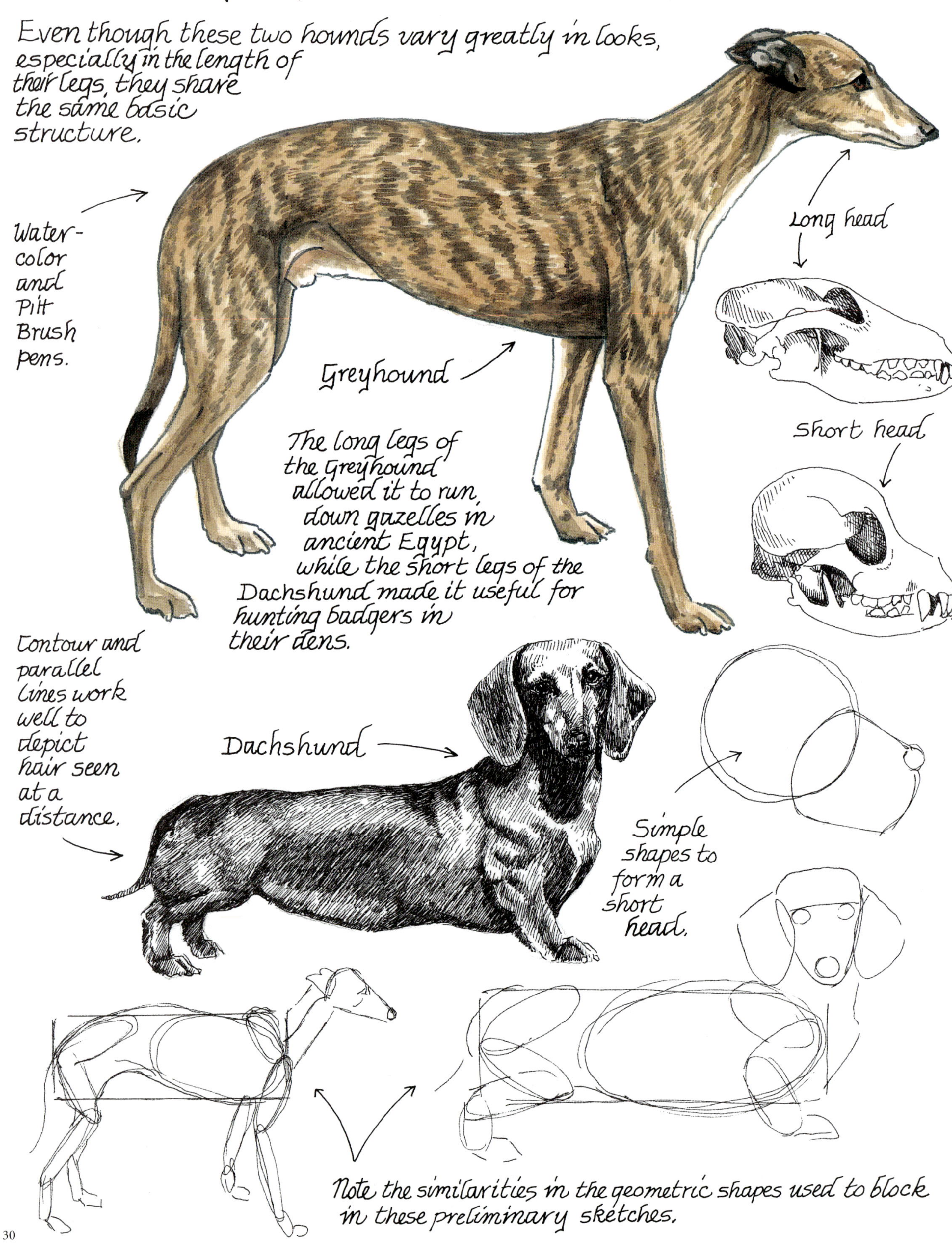

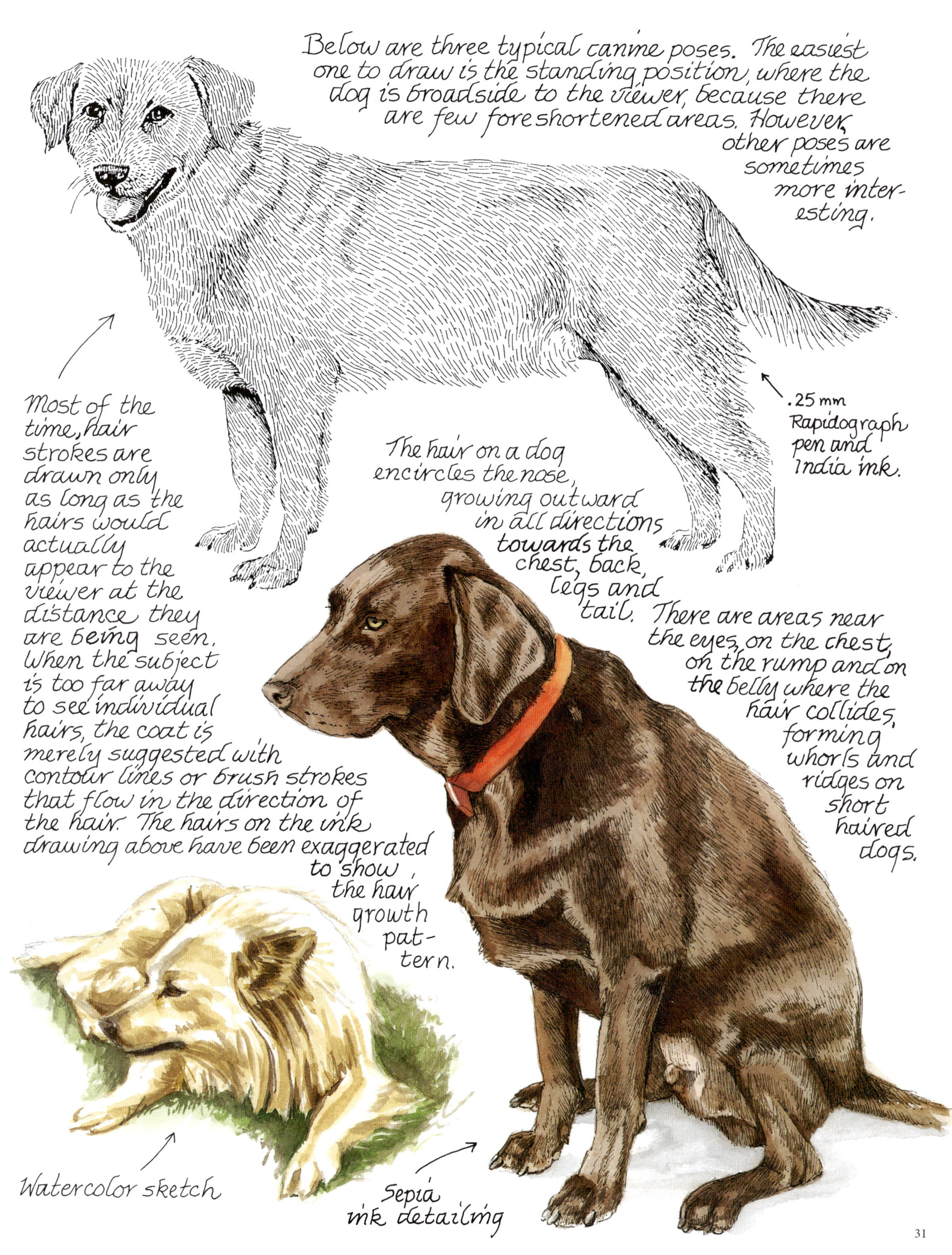
Below are three typical canine poses. The easiest one to draw is the standing position, where the dog is broadside to the viewer, because there are few foreshortened areas. However, other poses are sometimes more interesting.
.25 mm Rapidograph pen and India ink.
Most of the time, hair strokes are drawn only as long as the hairs would actually appear to the viewer at the distance they are being seen. When the subject is too far away to see individual hairs, the coat is merely suggested with contour lines or brush strokes that flow in the direction of the hair. The hairs on the ink drawing above have been exaggerated to show the hair growth pattern.
The hair on a dog encircles the nose, growing outward in all directions towards the chest, back, legs and tail. There are areas near the eyes, on the chest, on the rump and on the belly where the hair collides, forming whorls and ridges on short haired dogs.
Watercolor sketch
Sepia ink detailing

Facial Features

The eyes, more than any other feature of the face, gives the spark of life to the animal portrait. They reflect the spirit and the mood of the individual. Because of their importance, I usually start with the eyes when I paint a detailed portrait. If I am not happy with the result, I start over.

White hairs against a dark watercolor background can be preserved by masking them out (A), scratching in with a razor blade (B) or painting in using a white or pale colored acrylic paint (C). The latter method is mixed media.

B

A

C

Hair direction around the eye is from the eye outward.

A ridge is formed when the hair growing upward from the nose collides with the hair encircling outward from the eye.

Highlight dot

Eye lashes

Eye lid Shadow

Round pupil

Crescent of illumination

Moisture highlight

Tear duct

Iris

Third eye lid

In strong outdoor lighting a round highlight dot will form on the portion of the eye surface closest to the sun. The light passes through the eye orb, spreading out and causing illumination.

Illumination is represented by a crescent of lighter value on the opposite side of the iris from the highlight dot.

Pen, ink and watercolor

Indoor lighting may produce more than one highlight. Shapes may vary, reflecting the forms of the light sources.

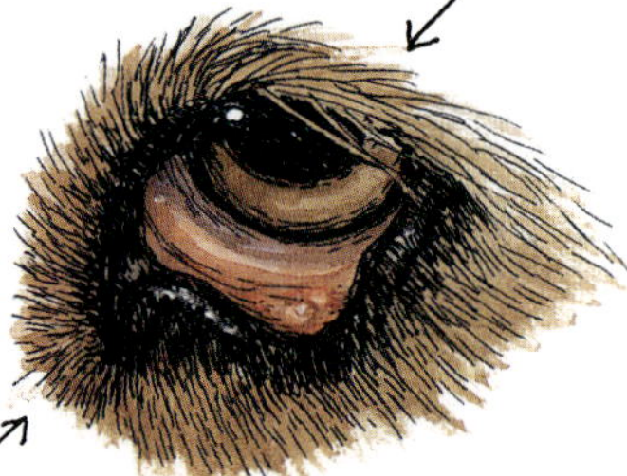

The drooping eye of the Basset Hound shows the pink flesh below the lower lid. Note moisture highlights.

Preliminary washes in Burnt Sienna and Sepia.

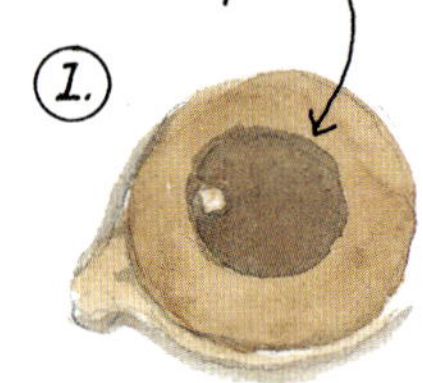

(1.)

Sepia glaze added

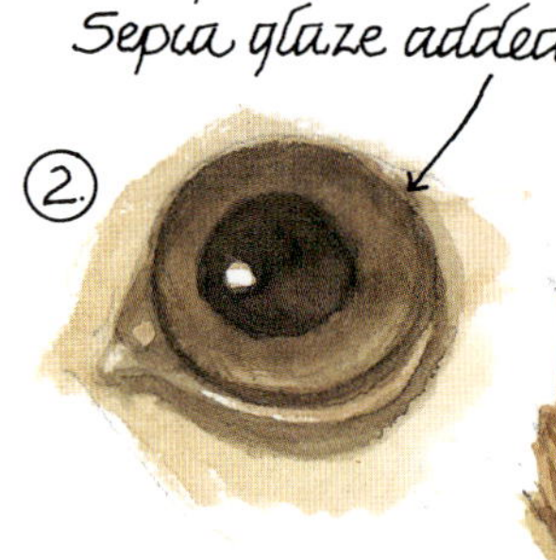

(2.)

Shadows and highlights added.

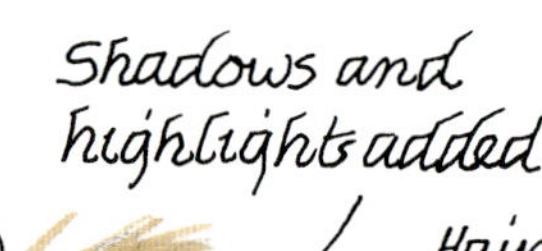

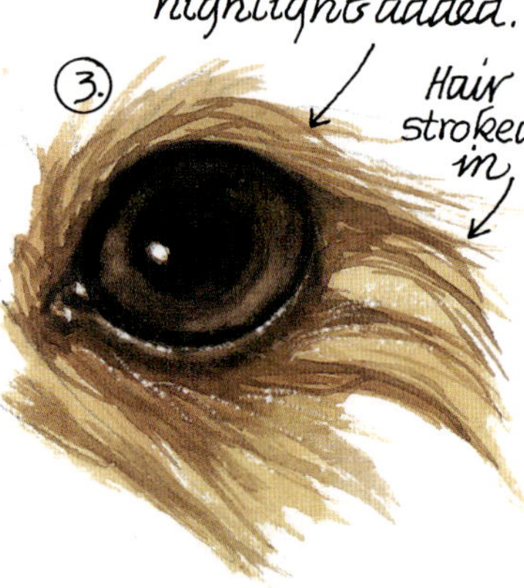

(3.)

Hair stroked in

A Yorkshire Terrier eye from start to finish, painted in watercolor.

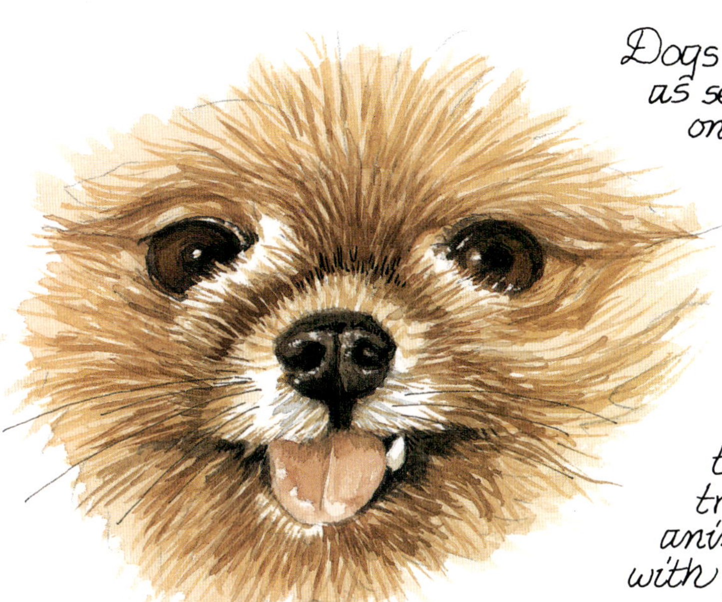

Dogs are capable of expressing a smile, as seen in the happy Pomeranian on the left and the sepia ink sketch of the Bulldog below. When a dog smiles, the eyes are lit with excitement. The jaws are open and pulled upward at the corners. The tongue is often protruding as the animal pants with pleasure.

Study the noses in the illustrations on this page. The line dividing the nose down the center is the septum. The nostrils are rounded near the septum, then they narrow and curve outward like commas.

If the nose is moist, it will show specks of highlight in the raised areas closest to the light source.

The texture of the dog nose ranges from smooth to covered with tiny bumps. Stippling or crosshatching works well to suggest the bumpy surfaces when working in pen and ink.

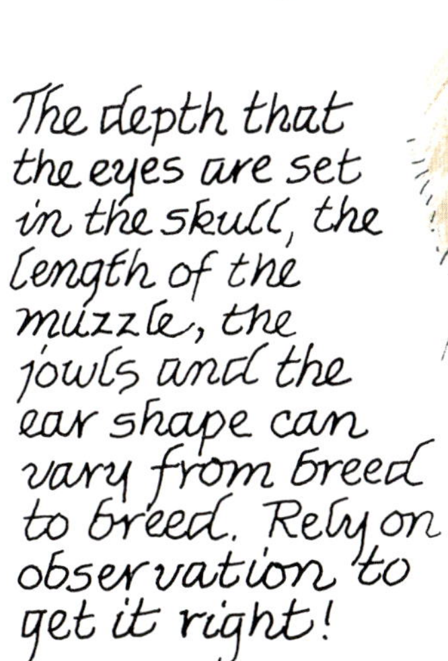

The depth that the eyes are set in the skull, the length of the muzzle, the jowls and the ear shape can vary from breed to breed. Rely on observation to get it right!

Both the Bulldog (left) and the Weimaraner (above) have looks of concentration on their faces. Note the eyes staring straight ahead.

The Ears

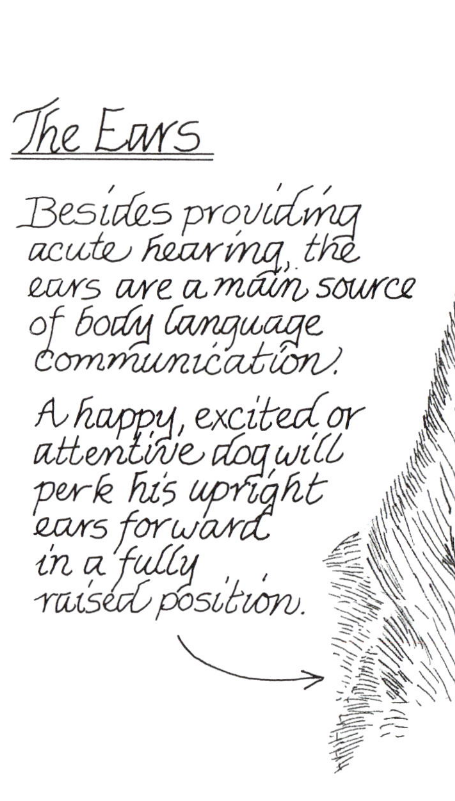

Besides providing acute hearing, the ears are a main source of body language communication.

A happy, excited or attentive dog will perk his upright ears forward in a fully raised position.

Left ears

When playing, howling, running, showing submisson or uncertainty, the dog will lower his ears to keep them out of the way.

When the ears are flattened tight to the head, the dog is feeling fear or apprehension.

Floppy ears are a little harder to read, although it's obvious that this Pointer is concentrating his attention on something.

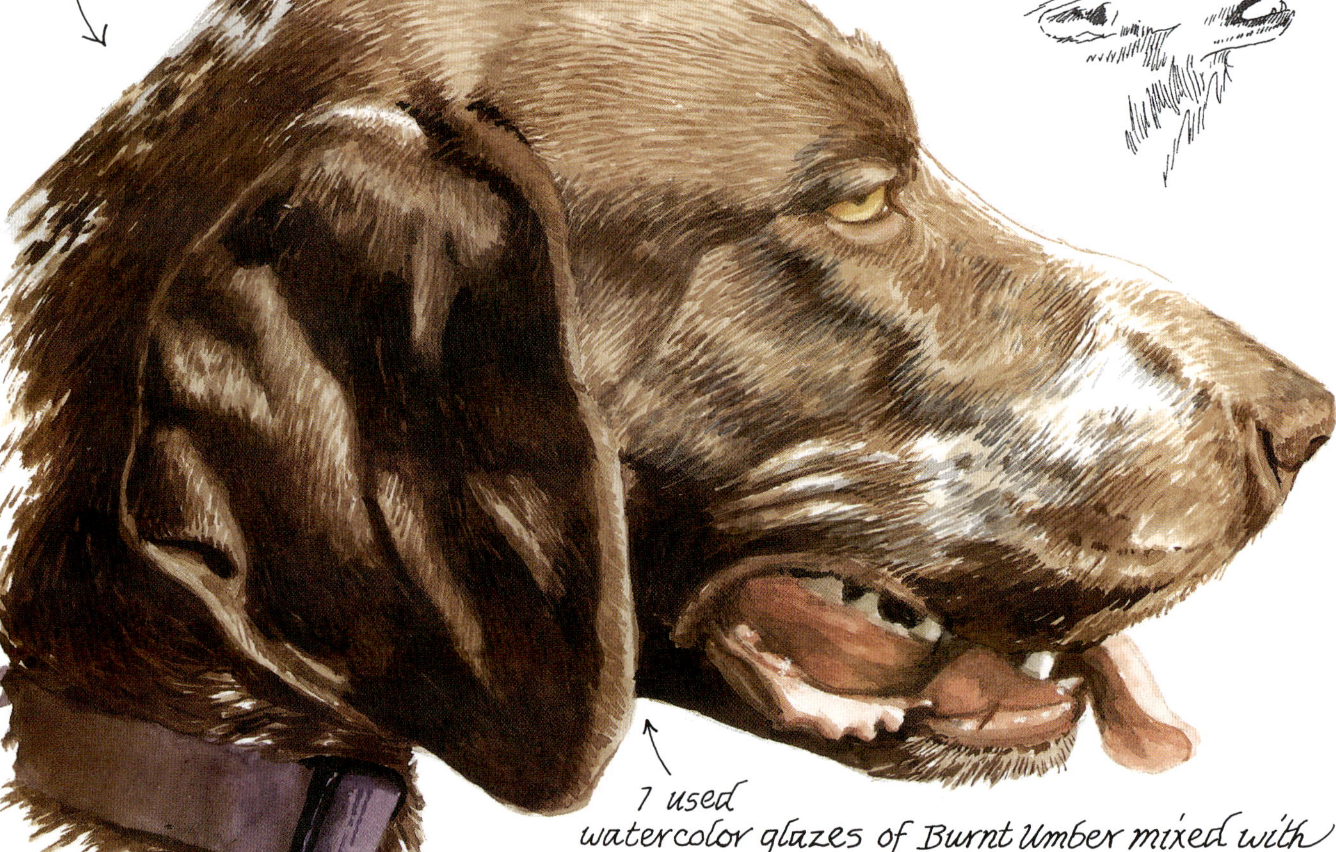

I used watercolor glazes of Burnt Umber mixed with Dioxazine Purple to create the brown coat in this painting. It was applied with a no.4 and no.2 round detail brush.

The Feet

Ulna
Radius
Pisiform
Carpus
Phalanges
Metacarpus
Bones of the forefoot
Left front foot
When I was young I handled the drawing of animal feet by hiding them in the grass. Now I consider them one of the most interesting parts of the animal to depict. It was a matter of becoming familiar with their shape.
Carpus pad
Left hind lower leg
Hock
Dew-claw
Pads
Back feet are narrower than front feet.
Pads have the texture of rough, grained leather.
Four lower toes
Four toes
Underside of claws
Front feet reclining

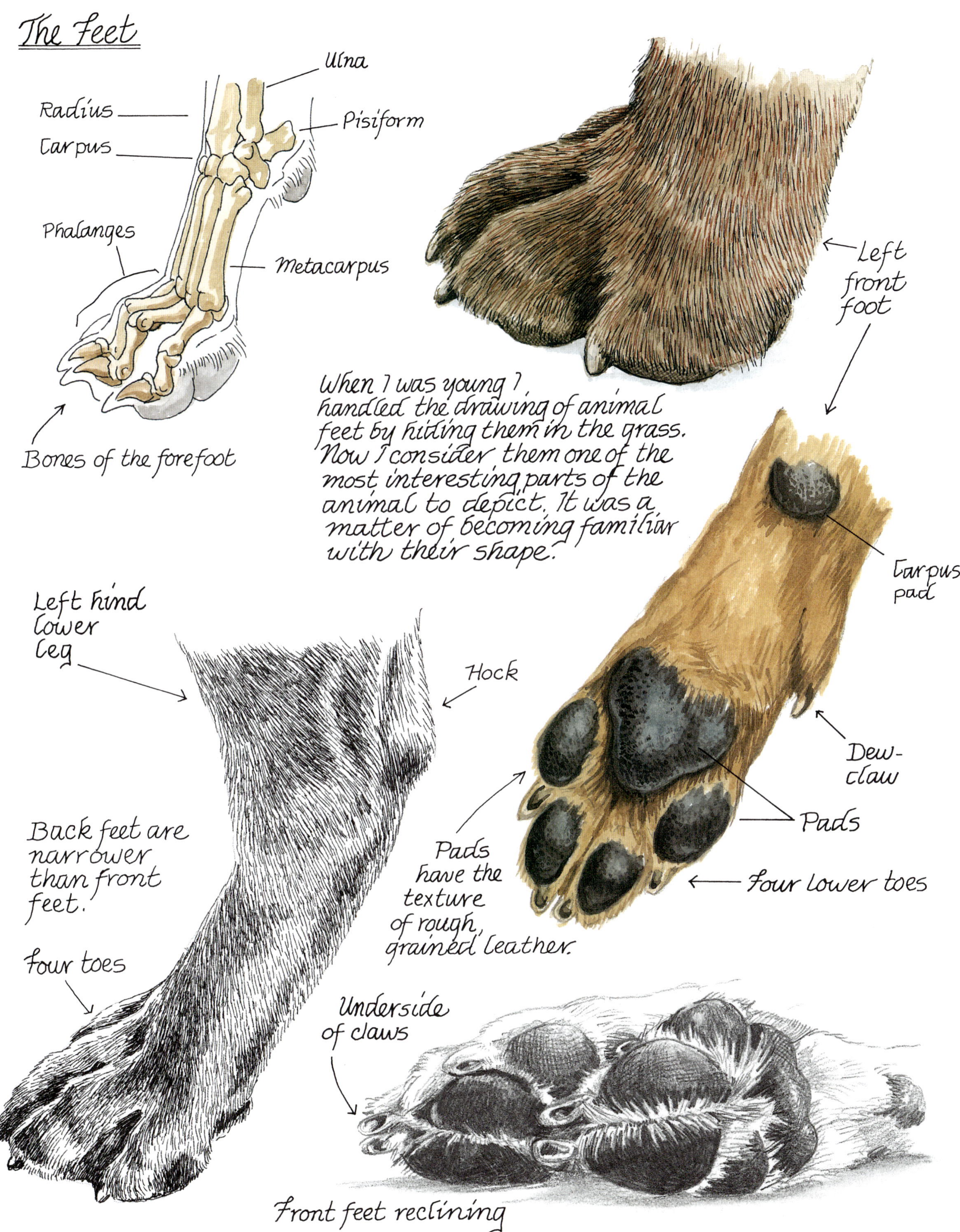

Puppies

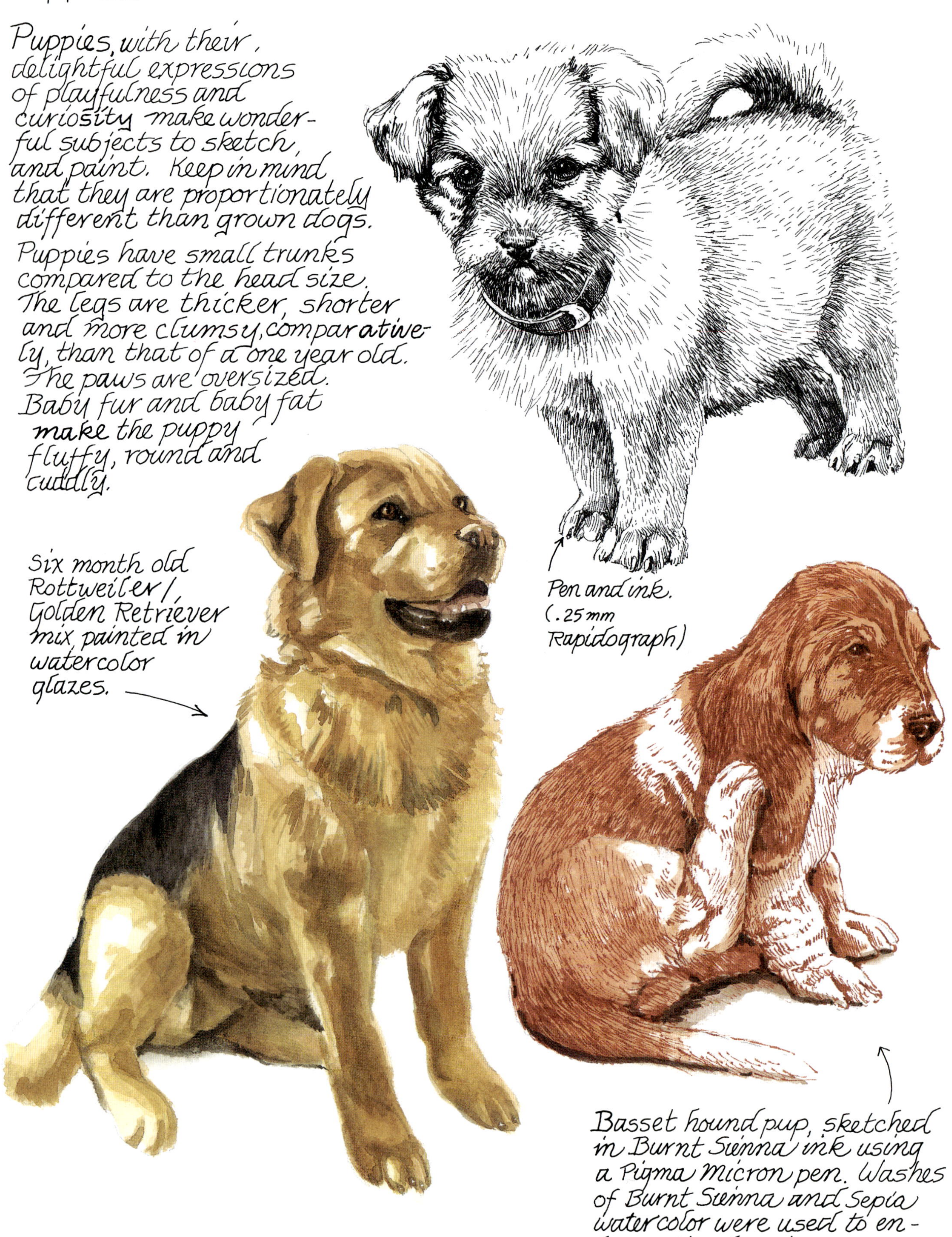

Puppies, with their delightful expressions of playfulness and curiosity make wonderful subjects to sketch and paint. Keep in mind that they are proportionately different than grown dogs.

Puppies have small trunks compared to the head size. The legs are thicker, shorter and more clumsy, comparatively, than that of a one year old. The paws are oversized. Baby fur and baby fat **make** the puppy fluffy, round and cuddly.

Pen and ink. (.25 mm Rapidograph)

Six month old Rottweiler/Golden Retriever mix painted in watercolor glazes.

Basset hound pup, sketched in Burnt Sienna ink using a Pigma Micron pen. Washes of Burnt Sienna and Sepia watercolor were used to enhance the drawing.

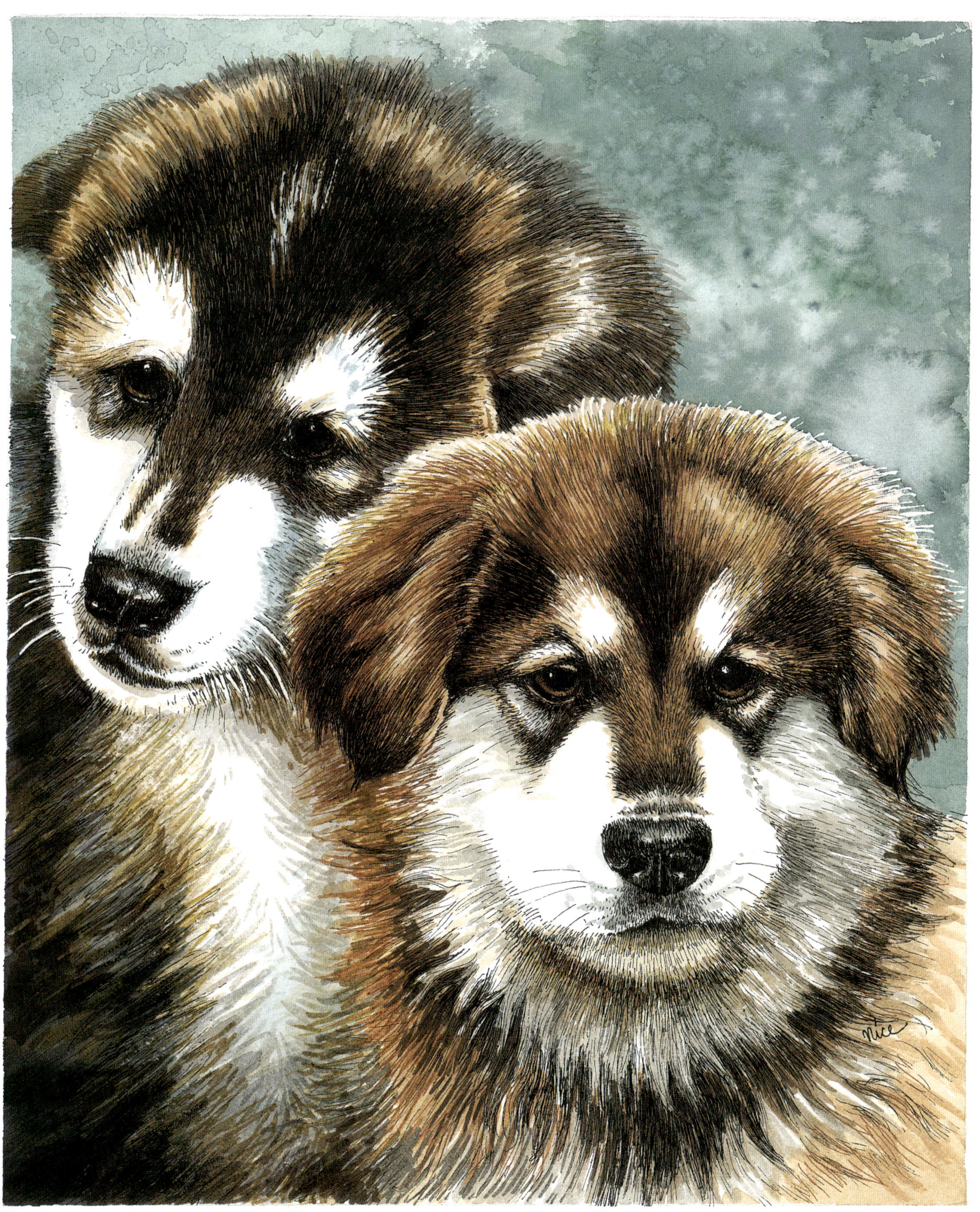

HARLEY AND STURGIS 8" x 10" (20.5cm x 25.5cm) Malamute mix puppies drawn in pen and India ink with watercolor and Pitt Brush Pens.

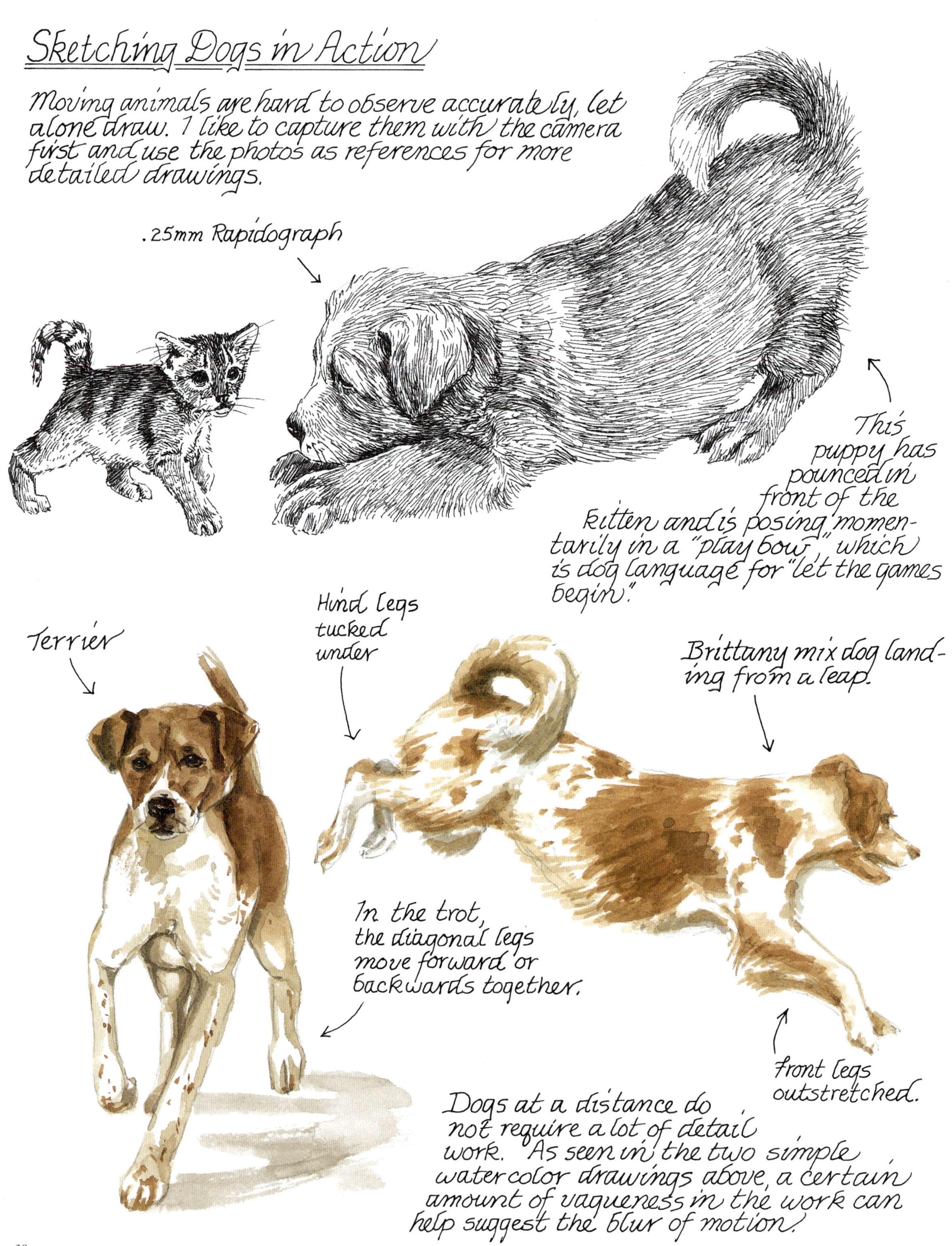
Sketching Dogs in Action
Moving animals are hard to observe accurately, let alone draw. I like to capture them with the camera first and use the photos as references for more detailed drawings.
.25mm Rapidograph
This puppy has pounced in front of the kitten and is posing momentarily in a "play bow," which is dog language for "let the games begin."
Terrier
Hind legs tucked under
Brittany mix dog landing from a leap.
In the trot, the diagonal legs move forward or backwards together.
Front legs outstretched.
Dogs at a distance do not require a lot of detail work. As seen in the two simple watercolor drawings above, a certain amount of vagueness in the work can help suggest the blur of motion.

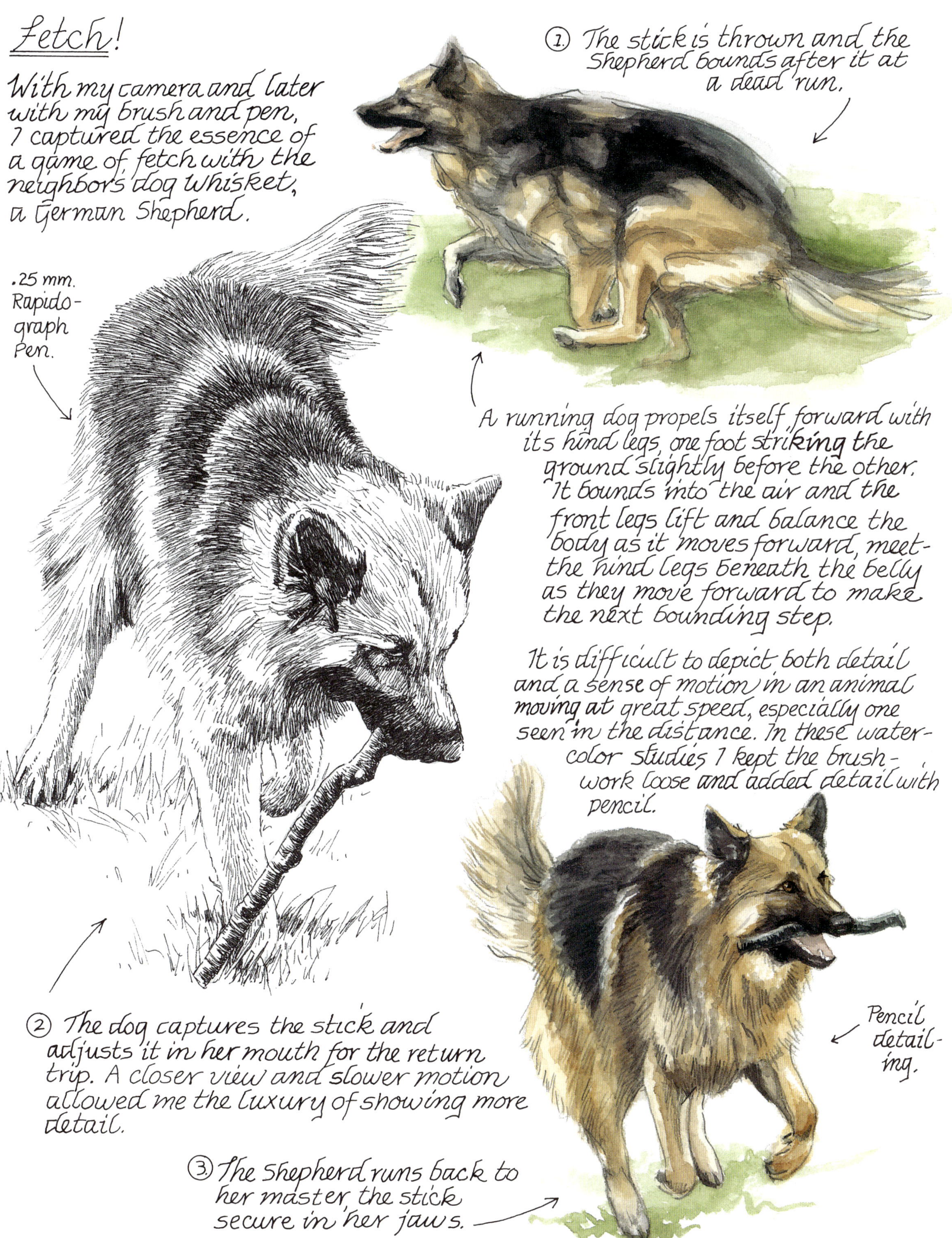
Fetch!
With my camera and later with my brush and pen, I captured the essence of a game of fetch with the neighbor's dog Whisket, a German Shepherd.
① The stick is thrown and the Shepherd bounds after it at a dead run.
.25 mm. Rapidograph Pen.
A running dog propels itself forward with its hind legs, one foot striking the ground slightly before the other. It bounds into the air and the front legs lift and balance the body as it moves forward, meet the hind legs beneath the belly as they move forward to make the next bounding step.
It is difficult to depict both detail and a sense of motion in an animal moving at great speed, especially one seen in the distance. In these watercolor studies I kept the brushwork loose and added detail with pencil.
② The dog captures the stick and adjusts it in her mouth for the return trip. A closer view and slower motion allowed me the luxury of showing more detail.
Pencil detailing.
③ The Shepherd runs back to her master, the stick secure in her jaws.

Creating a Pen, Ink and Watercolor Portrait

Project no. 2

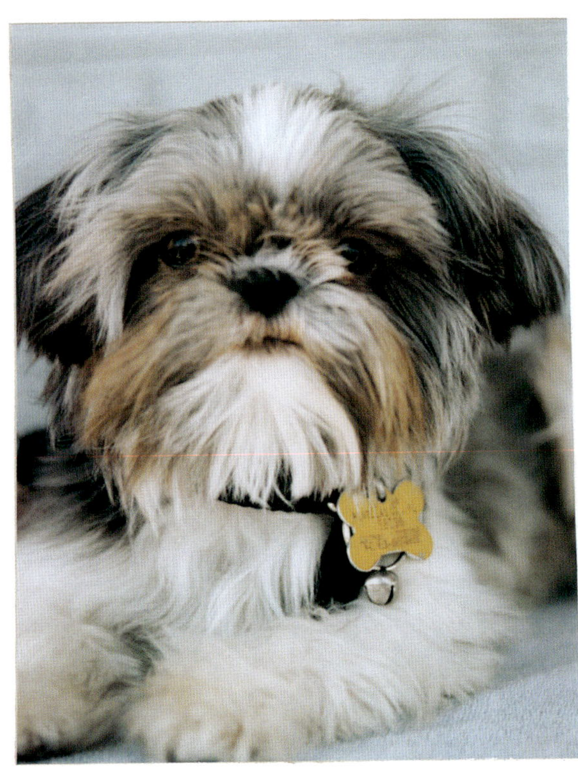

Pepe

① Begin with a clear, well cropped reference photo.

② Pick out the basic shapes within the photo image and pencil in a rough preliminary drawing.

③ Refine and correct the drawing.

④ Give depth and texture to the drawing by adding ink lines over the pencil outlines. Scribbly wavy lines, crosshatching and dots were used to complete this facsimile of the drawing on the opposite page.

⑤ Add washes of watercolor to tint the ink work. See the color mixture examples at the top of the following page.

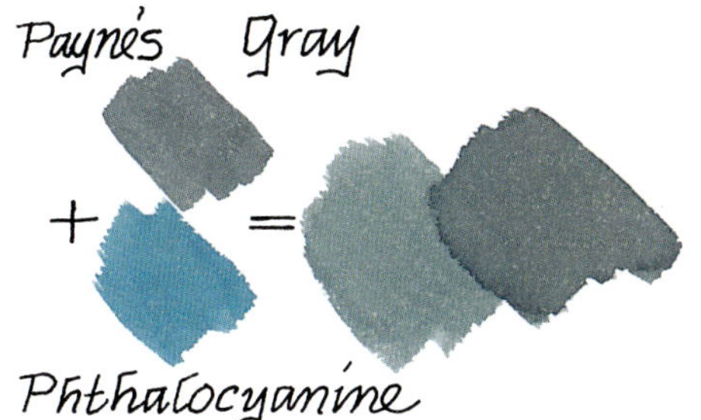

These are the main color mixtures used in the pen, ink and watercolor painting seen below.

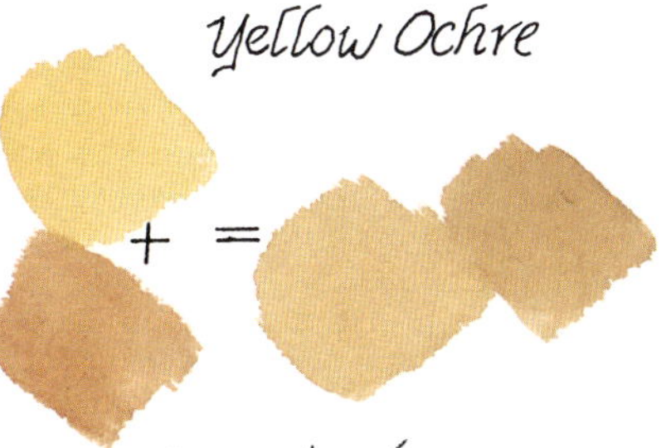

The background texture was created by daubing a crumpled tissue in the wet paint.

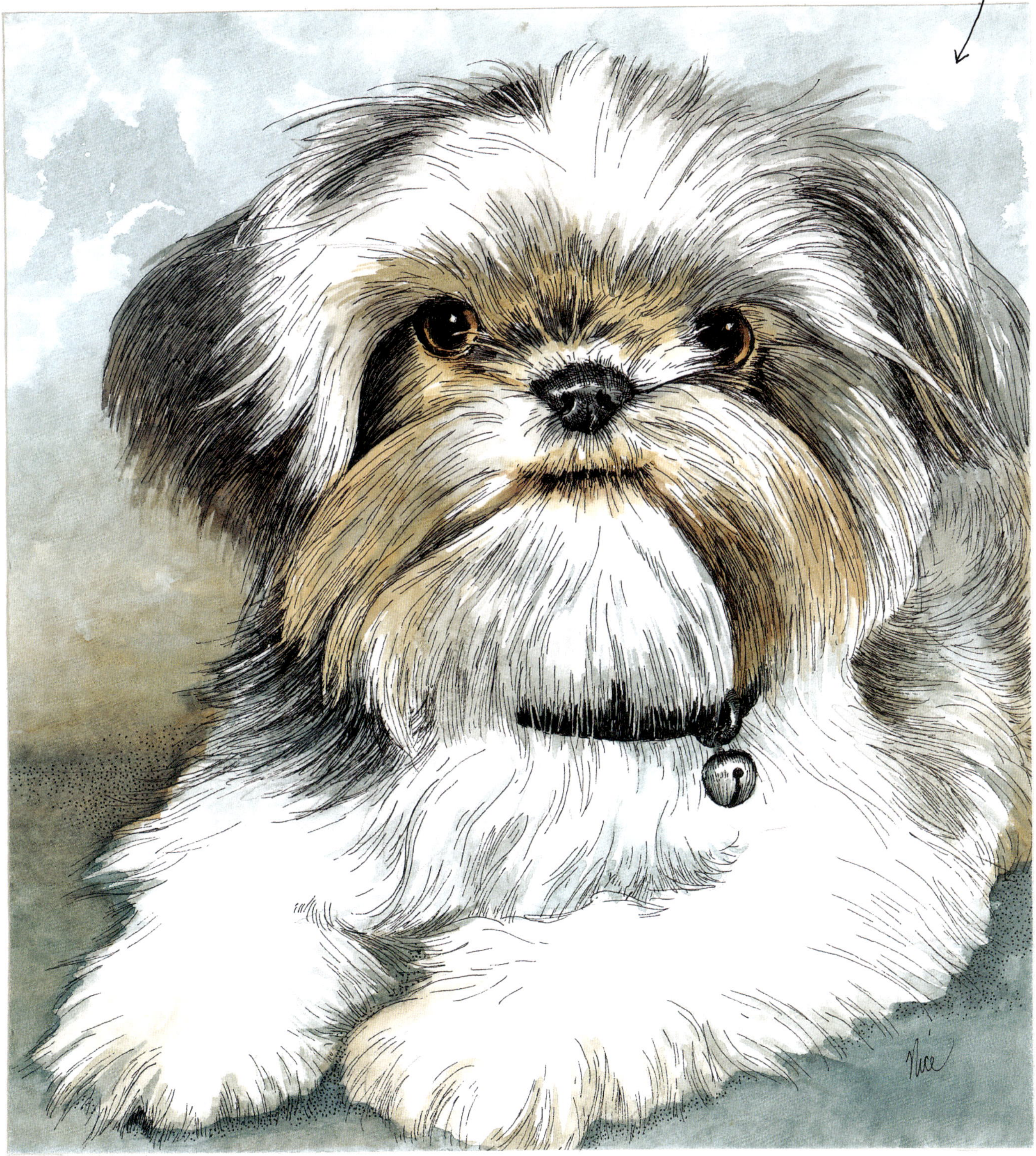

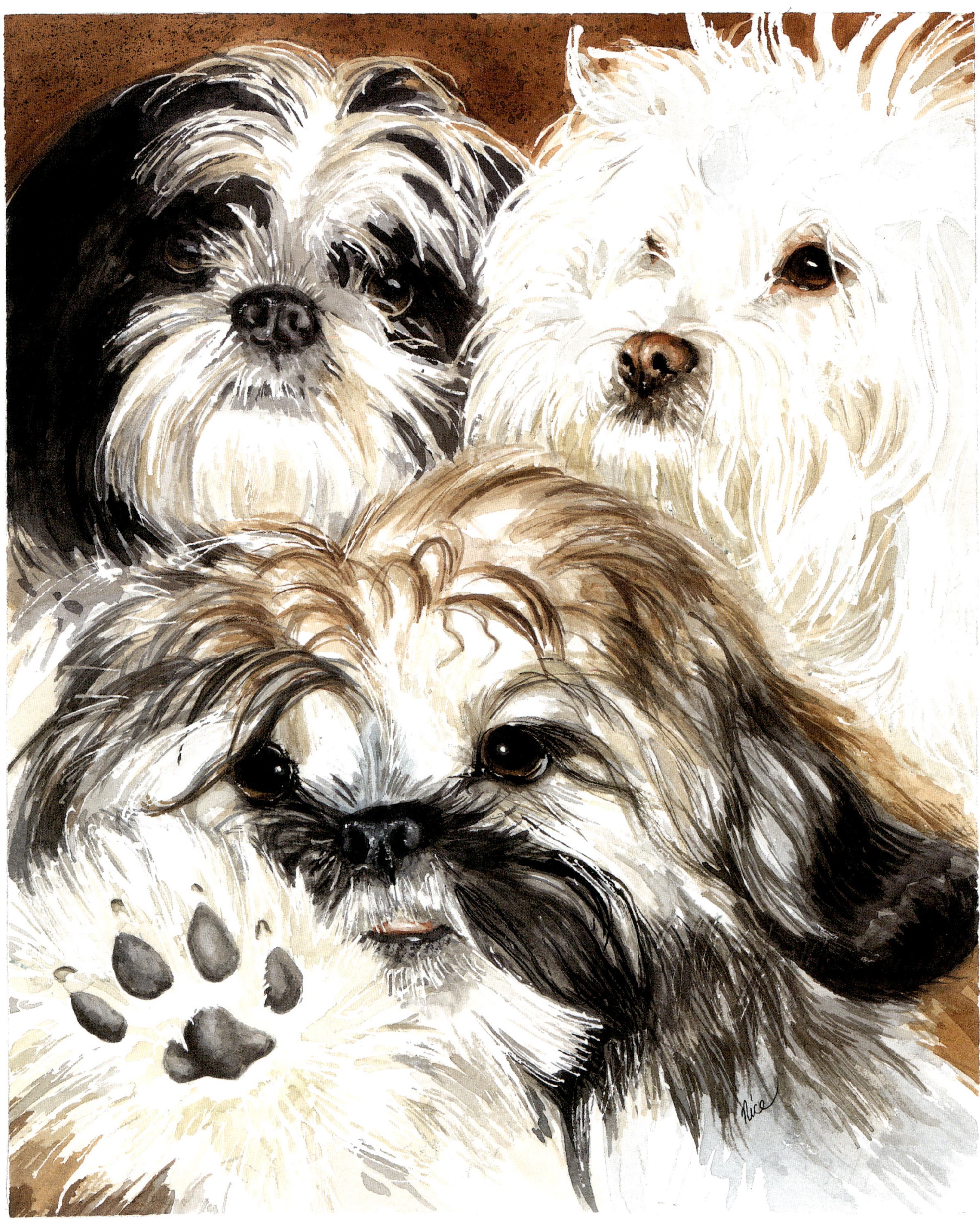

Small Companion Dogs

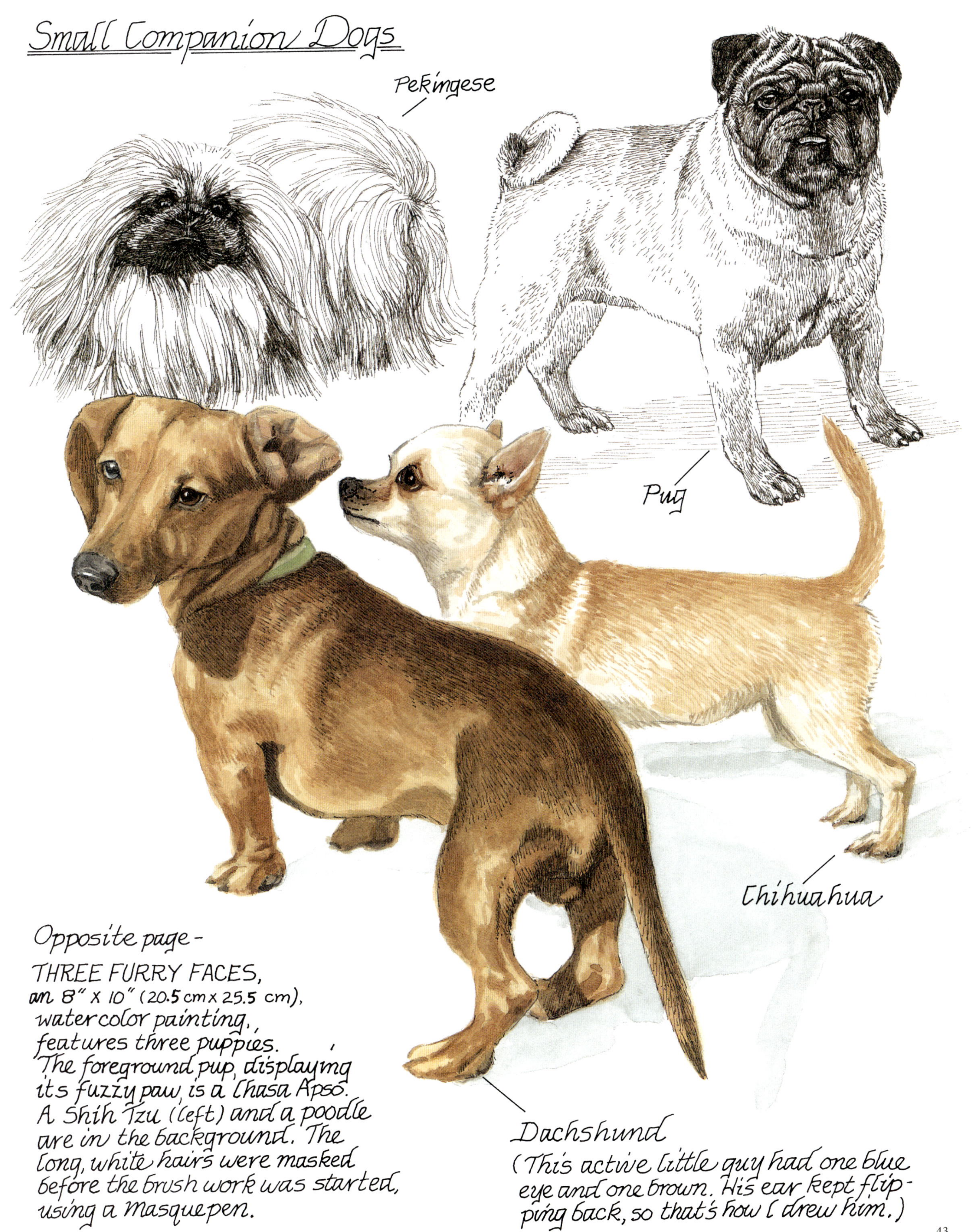

(This active little guy had one blue eye and one brown. His ear kept flipping back, so that's how I drew him.)

Opposite page-
THREE FURRY FACES, an 8" x 10" (20.5 cm x 25.5 cm), watercolor painting, features three puppies. The foreground pup, displaying its fuzzy paw, is a Lhasa Apso. A Shih Tzu (left) and a poodle are in the background. The long, white hairs were masked before the brush work was started, using a Masquepen.

Sporting Dogs

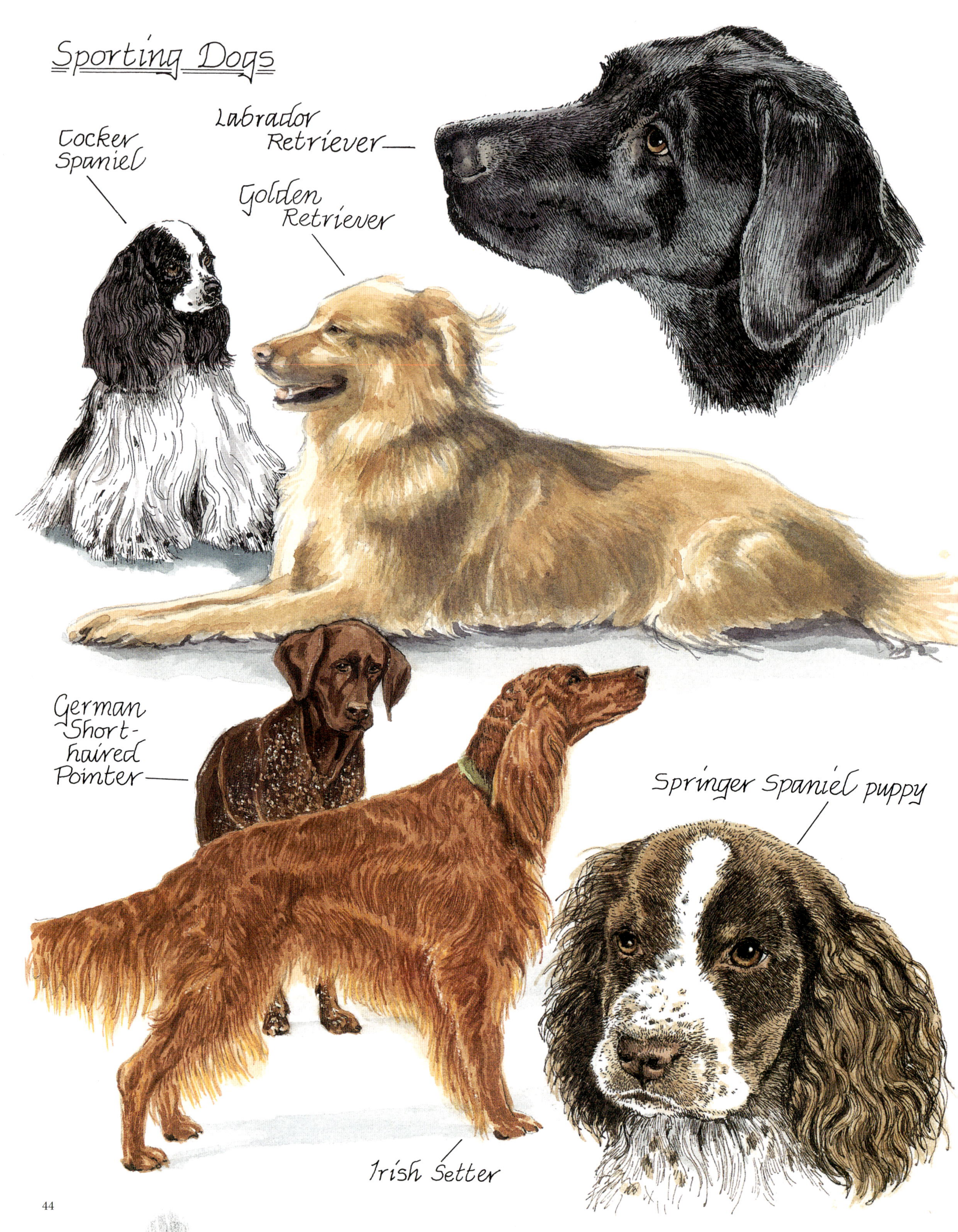

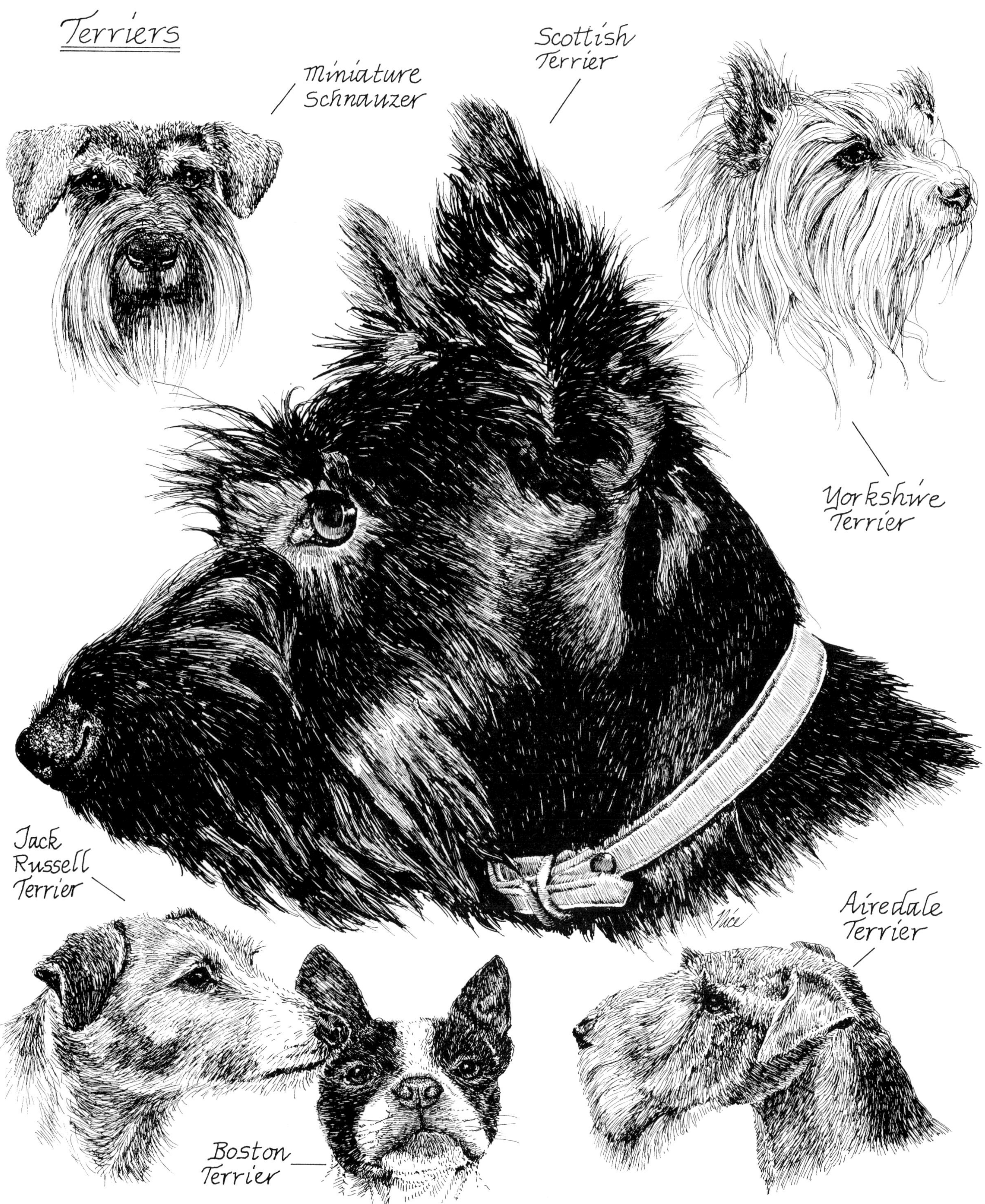
Terriers
Miniature Schnauzer
Scottish Terrier
Yorkshire Terrier
Jack Russell Terrier
Boston Terrier
Airedale Terrier

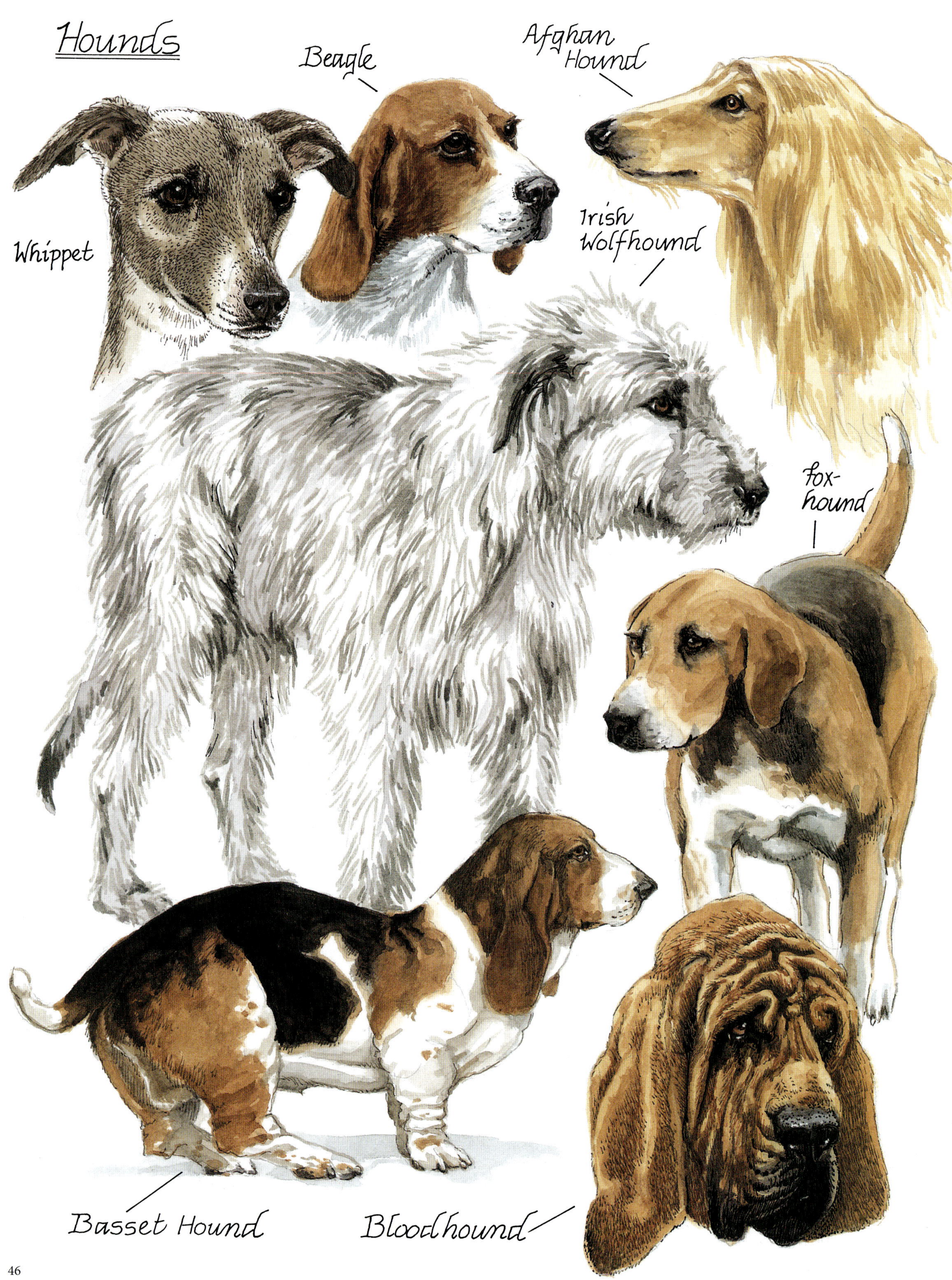
Hounds
Beagle
Afghan Hound
Whippet
Irish Wolfhound
Fox-hound
Basset Hound
Bloodhound

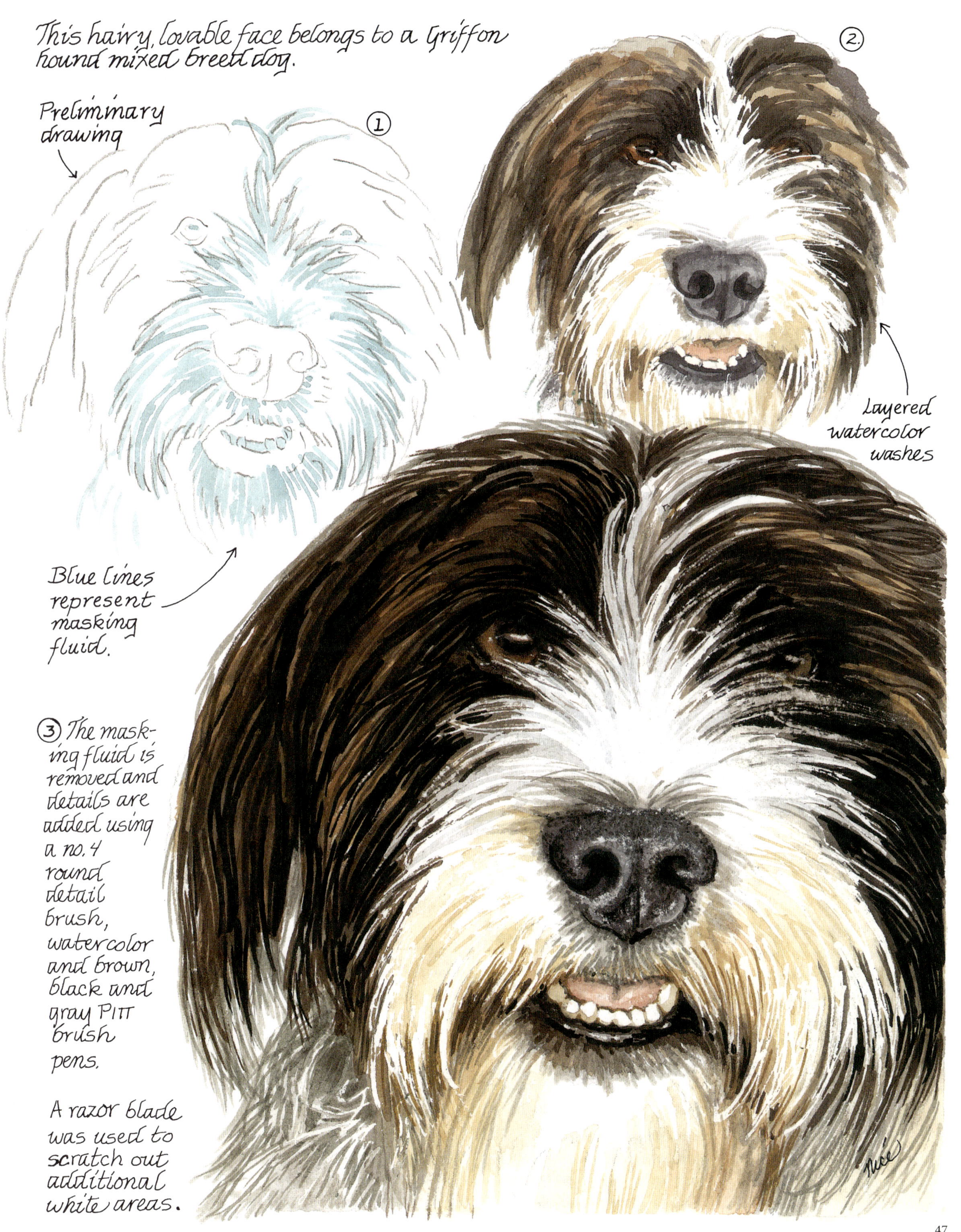
This hairy, lovable face belongs to a Griffon hound mixed breed dog.
Preliminary drawing
1
2.
Layered watercolor washes
Blue lines represent masking fluid.
3 The masking fluid is removed and details are added using a no. 4 round detail brush, watercolor and brown, black and gray PITT brush pens.
A razor blade was used to scratch out additional white areas.

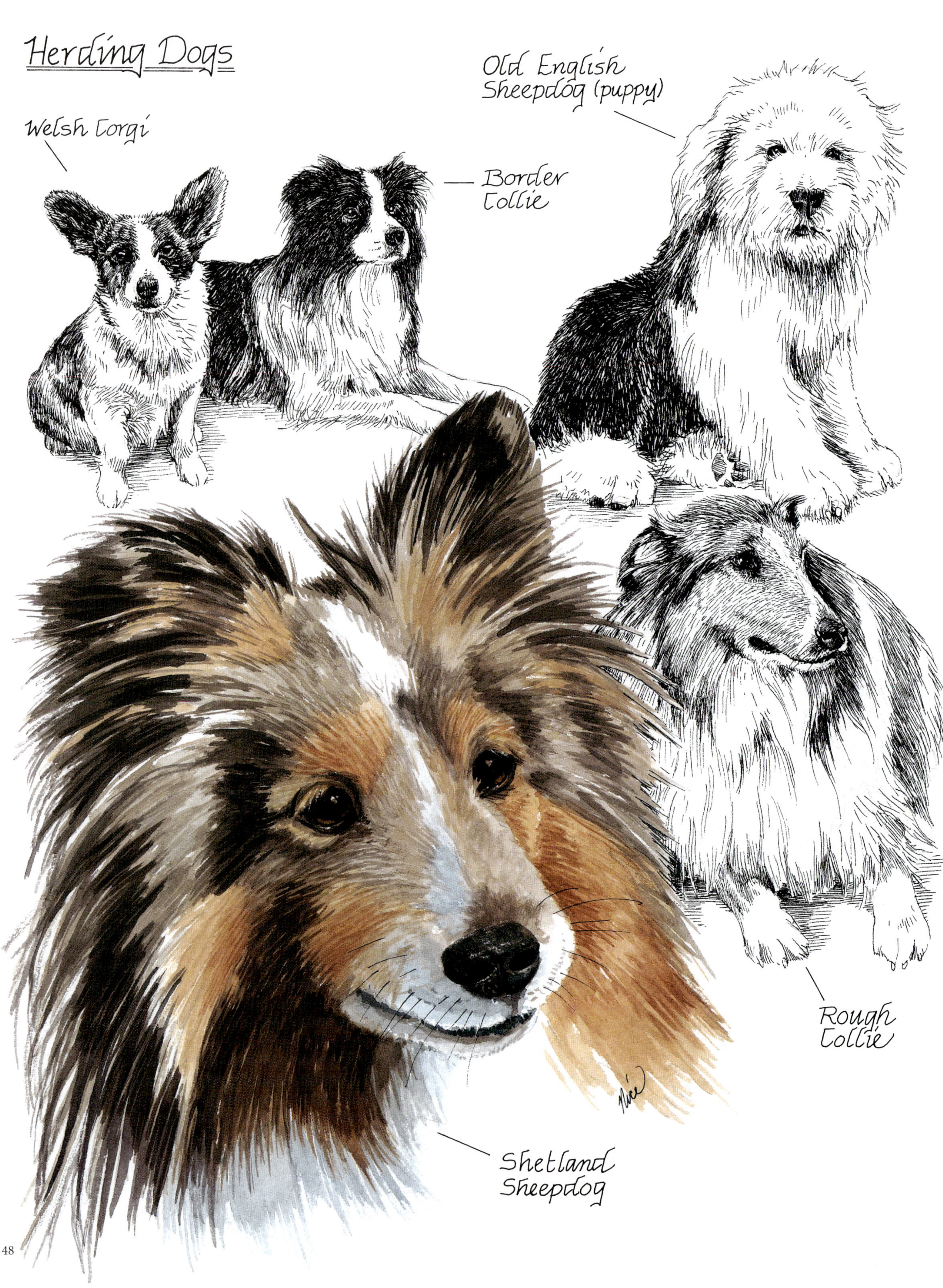
Herding Dogs
Old English
Sheepdog (puppy)
Welsh Corgi
Border
Collie
Rough
Collie
Shetland
Sheepdog

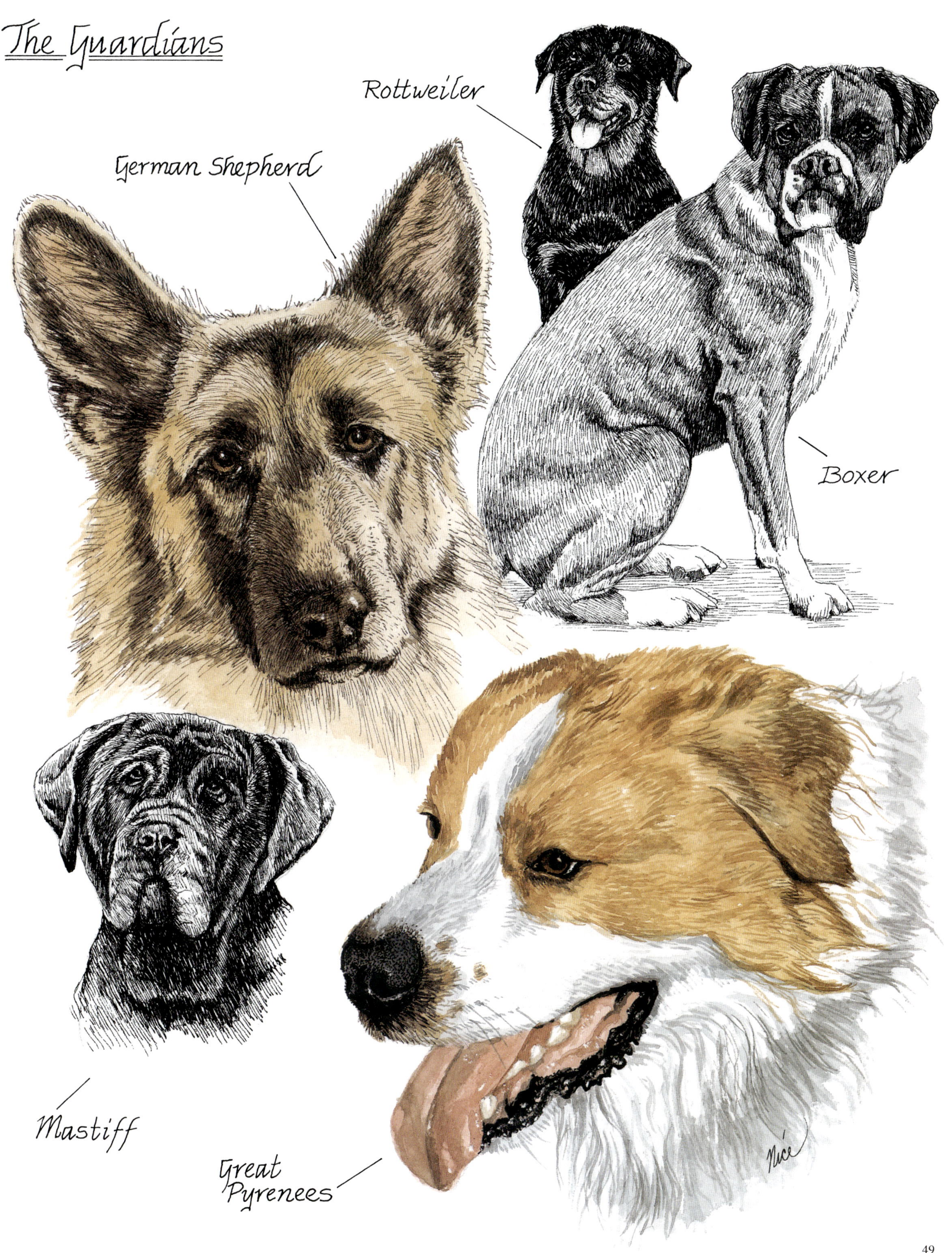
The Guardians
Rottweiler
German Shepherd
Boxer
Mastiff
Great Pyrenees

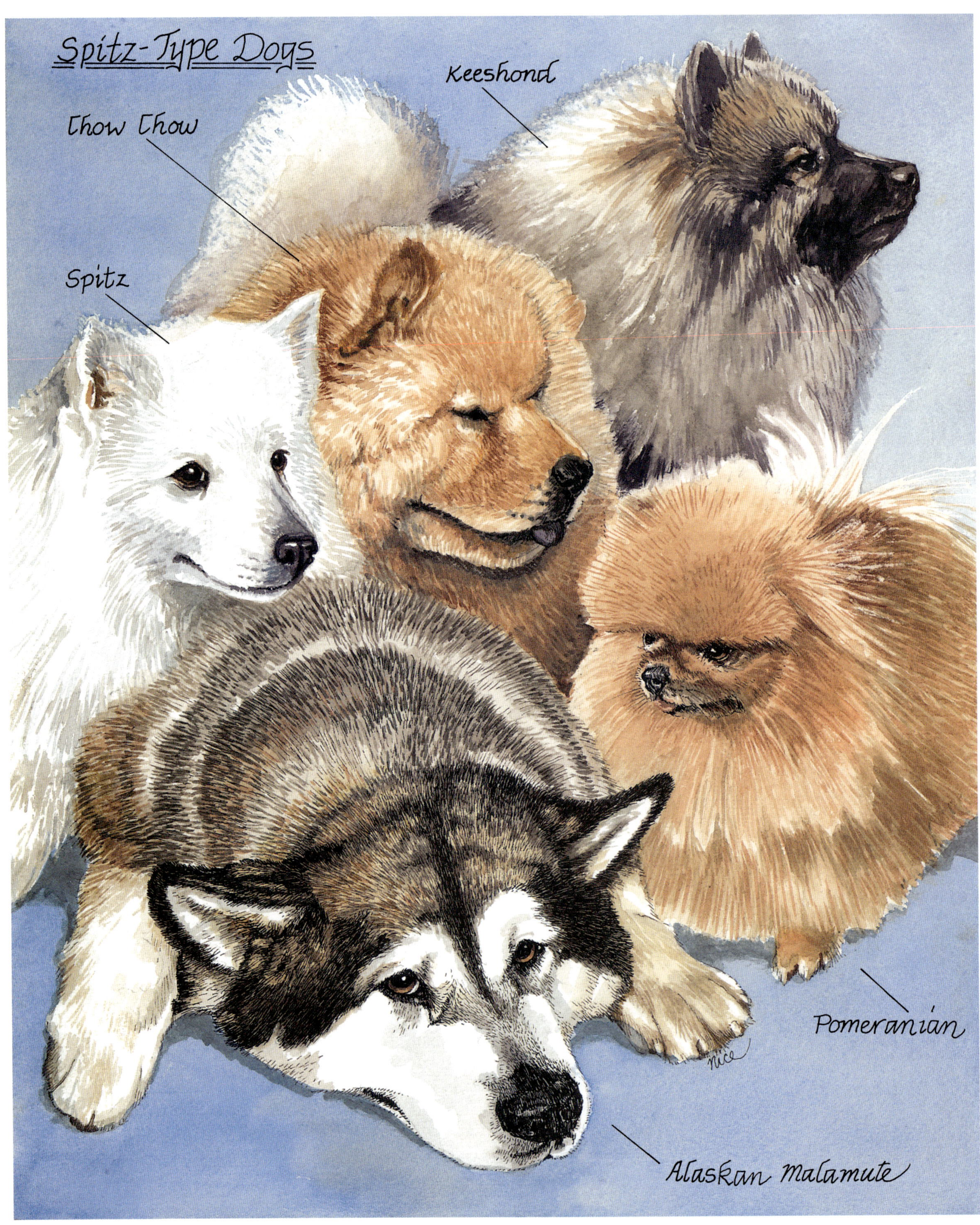
Spitz-Type Dogs
Keeshond
Chow Chow
Spitz
Pomeranian
Alaskan Malamute

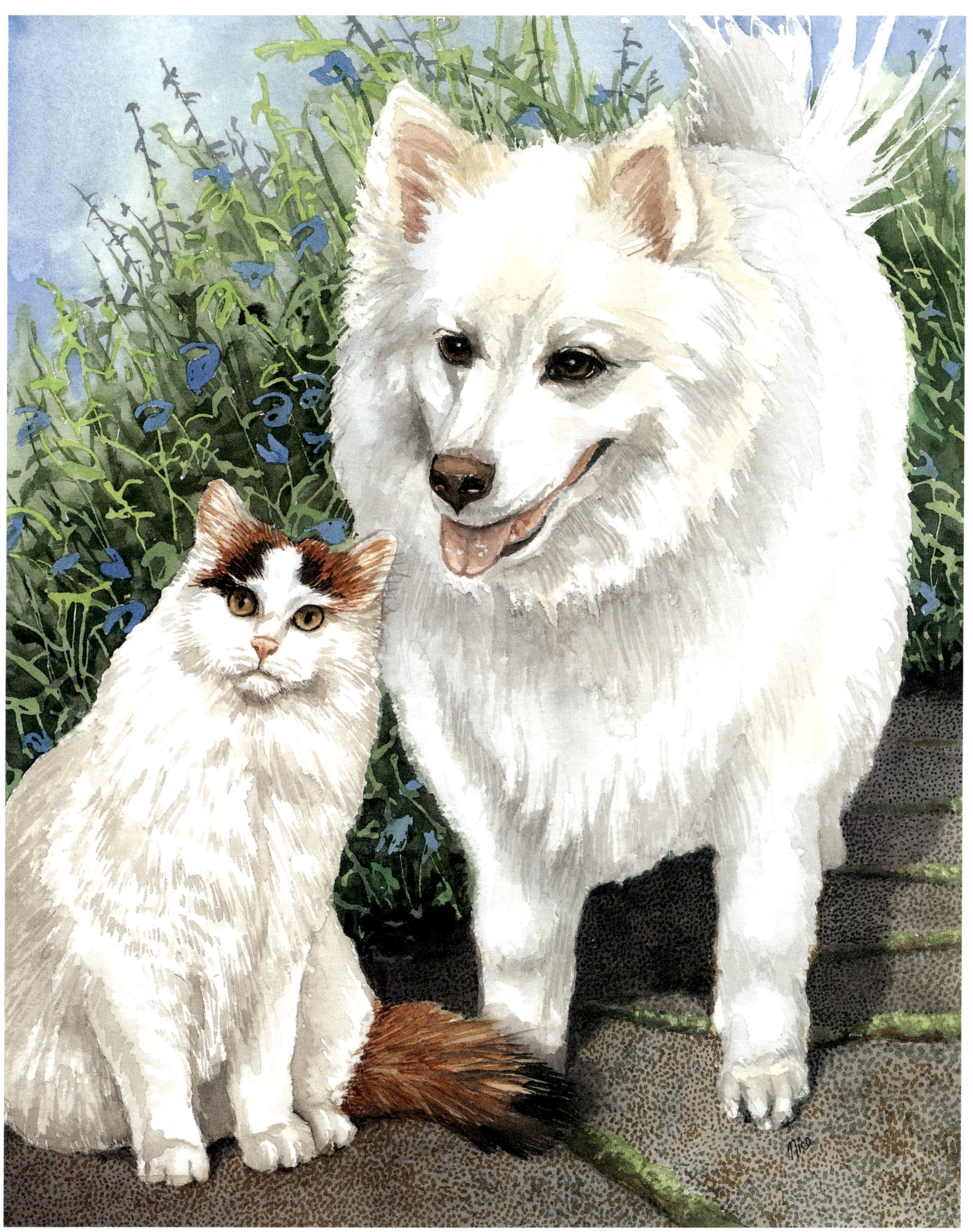

FRIENDS 8" x 10" (20.5cm x 25.5cm) Watercolor, with Pitt Brush Pen stippling on the foreground. The painting features an American Eskimo dog and a van-patterned cat. Van coloration is a white cat with patches of color above the eyes and a colored tail.

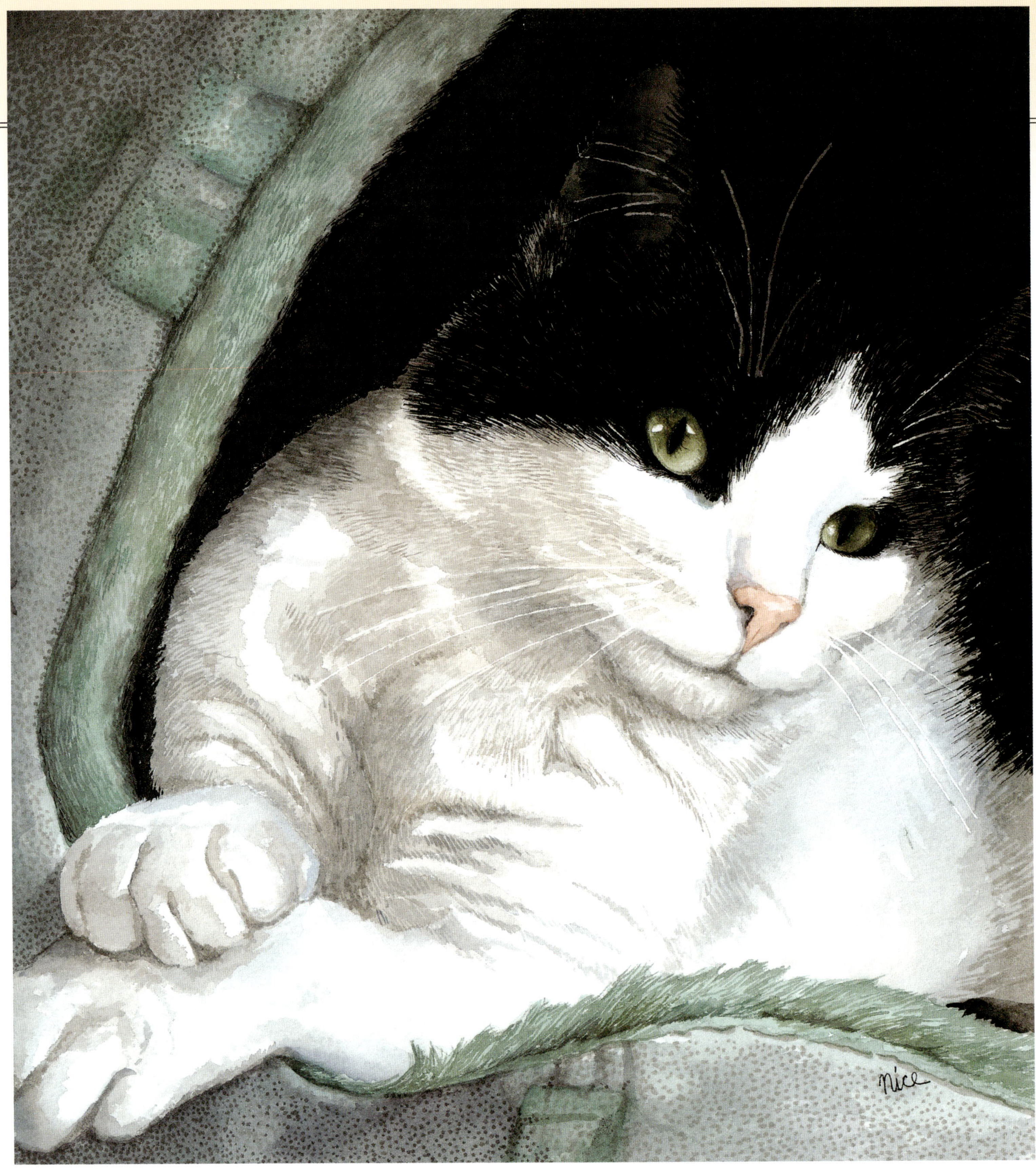

CATZILLA AT REST 8" x 9" (20.5cm x 23cm) Watercolor with pen and ink. The interior of the basket is India ink applied with a brush.

CAPTURING THE *character* of the CAT

3

WHEN I WAS A CHILD MY FAMILY ALWAYS HAD CATS and I adored them. I had forgotten how entertaining they could be until a frosty Halloween morning several years ago. I heard a pathetic, persistent yowl coming from the burn pile out by the barn. I found a tiny five week old kitten huddled in the ashes. I have no idea how she got there, as stray cats do not survive long in the mountain wilderness surrounding my home. After a bowl of food and a warm flea bath, my grubby foundling turned out to be a fluffy black and white menace, who quickly cuddled her way into my heart. I named her Sassy Catzilla. I was recovering from cancer at the time and her antics were just what I needed to lift my spirits. She made a great subject. You will find her likeness on the opposite page and throughout the rest of the chapter. It is true that the best subjects are those we know and love. I hope this chapter will prove helpful in capturing the likeness of the cat in your life.

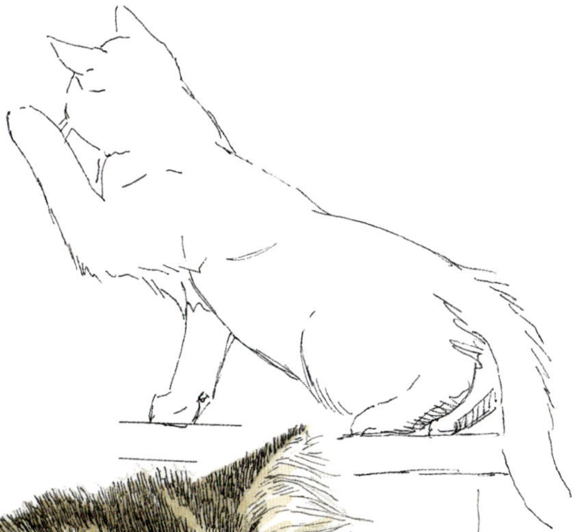

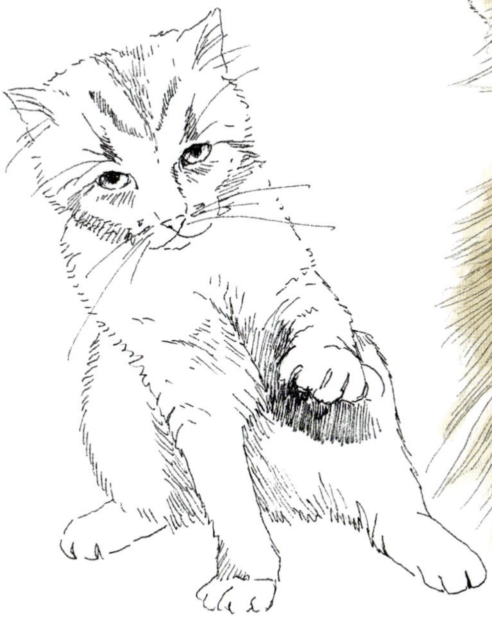

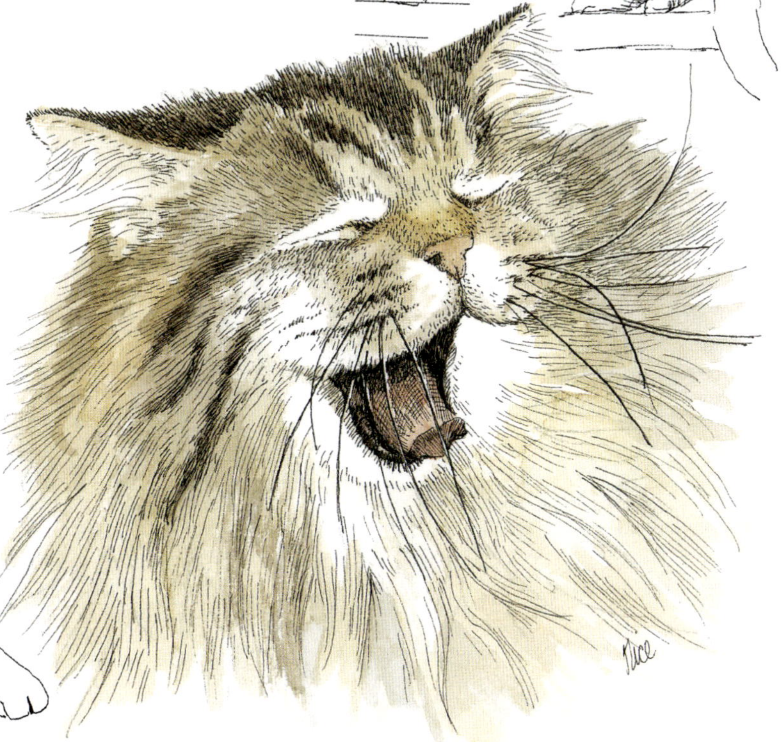

The Shape of the Cat

As you can see in the skull diagram shown below, the head of the cat is fairly oval when seen in profile and rather round when seen from the front. Oriental types have triangular faces, (bottom left.)

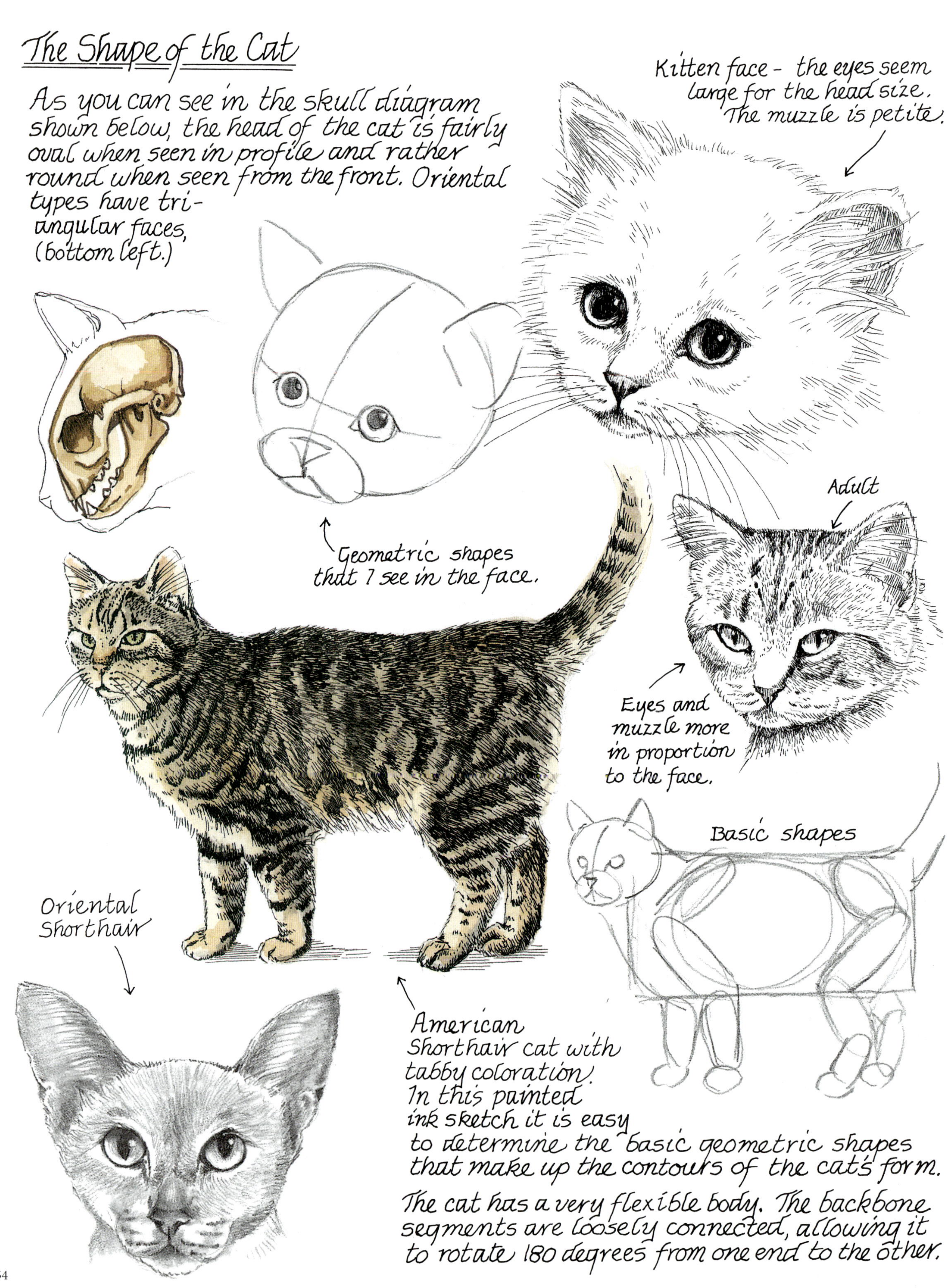

In this painted ink sketch it is easy to determine the basic geometric shapes that make up the contours of the cat's form.

The cat has a very flexible body. The backbone segments are loosely connected, allowing it to rotate 180 degrees from one end to the other.

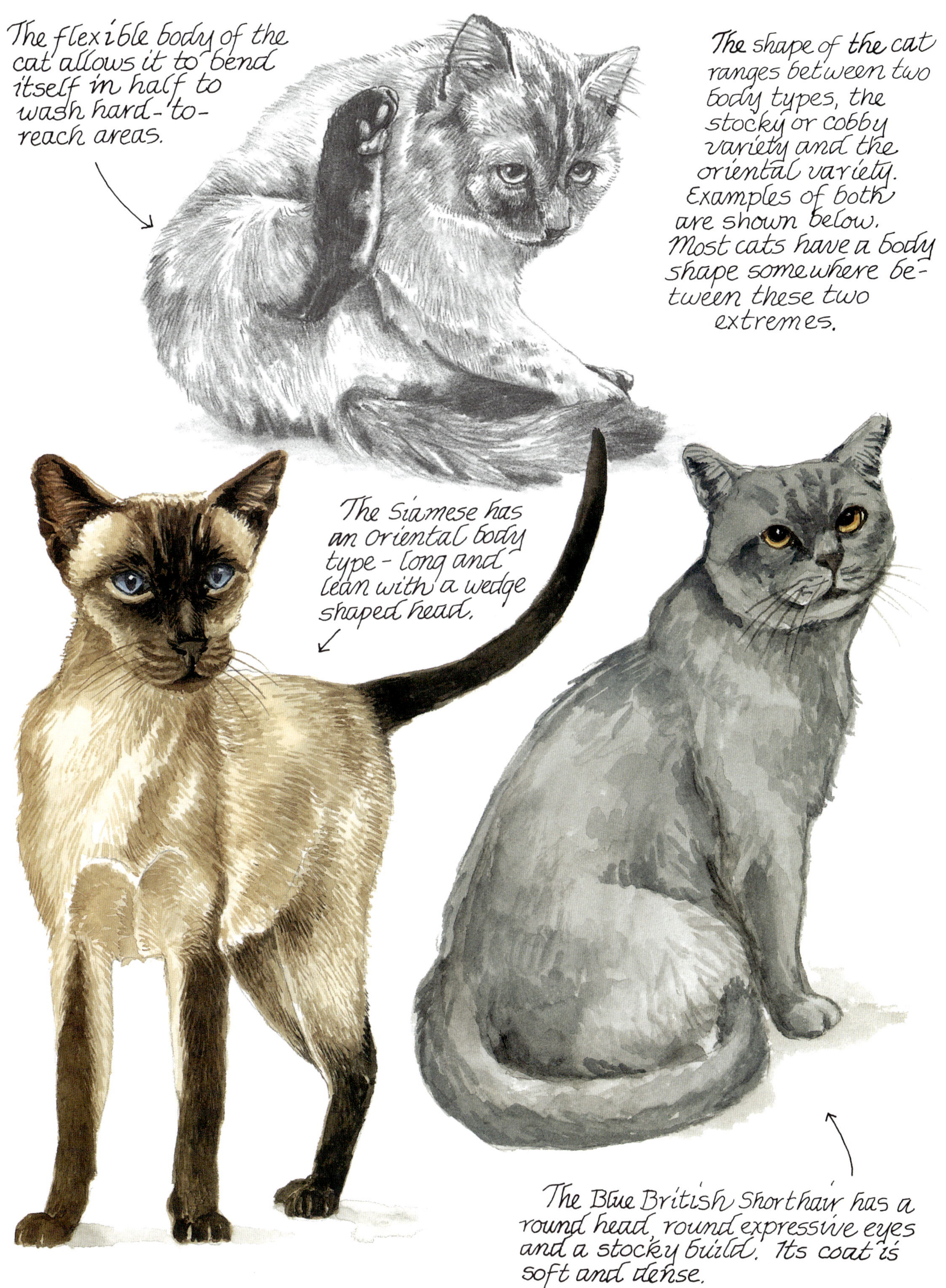
The flexible body of the cat allows it to bend itself in half to wash hard-to-reach areas.
The shape of the cat ranges between two body types, the stocky or cobby variety and the oriental variety. Examples of both are shown below. Most cats have a body shape somewhere between these two extremes.
The Siamese has an oriental body type - long and lean with a wedge shaped head.
The Blue British Shorthair has a round head, round expressive eyes and a stocky build. Its coat is soft and dense.

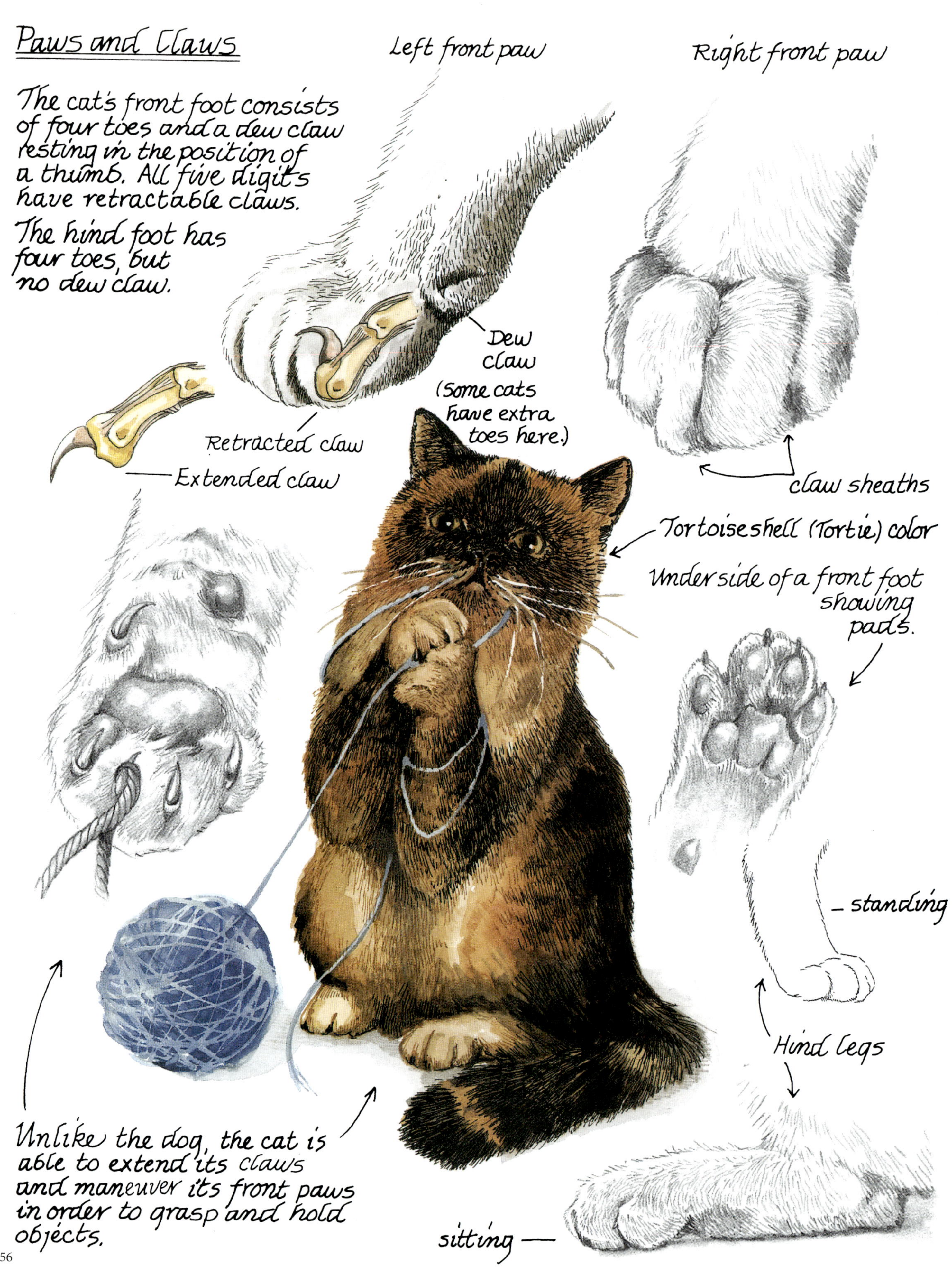
Paws and Claws
The cat's front foot consists of four toes and a dew claw resting in the position of a thumb. All five digits have retractable claws.
The hind foot has four toes, but no dew claw.
Left front paw
Right front paw
Dew claw
(Some cats have extra toes here.)
Retracted claw
Extended claw
claw sheaths
Tortoiseshell (Tortie) color
Underside of a front foot showing pads.
standing
Hind legs
sitting
Unlike the dog, the cat is able to extend its claws and maneuver its front paws in order to grasp and hold objects.

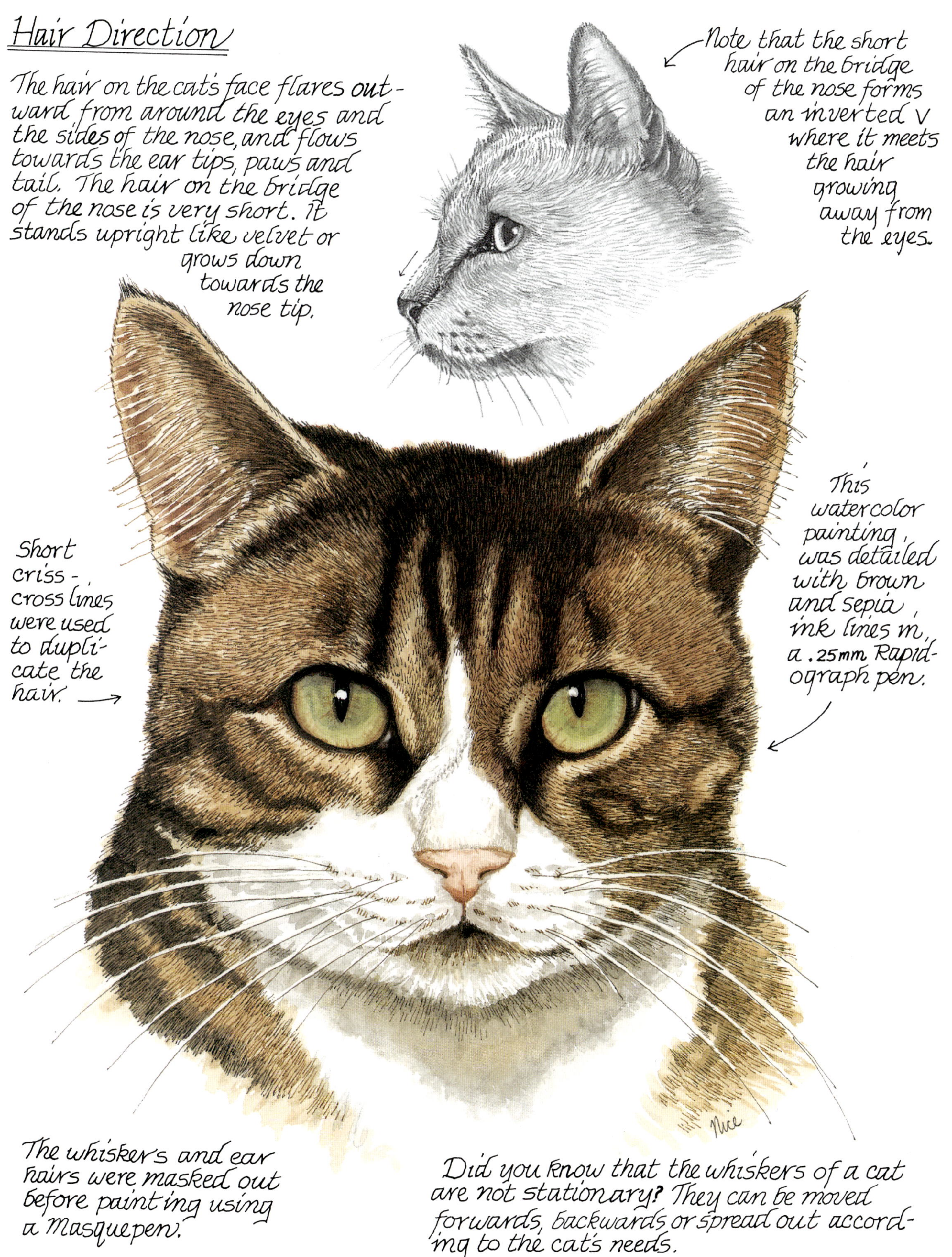

Hair Direction
The hair on the cat's face flares outward from around the eyes and the sides of the nose, and flows towards the ear tips, paws and tail. The hair on the bridge of the nose is very short. It stands upright like velvet or grows down towards the nose tip.
Note that the short hair on the bridge of the nose forms an inverted V where it meets the hair growing away from the eyes.
Short criss-cross lines were used to duplicate the hair.
This watercolor painting was detailed with brown and sepia ink lines in a .25mm Rapidograph pen.
Nice
The whiskers and ear hairs were masked out before painting using a Masquepen.
Did you know that the whiskers of a cat are not stationary? They can be moved forwards, backwards or spread out according to the cat's needs.

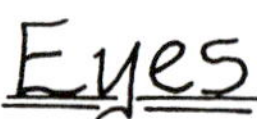

Eyes

In strong light, the pupil in a cat's eye is a vertical slit. As the light dims, the pupil widens, becoming circular.

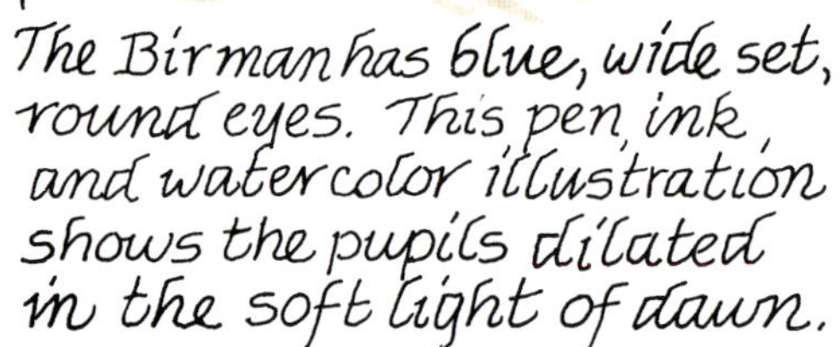

The Birman has blue, wide set, round eyes. This pen, ink and watercolor illustration shows the pupils dilated in the soft light of dawn.

The Exotic Shorthaired Persian has prominent, round eyes.

The Oriental Shorthair has slanted, almond shaped eyes. Note the pupils, constricted by strong light.

A cat's pupils can also dilate when it's excited or frightened.

(.25 mm pen)

Side view of a Russian Blue cat painted in watercolor.

Step-by-step example

① Pencil sketch

② Preliminary watercolor washes.

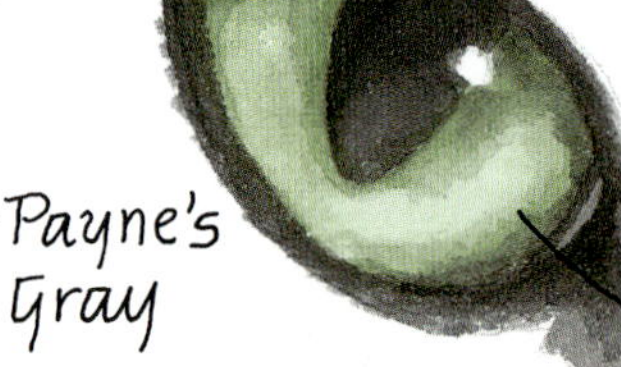

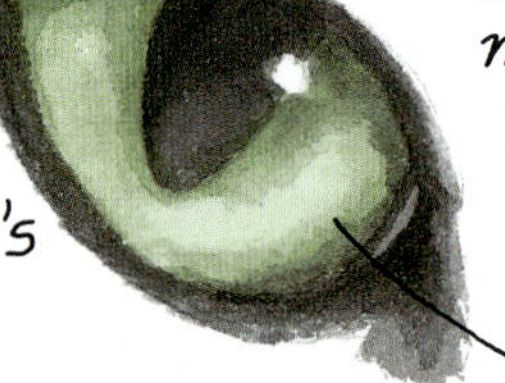

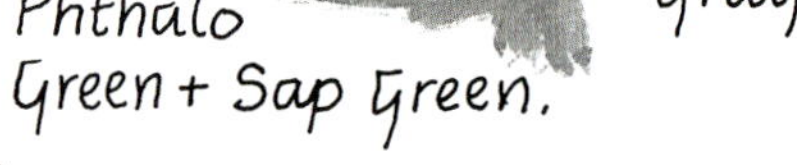

Phthalo Green + Sap Green.

Payne's Gray

③ Blend more paint into shadow areas.

④ Glaze with thin red-orange wash.

⑤ Add fine details.

Scratch in highlights on lower eye lid.

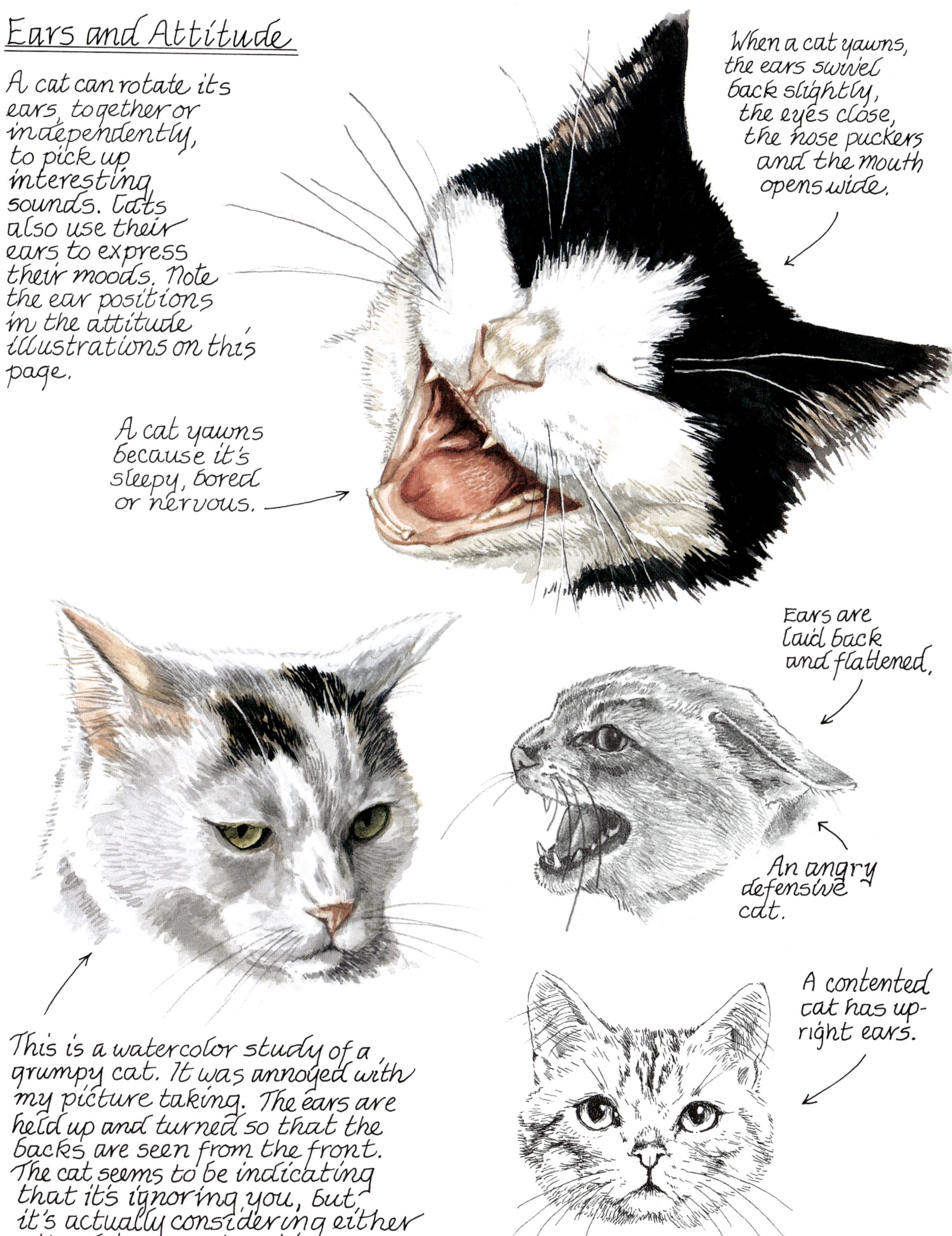
Ears and Attitude
A cat can rotate its ears, together or independently, to pick up interesting sounds. Cats also use their ears to express their moods. Note the ear positions in the attitude illustrations on this page.
When a cat yawns, the ears swivel back slightly, the eyes close, the nose puckers and the mouth opens wide.
A cat yawns because it's sleepy, bored or nervous.
Ears are laid back and flattened.
An angry defensive cat.
A contented cat has upright ears.
This is a watercolor study of a grumpy cat. It was annoyed with my picture taking. The ears are held up and turned so that the backs are seen from the front. The cat seems to be indicating that it's ignoring you, but it's actually considering either attacking or retreating.

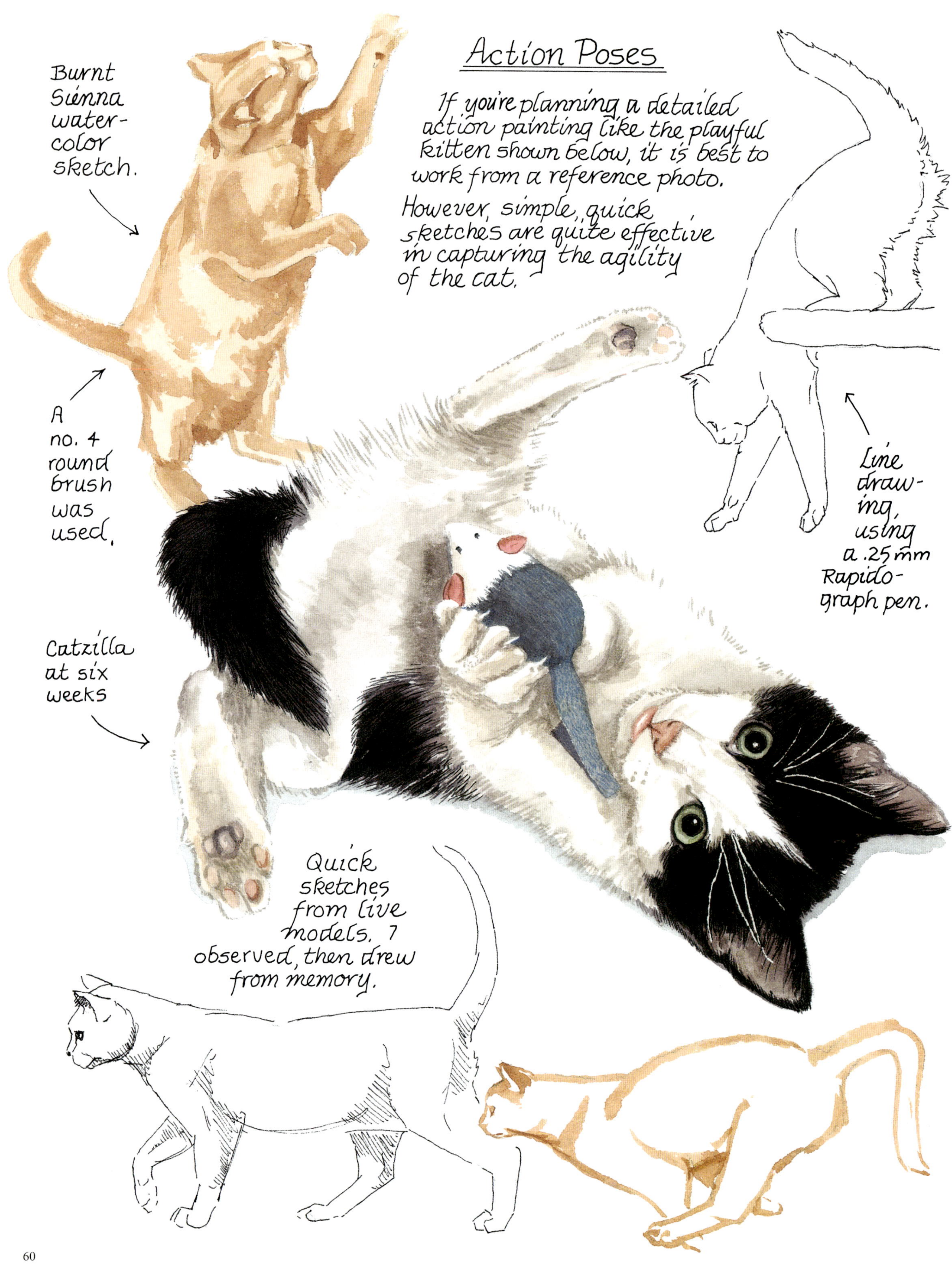
Action Poses
If you're planning a detailed action painting like the playful kitten shown below, it is best to work from a reference photo.
However, simple, quick sketches are quite effective in capturing the agility of the cat.
Burnt Sienna water-color sketch.
A no. 4 round brush was used.
Line drawing, using a .25 mm Rapidograph pen.
Catzilla at six weeks
Quick sketches from live models. I observed, then drew from memory.

The Sleeping Cat

The cat spends two-thirds of its life sleeping. It is the easiest pose to catch cats enacting, but not necessarily the easiest pose to draw or paint. The feline is fond of curling and twisting its body into unlikely positions that will give the artist plenty of practice drawing foreshortened limbs and upside-down heads. Keep in mind that the body parts resting beneath the cat will be flattened by the cat's weight.

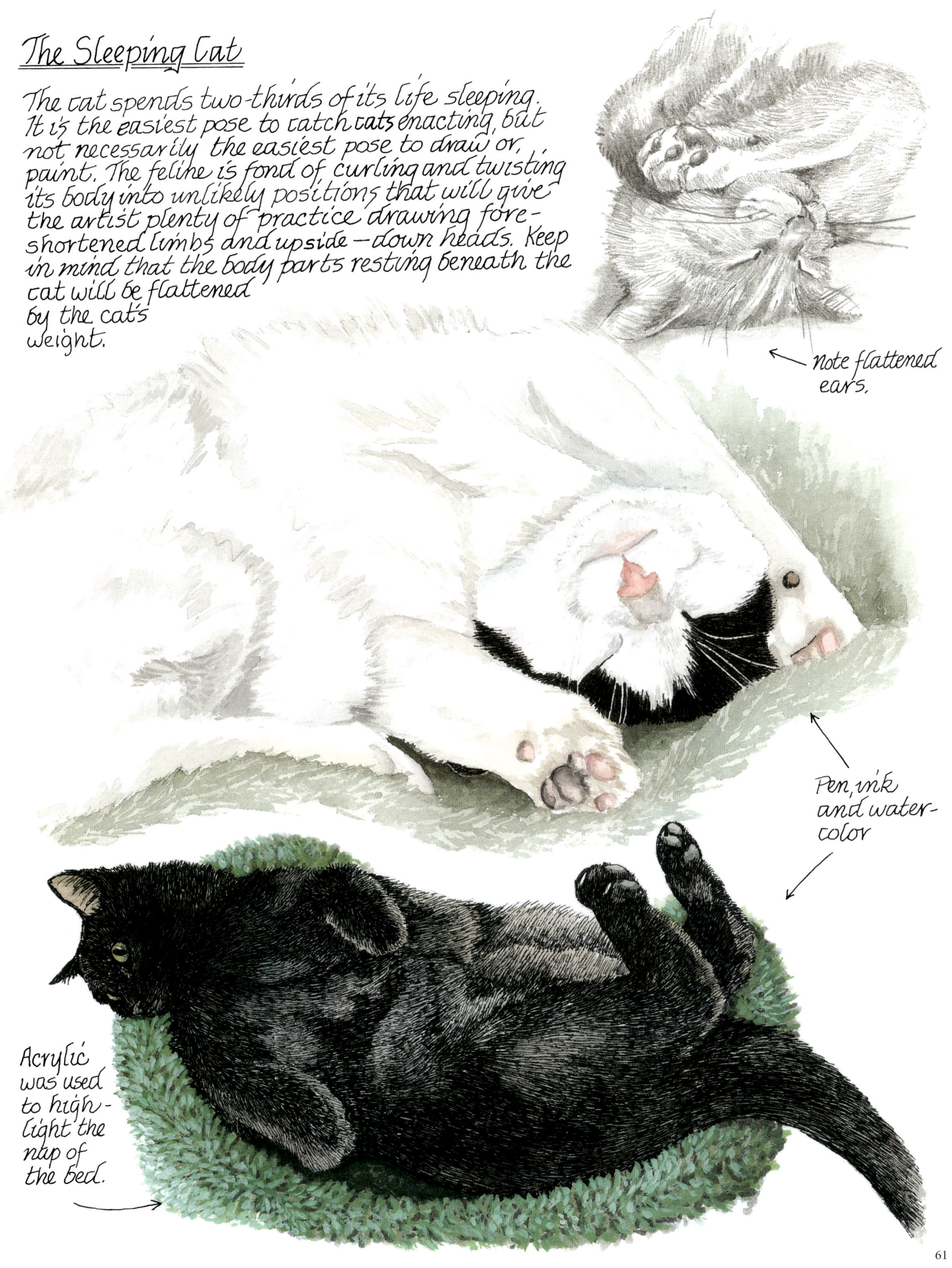

Popular Cat Breeds

The cat breeds on this page come in almost all the typical feline colors and patterns.

Scottish Fold

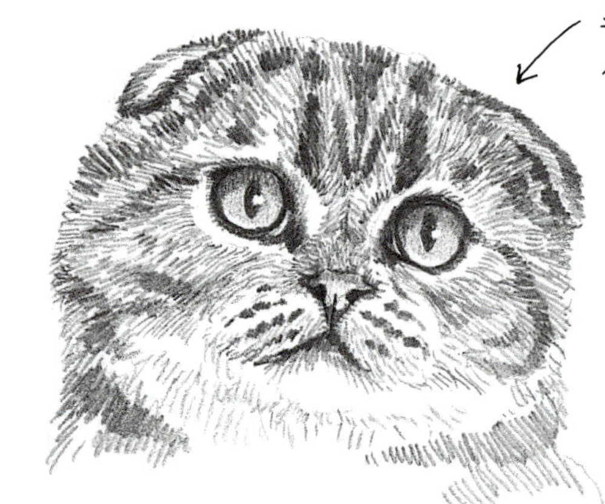

This distinctive breed has a rounded head and ears folded flat against the head.

Manx

This cat has a short tail or most often, no tail at all.

Hind legs are longer than forelegs.

Round face and large round eyes.

American Shorthair

These are large, robust cats.

British Shorthair

This cat is noted for its strong, cobby body and dense coat.

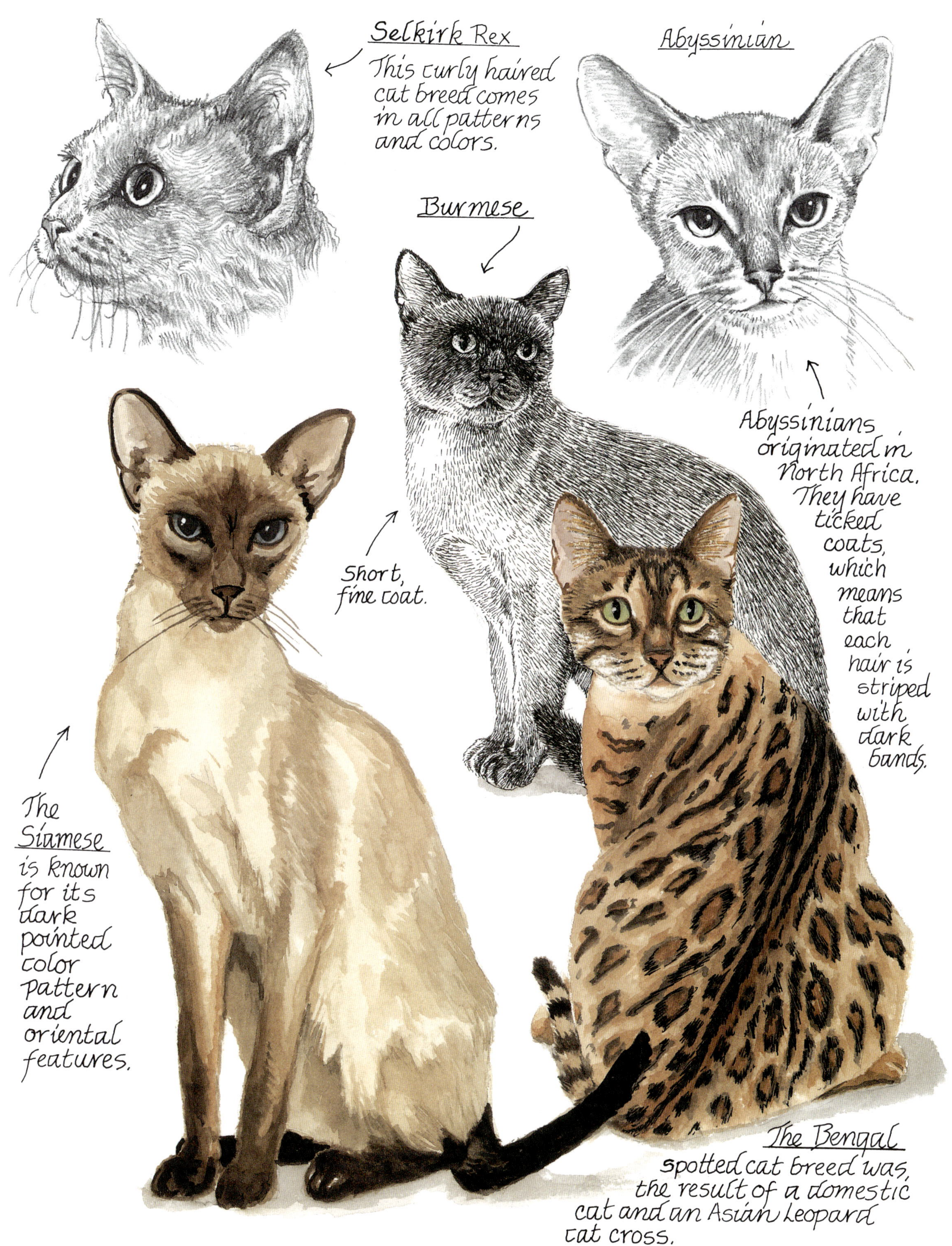
Selkirk Rex
This curly haired cat breed comes in all patterns and colors.
Abyssinian
Burmese
Abyssinians originated in North Africa. They have ticked coats, which means that each hair is striped with dark bands.
Short, fine coat.
The Siamese is known for its dark pointed color pattern and oriental features.
The Bengal
spotted cat breed was the result of a domestic cat and an Asian Leopard cat cross.

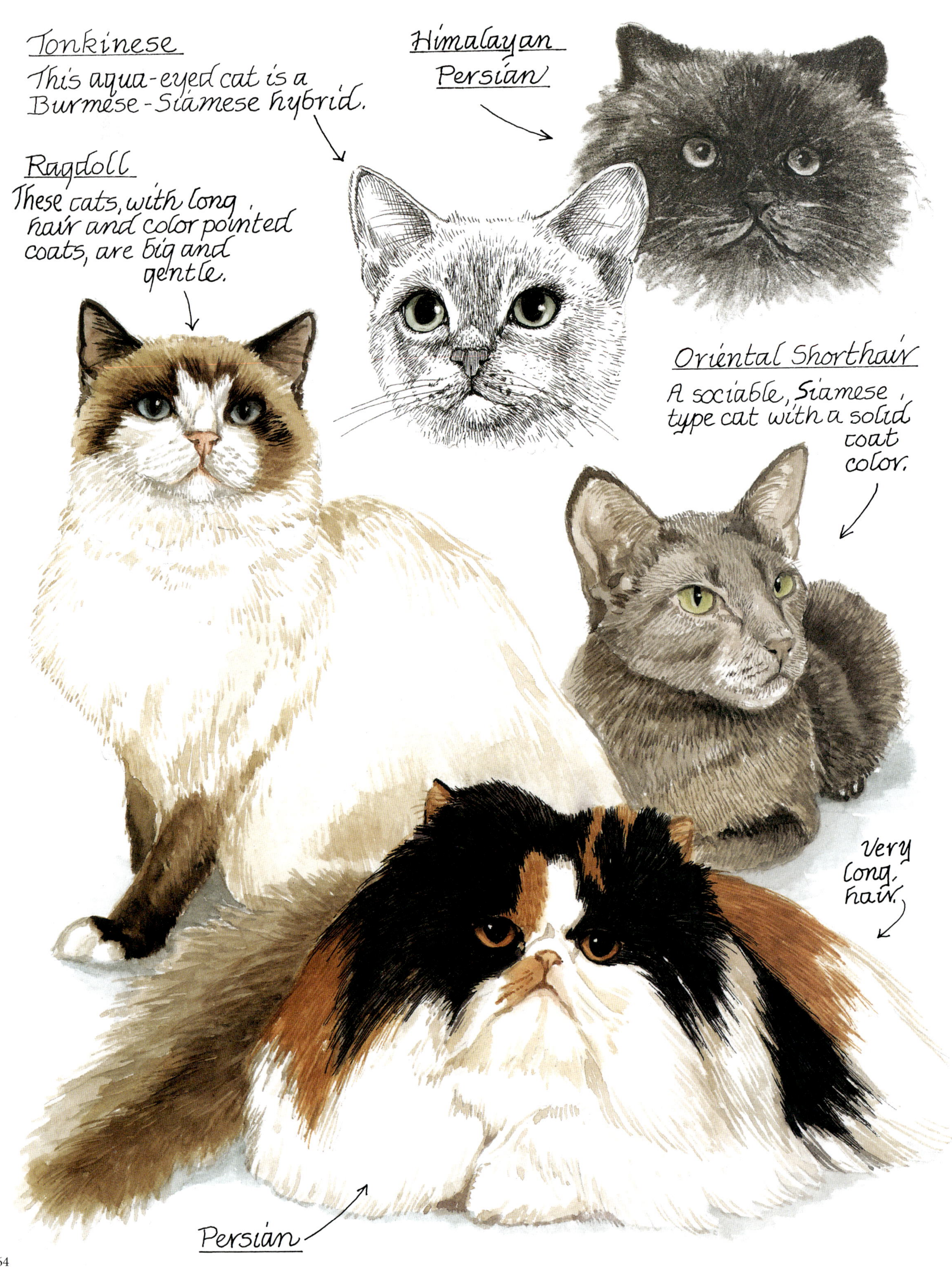
Tonkinese
This aqua-eyed cat is a Burmese-Siamese hybrid.
Himalayan Persian
Ragdoll
These cats, with long hair and color pointed coats, are big and gentle.
Oriental Shorthair
A sociable, Siamese type cat with a solid coat color.
Very long hair.
Persian

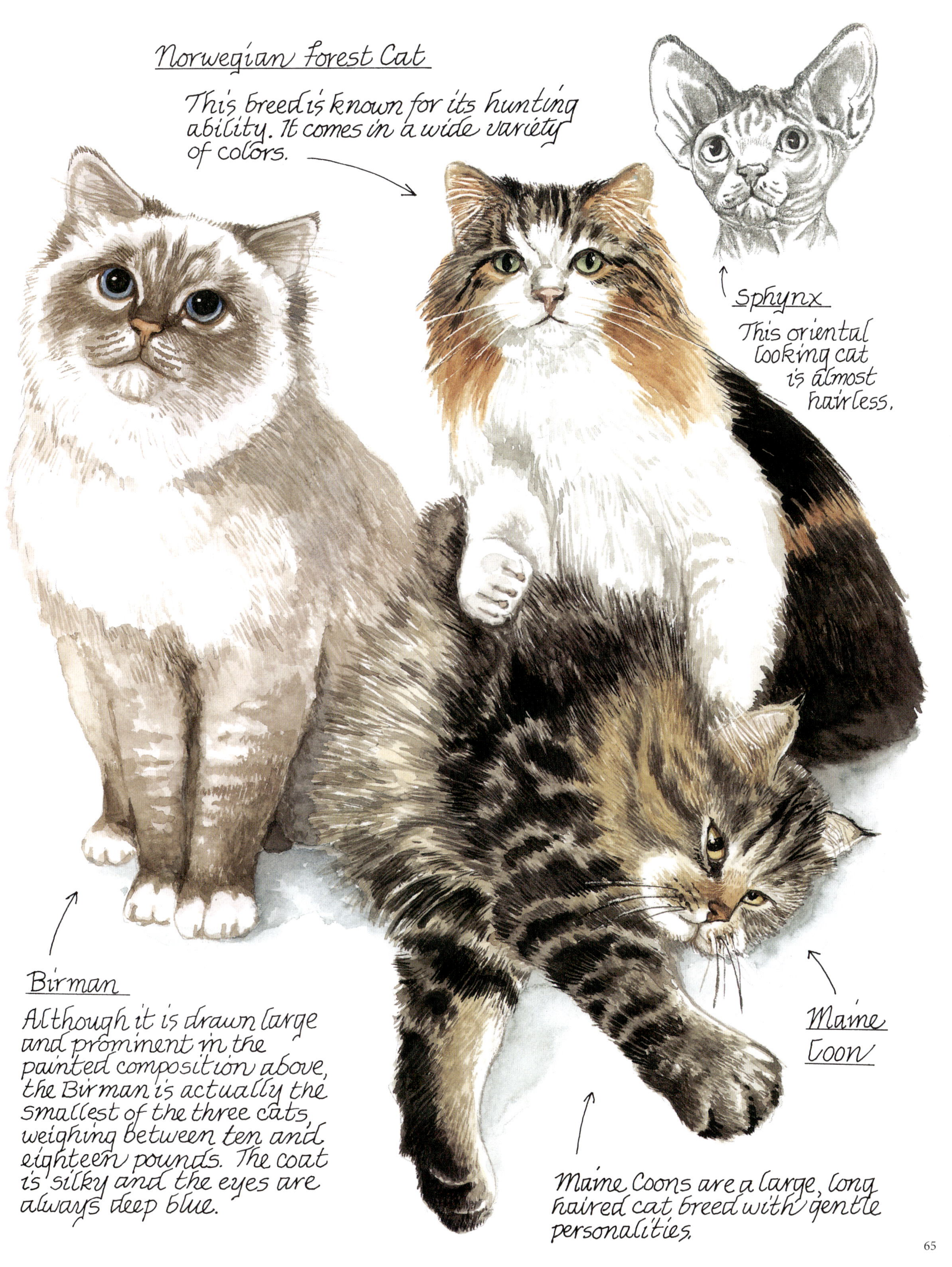
Norwegian Forest Cat
This breed is known for its hunting ability. It comes in a wide variety of colors.
Sphynx
This oriental looking cat is almost hairless.
Birman
Although it is drawn large and prominent in the painted composition above, the Birman is actually the smallest of the three cats, weighing between ten and eighteen pounds. The coat is silky and the eyes are always deep blue.
Maine Coon
Maine Coons are a large, long haired cat breed with gentle personalities.

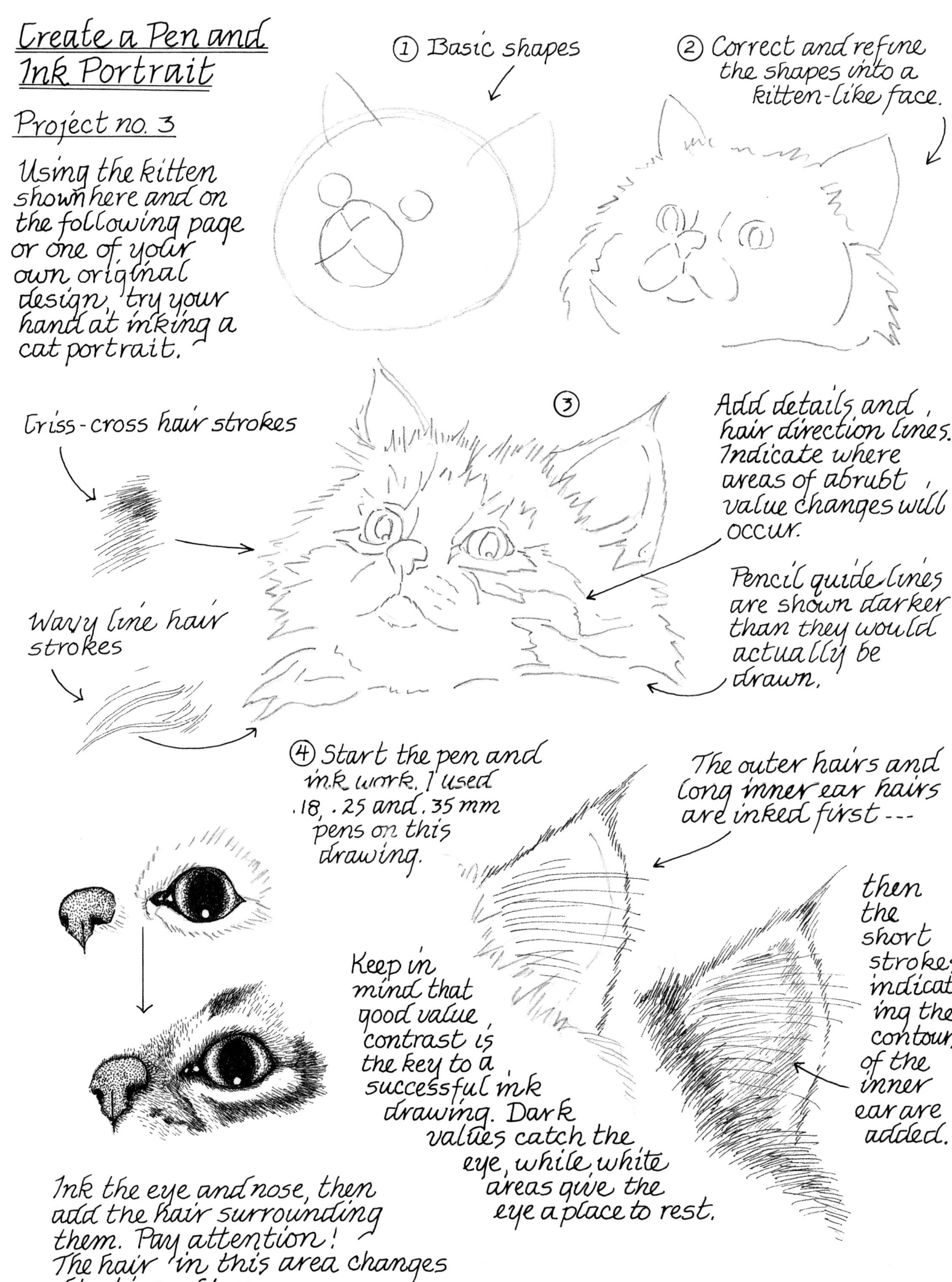
Create a Pen and Ink Portrait
Project no. 3
Using the kitten shown here and on the following page or one of your own original design, try your hand at inking a cat portrait.
① Basic shapes
② Correct and refine the shapes into a kitten-like face.
③
Criss-cross hair strokes
Add details and hair direction lines. Indicate where areas of abrubt value changes will occur.
Pencil guide lines are shown darker than they would actually be drawn.
Wavy line hair strokes
④ Start the pen and ink work. I used .18, .25 and .35 mm pens on this drawing.
The outer hairs and long inner ear hairs are inked first ---
then the short strokes indicating the contours of the inner ear are added.
Keep in mind that good value contrast is the key to a successful ink drawing. Dark values catch the eye, while white areas give the eye a place to rest.
Ink the eye and nose, then add the hair surrounding them. Pay attention! The hair in this area changes direction often.

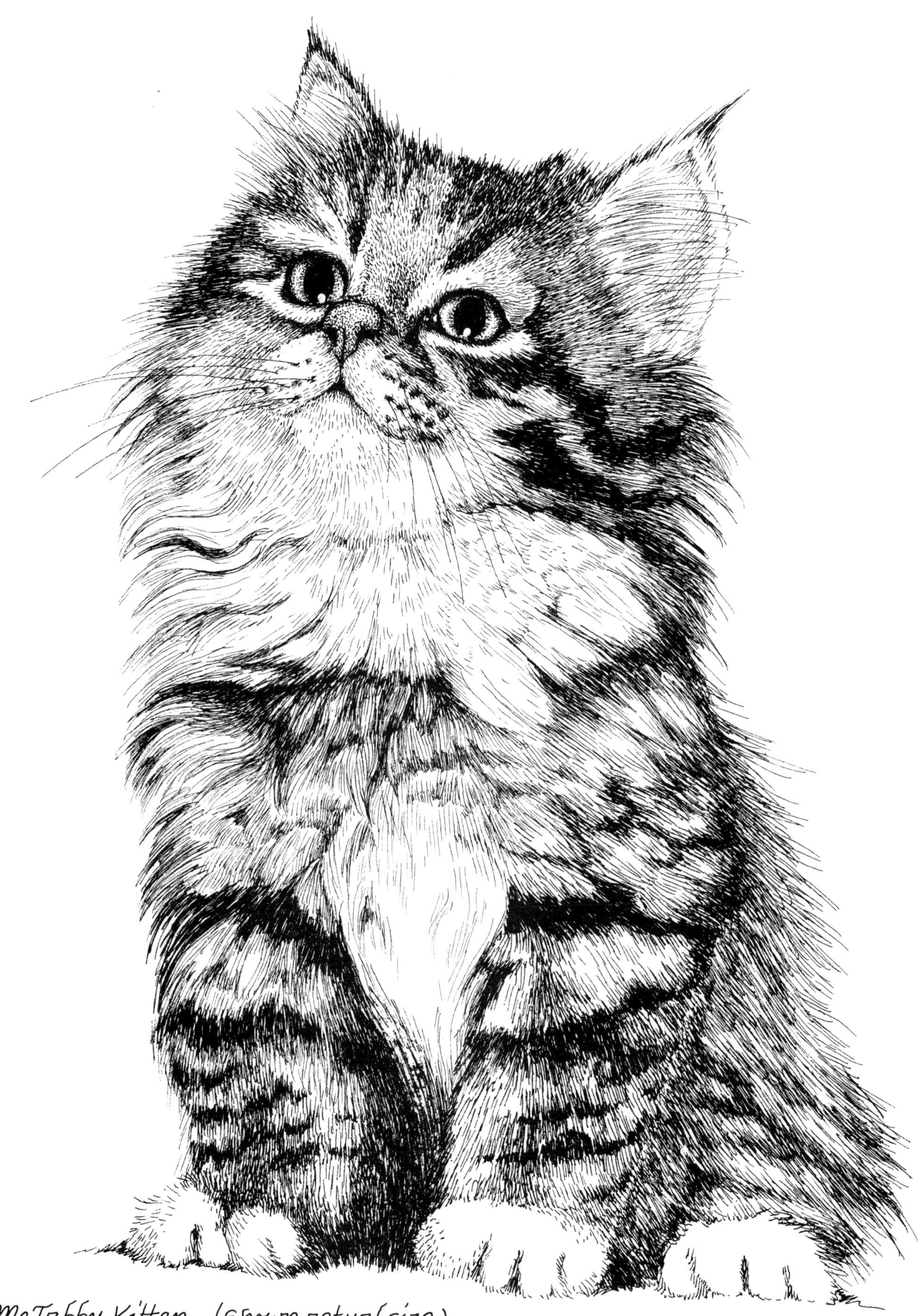

McTabby Kitten (Shown actual size)

A pen and ink drawing of a Siberian kitten, bred by Emerald Forest Siberians. The internet is a good place to find cute animal photos, but don't forget to get permission before copying them.

Watercolor Cat Portrait – Project no. 4

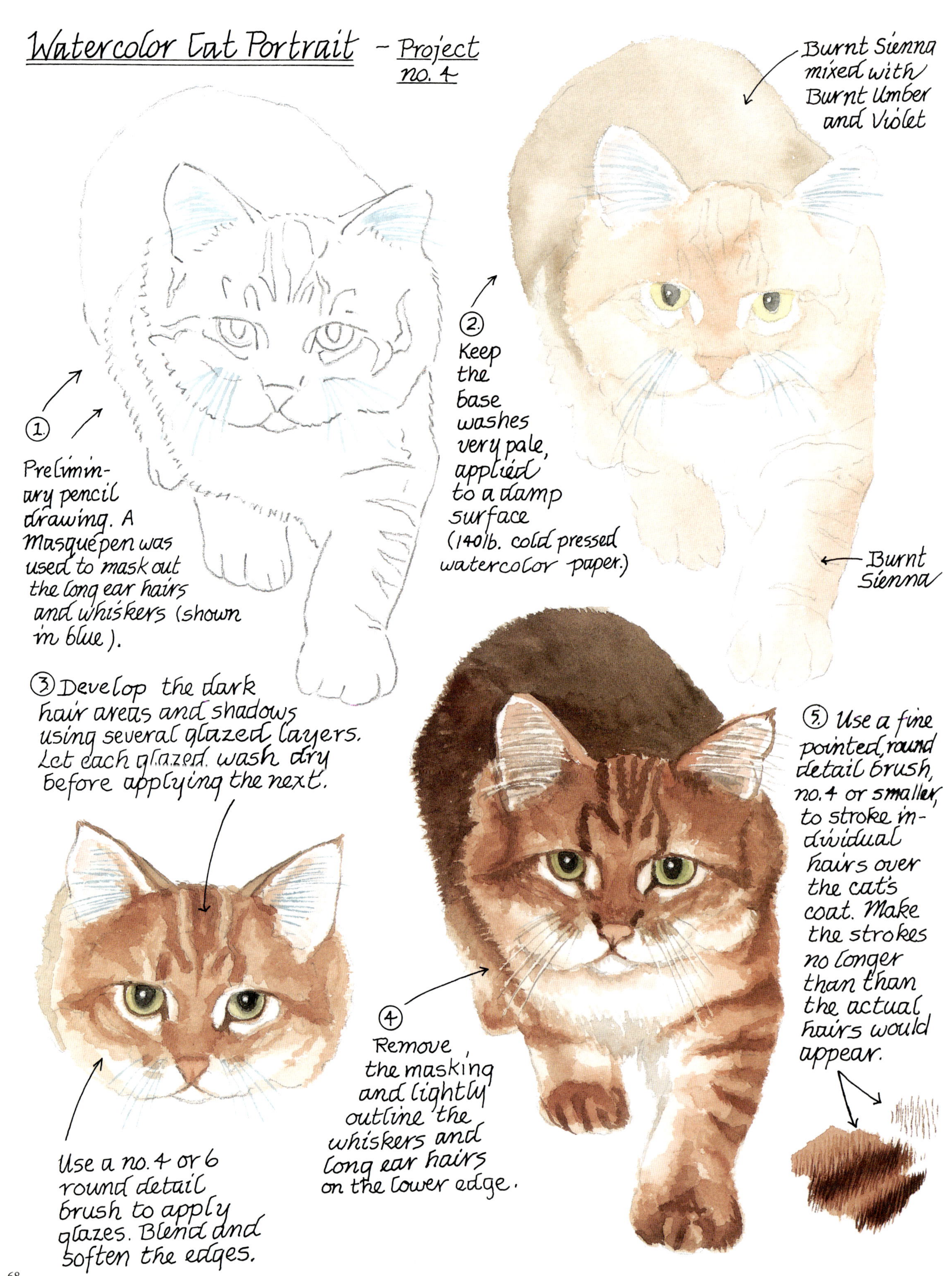

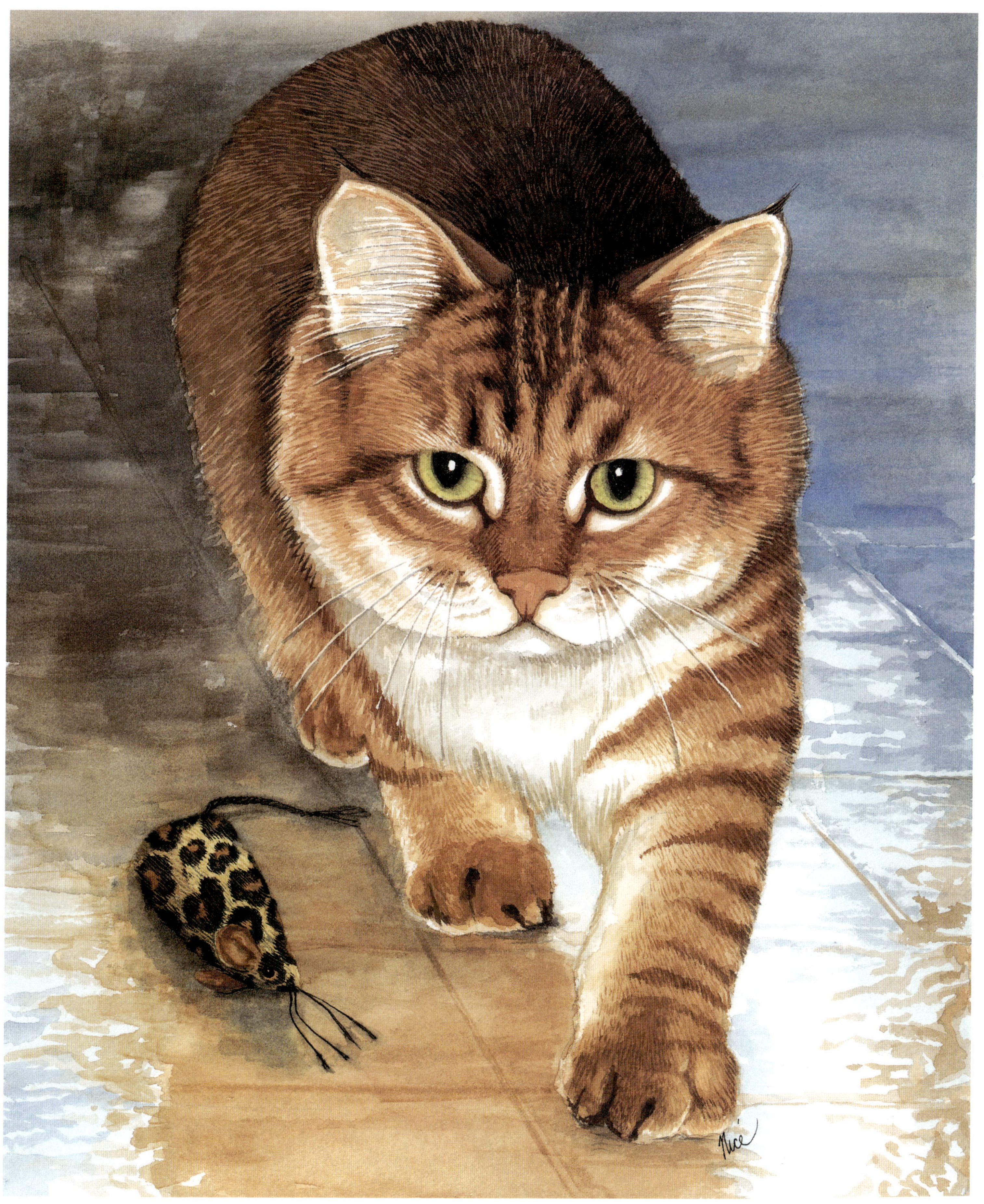

ELIZAVETA, TIGER IN THE KITCHEN 8" x 10" (20.5cm x 25.5cm) Watercolor painting. Painted from a photo supplied by Emerald Forest Siberians.

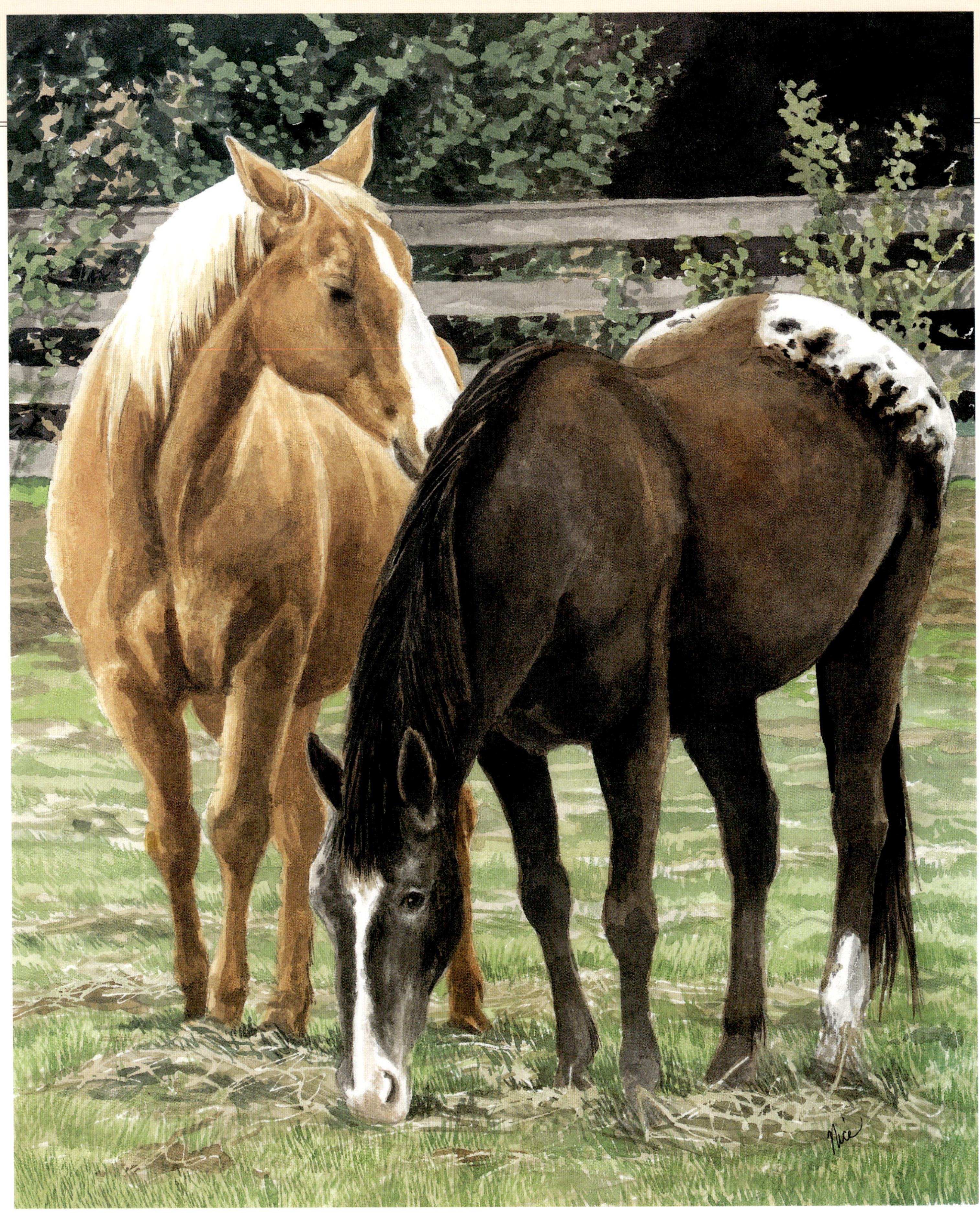

OLD FRIENDS IN SPRING PASTURE 8" x 10" (20.5cm x 25.5cm) Watercolor. The horse on the left is Sundancer's Dare, a palomino Quarter Horse/American Saddlebred gelding. The dark spotted mare is an Appaloosa (American Indian Horse Registry). Her name is Lady Ta Wi.

THE *elegant* EQUINE

4

AS A CHILD, I WAS AS HORSE CRAZY as any little girl could be. We didn't have a place where I could keep a horse of my own, but I spent endless hours galloping up and down the sidewalks with my friends, mounted on "stick horses." A good portion of my allowance was put towards hours at the riding stable. I collected horse statues; read about horses, and of course, I drew them. I saw them in my mind as powerful, majestic creatures, with noble, sculptured heads, rippling muscles and flowing manes and tails. The horses I drew were rather blocky creatures, with disproportioned heads and legs. However, I did manage the flowing manes and tails, guaranteed to trip any horse unfortunate enough to grow them that long. The general method I used to draw a horse was to begin with one of the ears, proceed around the head and then down the neck and around the rest of the body. With any luck, I would end up with the second ear somewhere in the vicinity of the first ear. Since then, I have increased my observation skills and developed better ways to draw a lifelike, believable horse. In this chapter I will share these drawing discoveries with you.

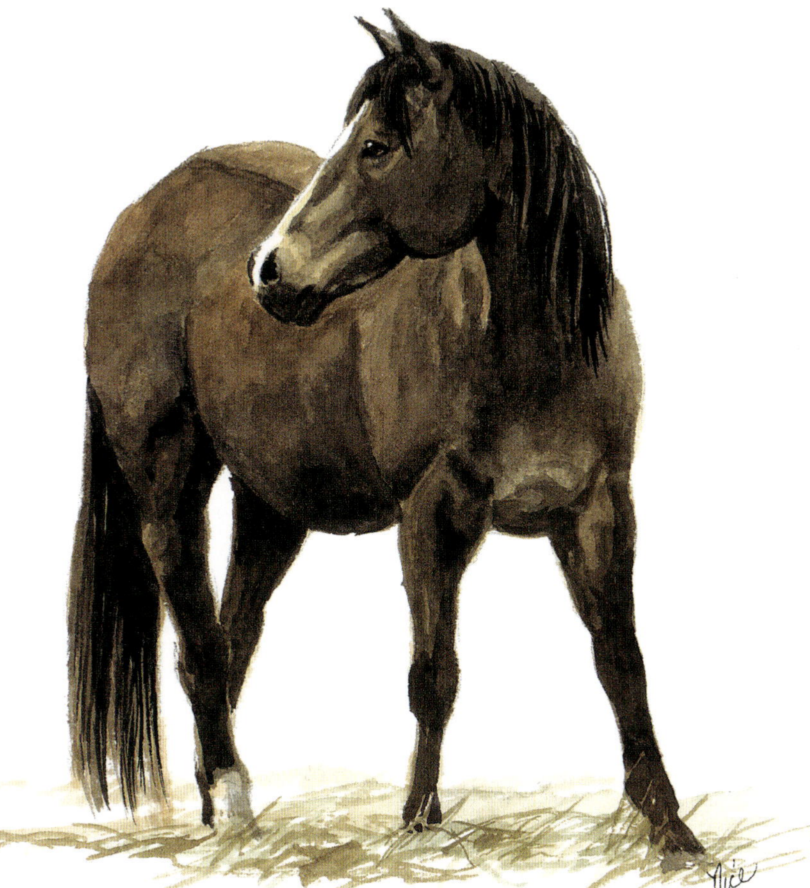

Smokey Doe - a dun colored Quarter Horse mare.

Conformation

In order to draw or paint a realistic horse one needs to become familiar with the body parts and how they relate to each other. In a well formed horse, the length of the head (marked with red lines in the drawing below) should be the same as the girth measurement. It should also equal the length of the hind leg from the hock to the ground, from the hock to the stifle, from the stifle to the point of the croup and the front legs from the chestnut to the ground. Although most horses don't quite measure up to these standards, it provides a good base for checking the proportions of your equine renderings.

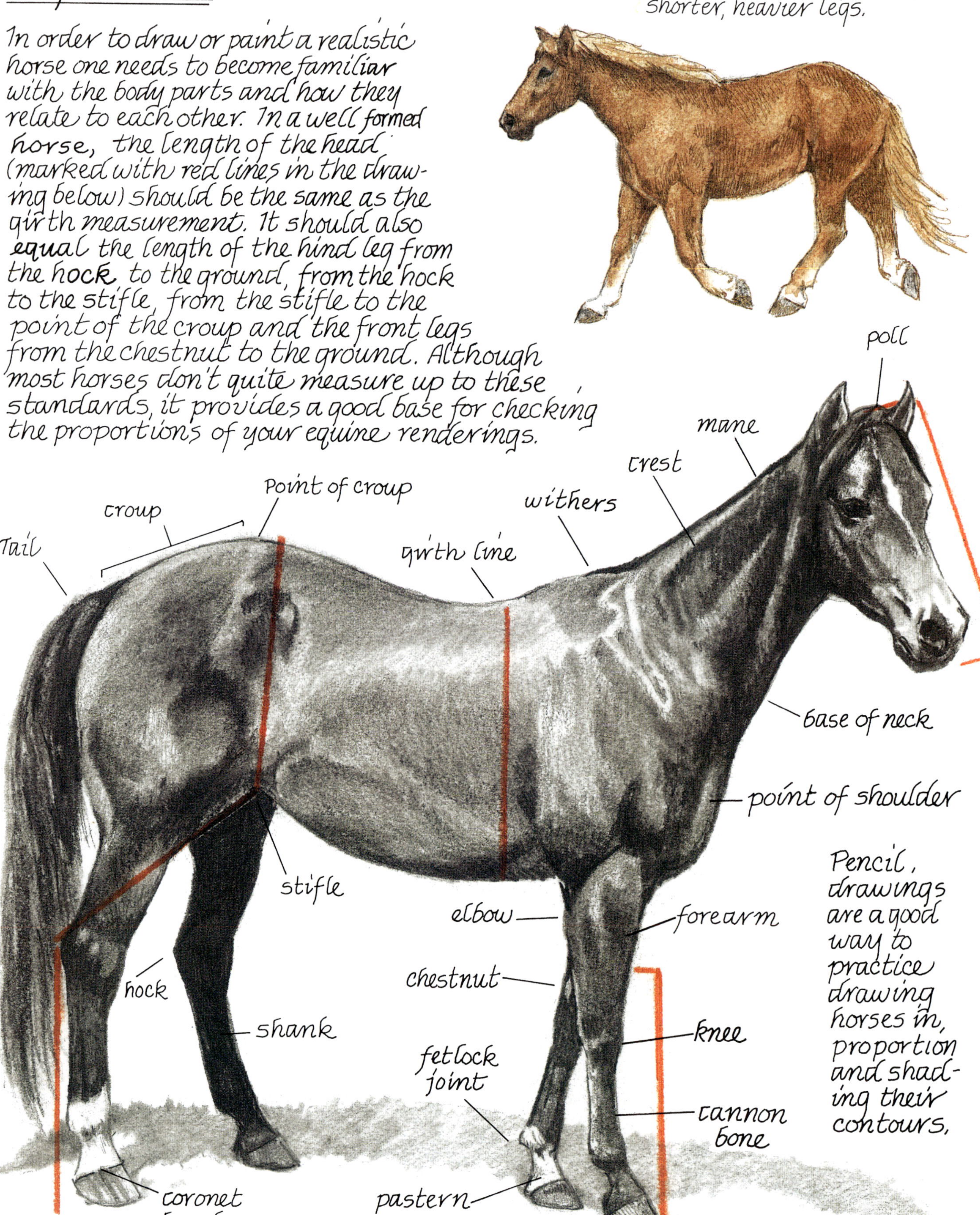

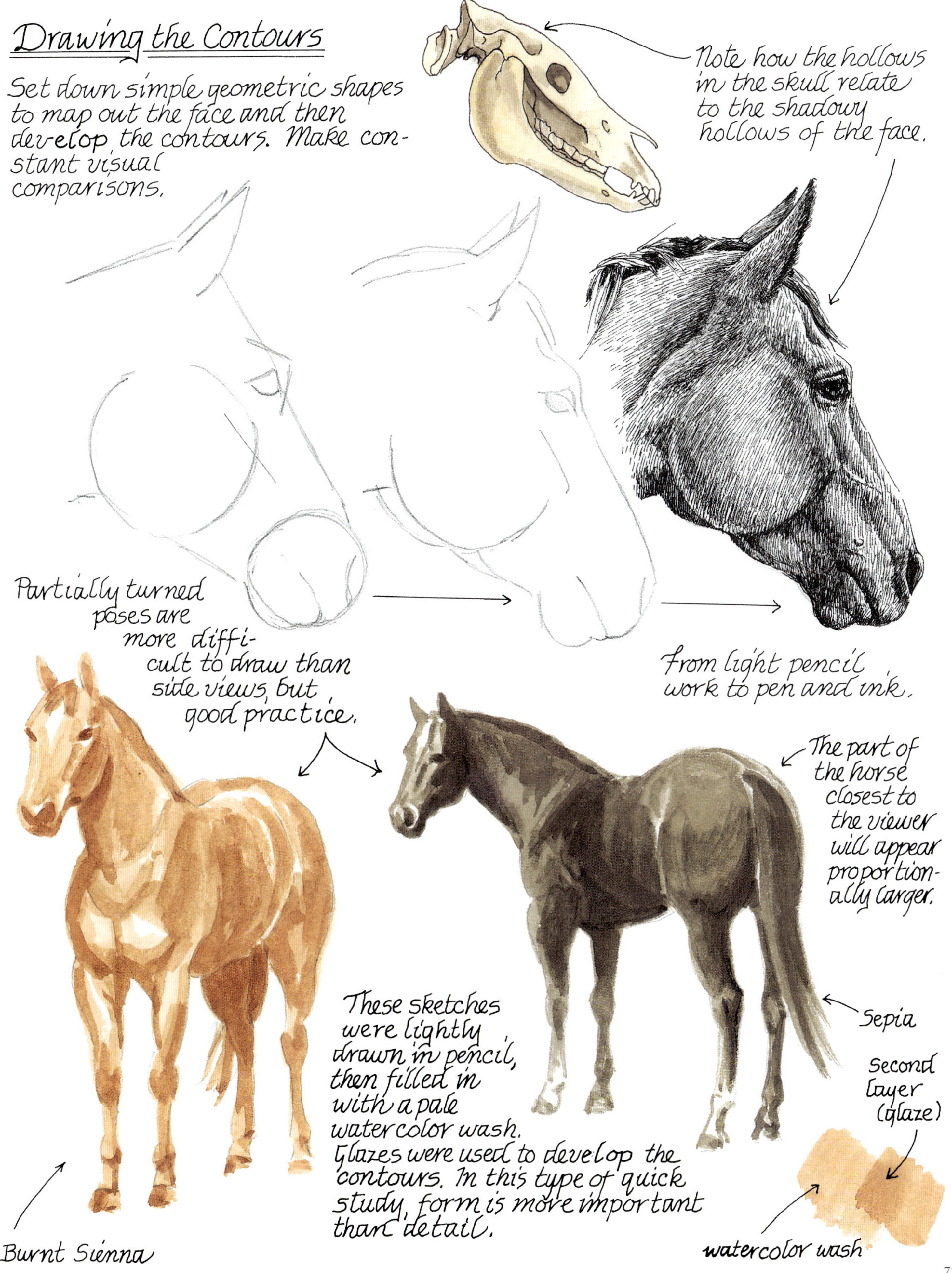
Drawing the Contours
Set down simple geometric shapes to map out the face and then develop the contours. Make constant visual comparisons.
Note how the hollows in the skull relate to the shadowy hollows of the face.
Partially turned poses are more difficult to draw than side views, but good practice.
From light pencil work to pen and ink.
The part of the horse closest to the viewer will appear proportionally larger.
These sketches were lightly drawn in pencil, then filled in with a pale watercolor wash. Glazes were used to develop the contours. In this type of quick study, form is more important than detail.
Sepia
Second layer (glaze)
watercolor wash
Burnt Sienna

The Eyes and Hair

This eye was painted with watercolor glazes and detailed with a fine brush and some Sepia pen work. Note that the eye is positioned to the side, but well forward on the face.

Left eye, viewed towards the front of the face.

The horse has capsule shaped pupils which lay horizontally across the eye. They can be closed to a slit in bright light and still allow the horse to see to the front and to the rear. In dim light the pupils expand to an almost circular shape.

① Pencil sketch with first watercolor washes applied.

This is a side view of an Appaloosa's eye. The white sclera at the edge of the eye is a characteristic of the breed.

Sclera

②

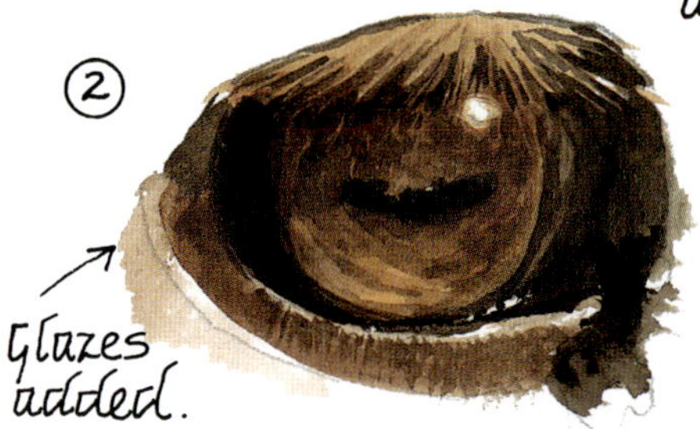

Glazes added.

③

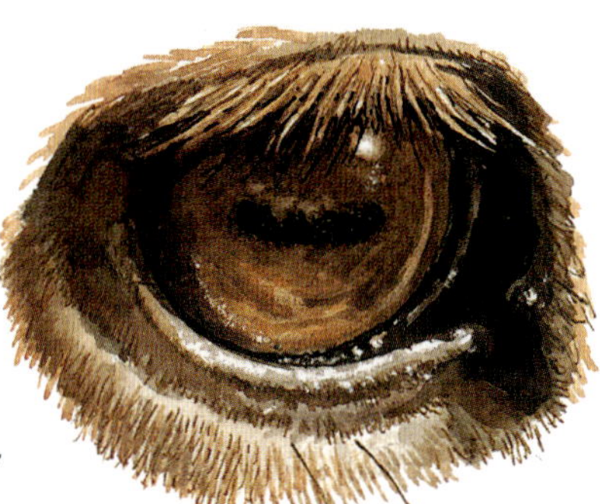

Details added with pen and brush.

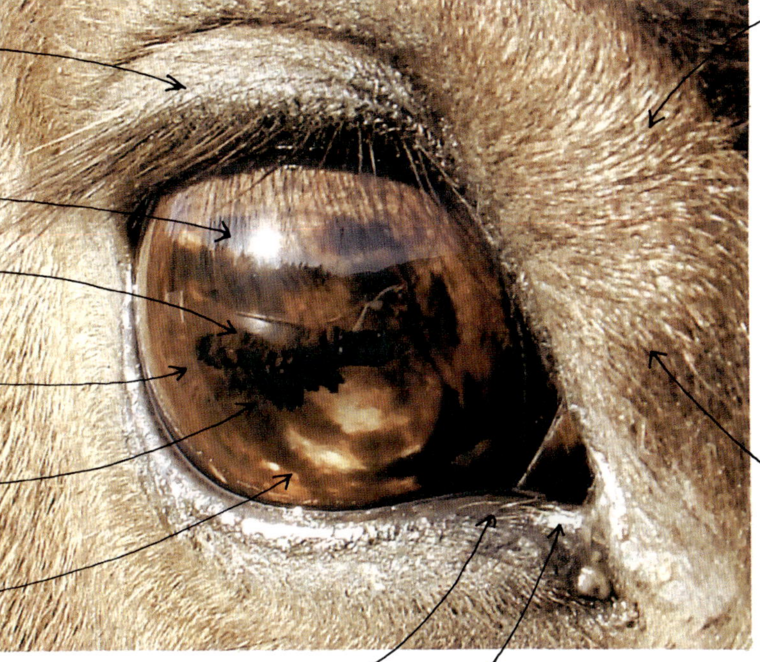

This photograph clearly shows the light play in a horse's eye on a sunny day. The brown mossy looking substance at the edge of the pupil is called the Corpora Nigra. It is a normal occurence and does not affect the sight.

Notice how the hair grows away from the eye in all directions.

Pupil fully open.

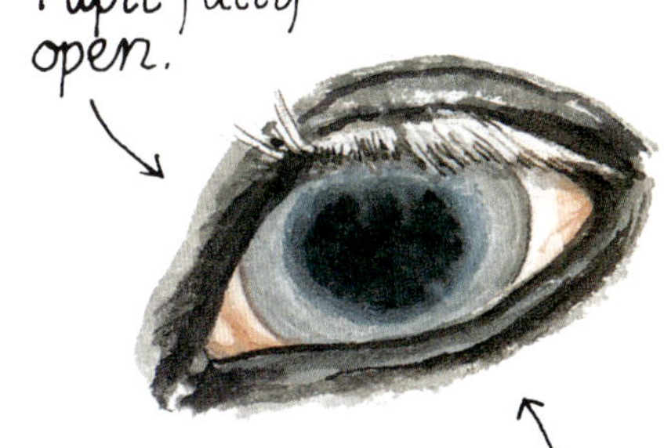

Blue eyes are a common occurence in spotted horses (Paints and Pintos).

The hair on a horse's face spreads out from a whorl of hair located between and a little above the eyes. From this point it flows towards the poll (between the ears), the cheeks and the muzzle. There is an area just forward of the eye where the hair growing outward collides with the hair growing down from the whorl. Study the photo on the opposite page (top left).

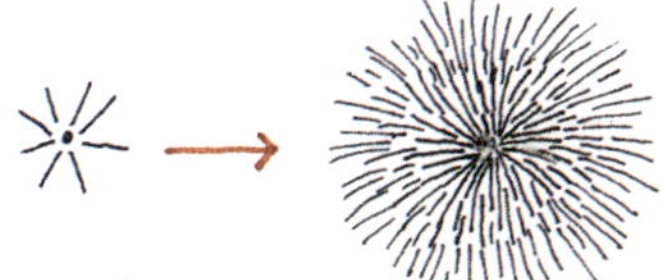

When ink sketching a whorl, start with a dot and some guide lines, then fill it in.

Painted whorls begin with a directional wash, then individual hairs are added.

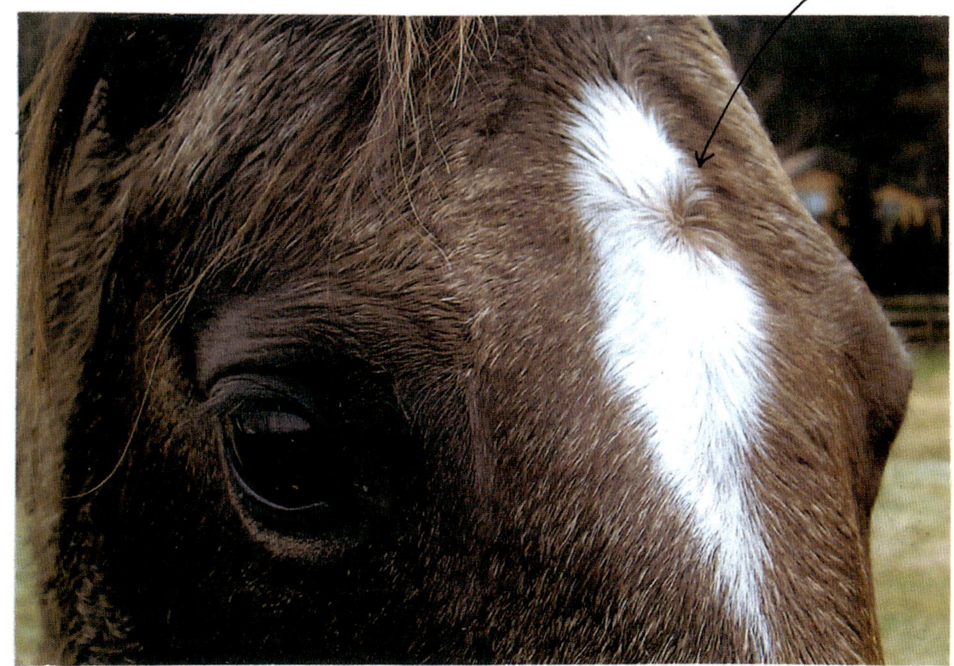

Note that the hairs making up the horse's coat are not one color, but many varying shades.

Ears and Muzzles

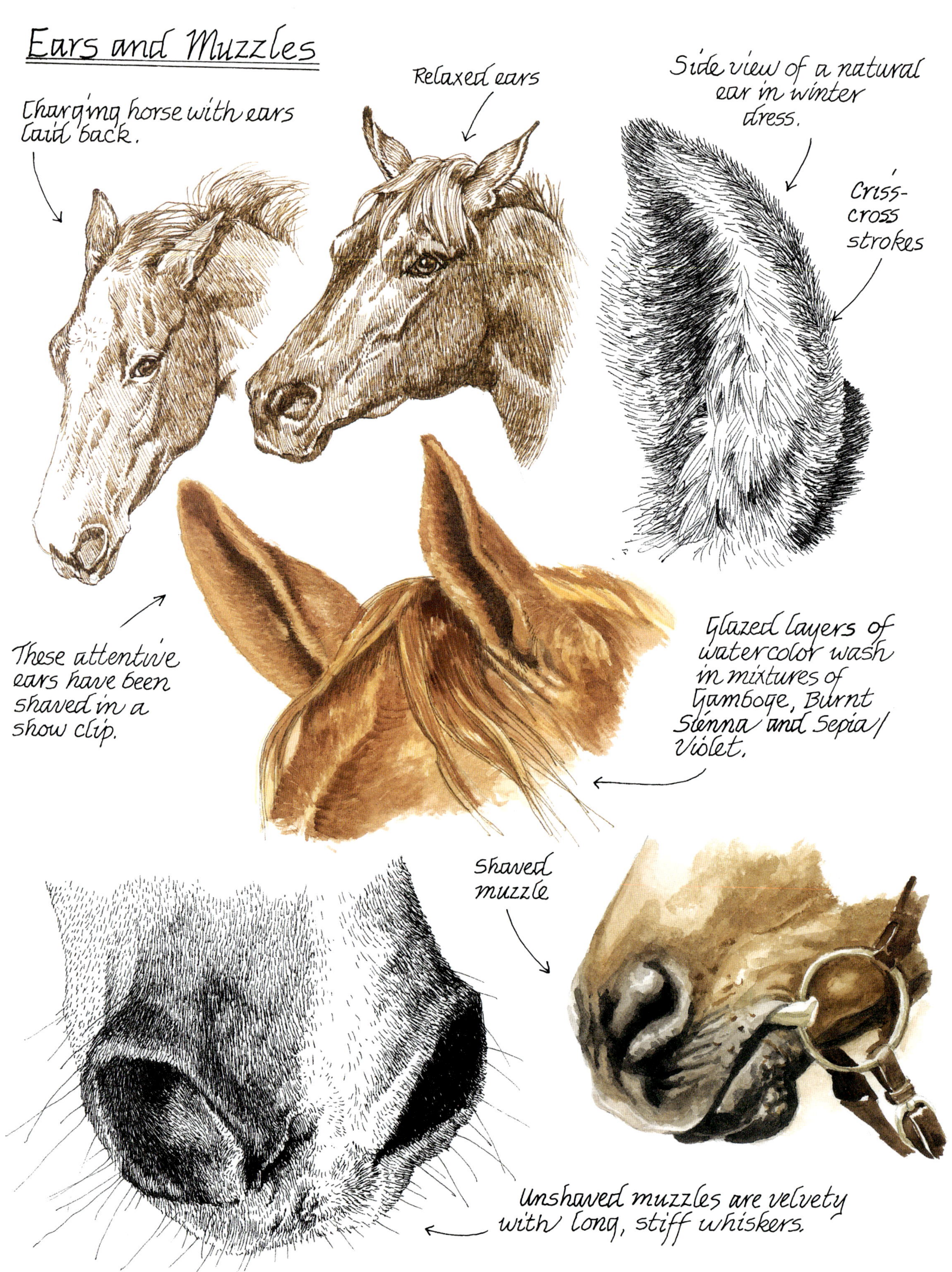

Project no. 5

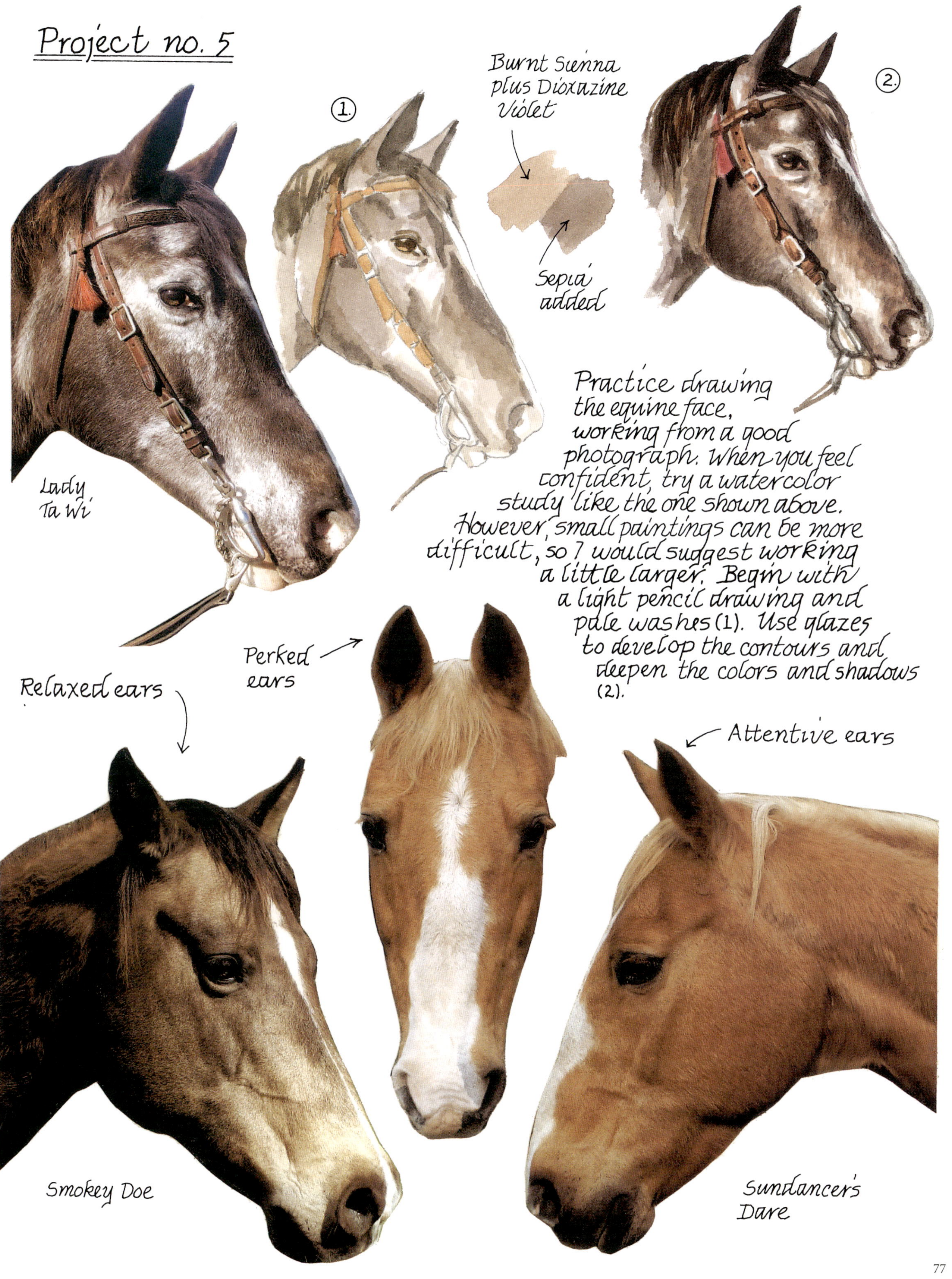

Practice drawing the equine face, working from a good photograph. When you feel confident, try a watercolor study like the one shown above. However, small paintings can be more difficult, so I would suggest working a little larger. Begin with a light pencil drawing and pale washes (1). Use glazes to develop the contours and deepen the colors and shadows (2).

Legs and Hooves

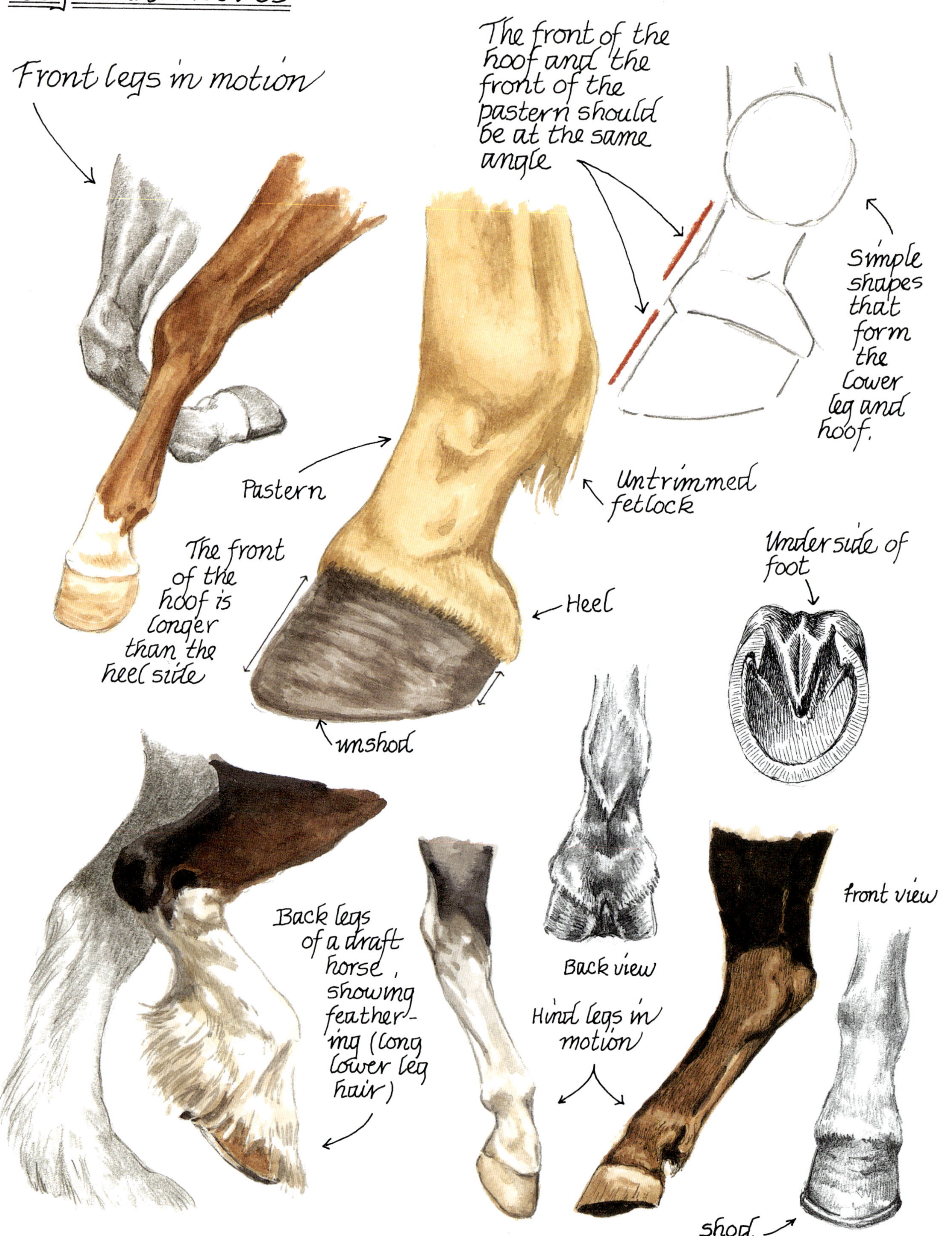

The Flowing Mane and Tail

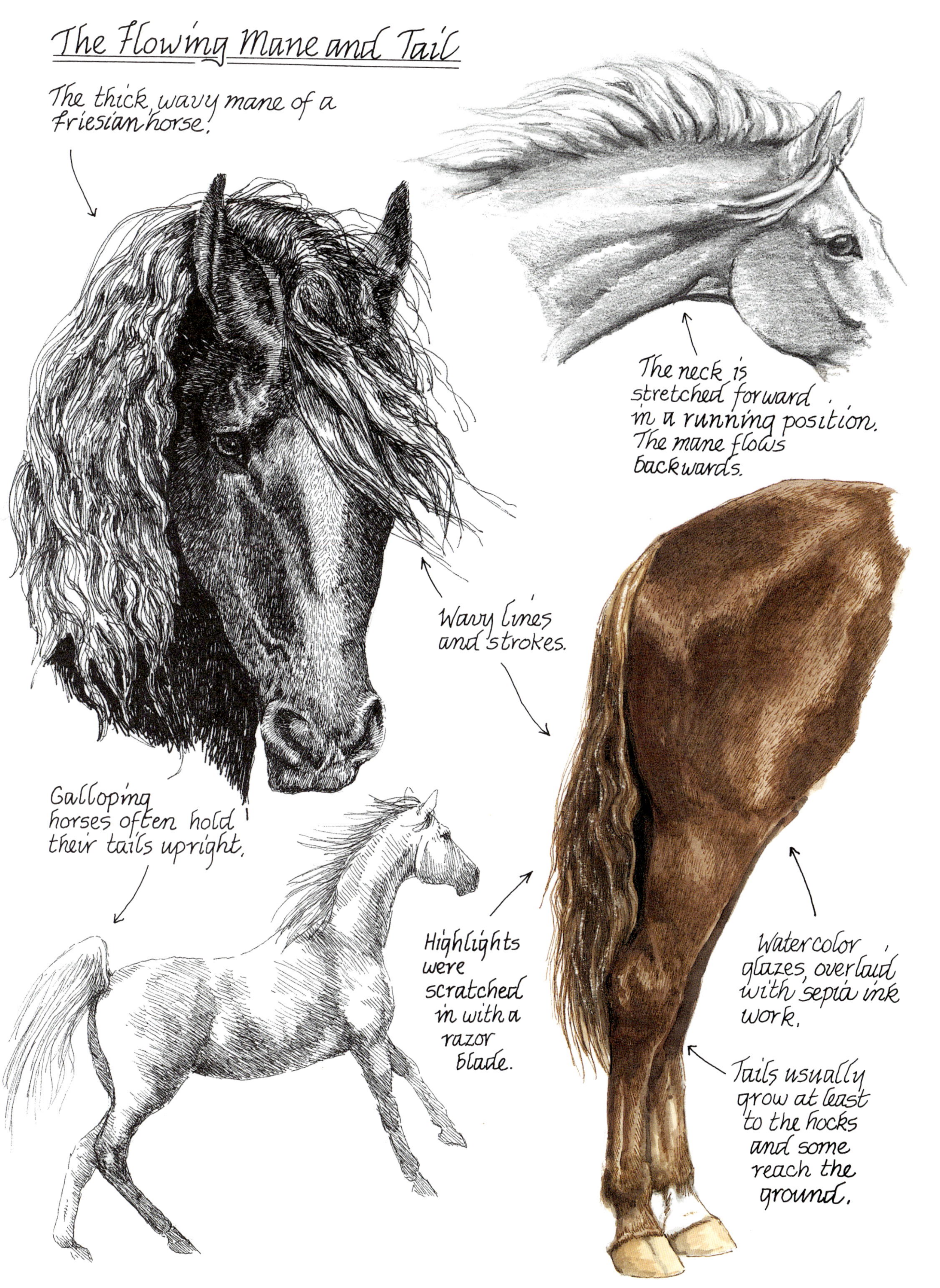

Drawing the Complete Horse

Project no. 6

I couldn't resist photographing this Appaloosa gelding as he happily basked in the spring sunshine. It's an unusual horse pose full of wonderful curves and angles. I found it fun to work from. See what you can do with it.

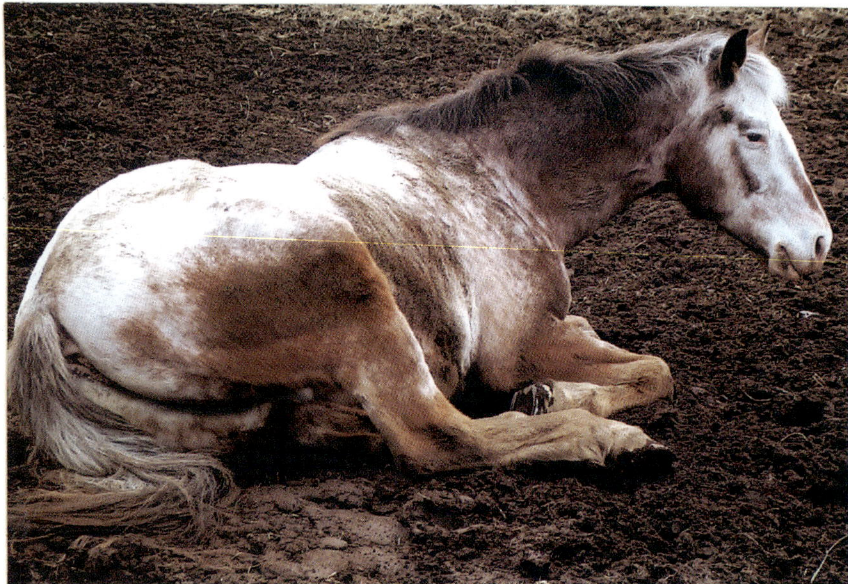

An "Appy" named Statton

① Study the photo and make some comparisons. Note that the angle of the face is almost the same as the angle of the upper rear leg (green lines). See what lines up vertically and horizontally.

② Block in the shapes

The brown lines will help you see how the body parts line up.

③ Refine and correct the pencil drawing.

④ Work the ink lines over the pencil drawing. I used contour ink lines which followed the curve of the body rather than criss-cross hair strokes, because of the horse's distance.

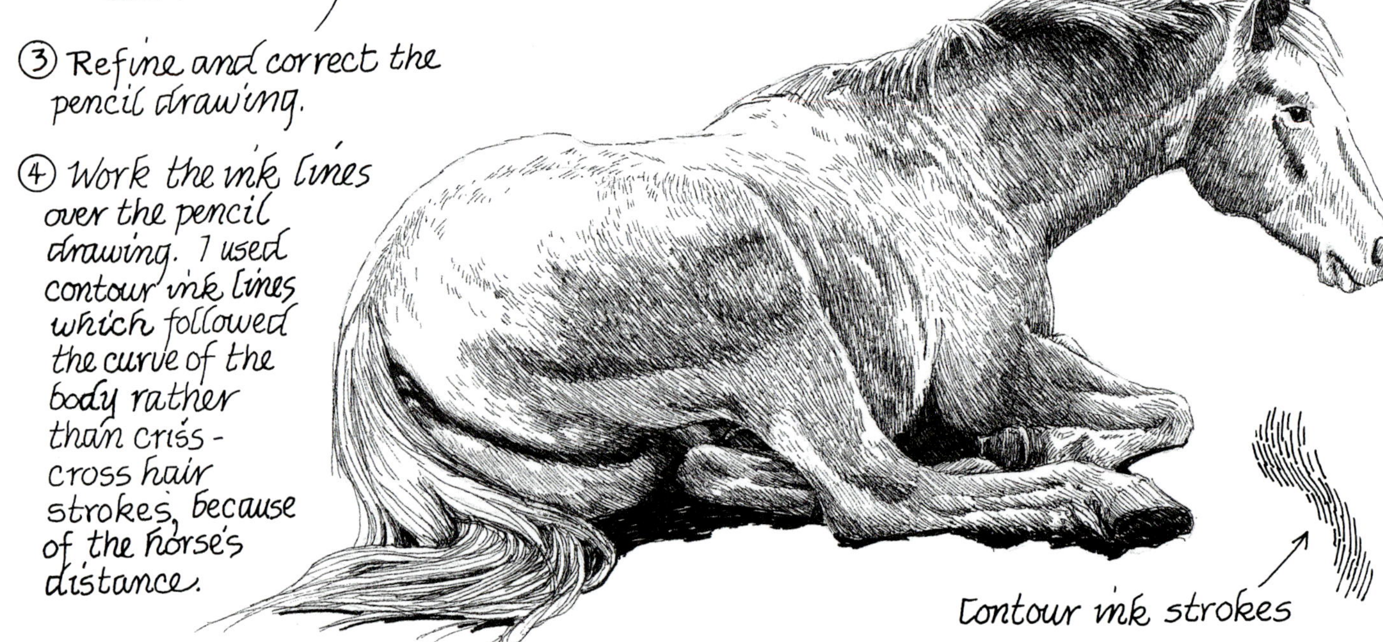

Contour ink strokes

Placing Riders on Horses

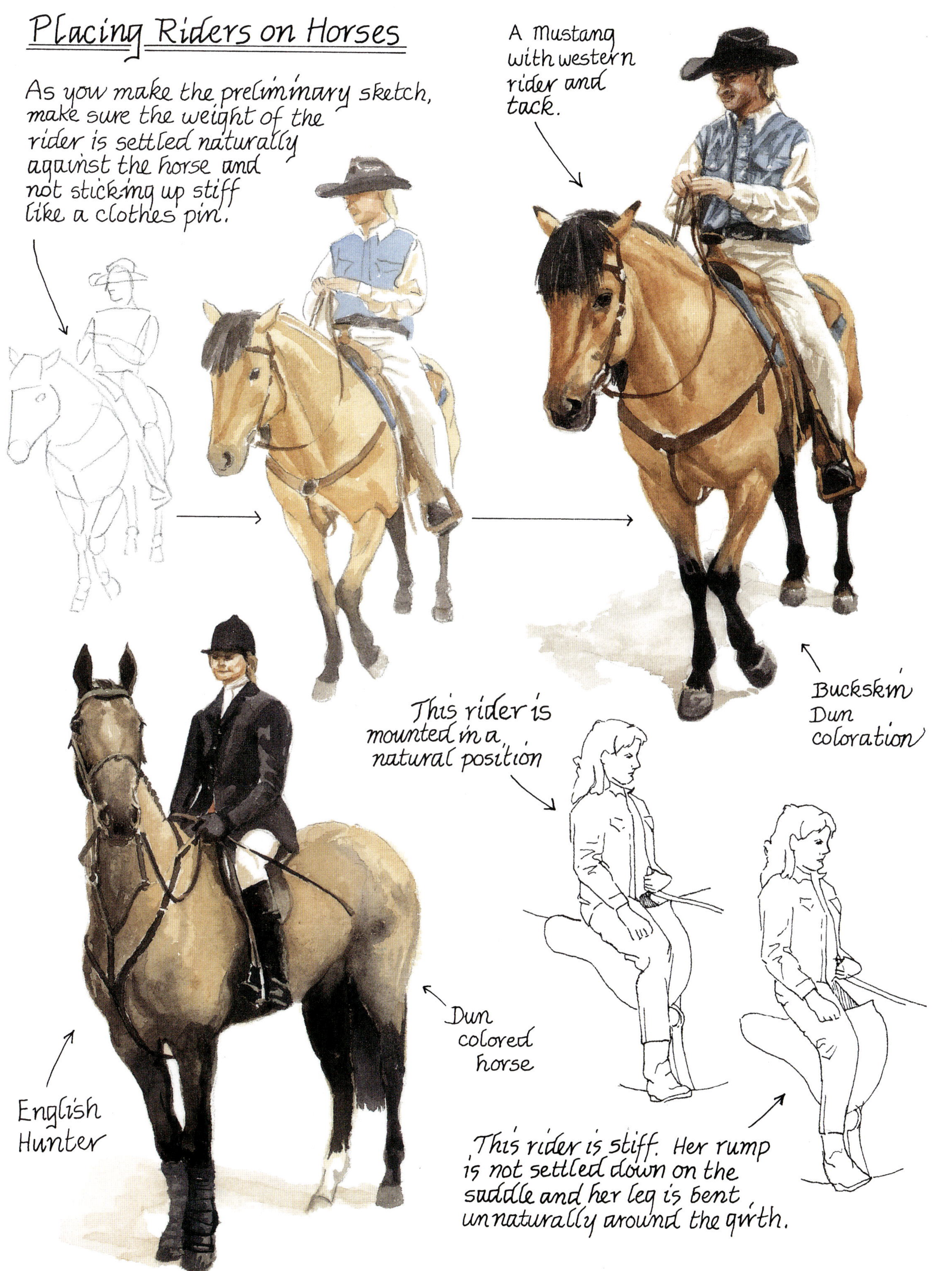

The Horse in Motion

At the walk each foot touches the ground separately creating four distinct beats. The sequence is left hind, left fore, right hind and right fore.

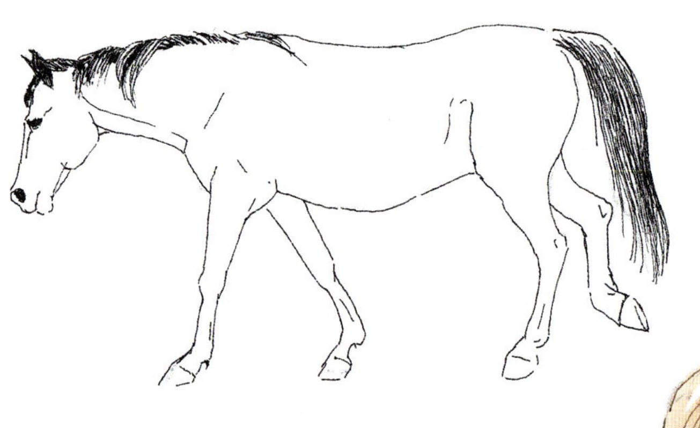

Light ink wash and pen outline

The trotting horse moves the diagonal legs together creating a two beat foot-fall. The hind legs should reach well under the body at the faster speed.

Diagonal legs move forward together.

Layered watercolor washes

The canter is a three beat gait. If the horse pushes off with the right hind foot, the right fore leg and the left hind will touch the ground next, simultaneous-ly, and then the left fore leg.

As the horse increases his speed, the canter becomes a gallop which is a four beat gait. The horse pushes off with a hind foot, but the sequence depends on the speed. There is a moment when all four feet are off the ground.

Portraying the Foal

The new born foal is quite different proportionally when compared to the adult horse. The foal's head and girth measurement should still be about the same, but the trunk is small and compact. The legs are long and slender with large joints. The hooves are tiny. The muzzle is covered with fuzzy "milk hairs." The mane and tail are short, with silky hairs. Often the stance is awkward and endearing.

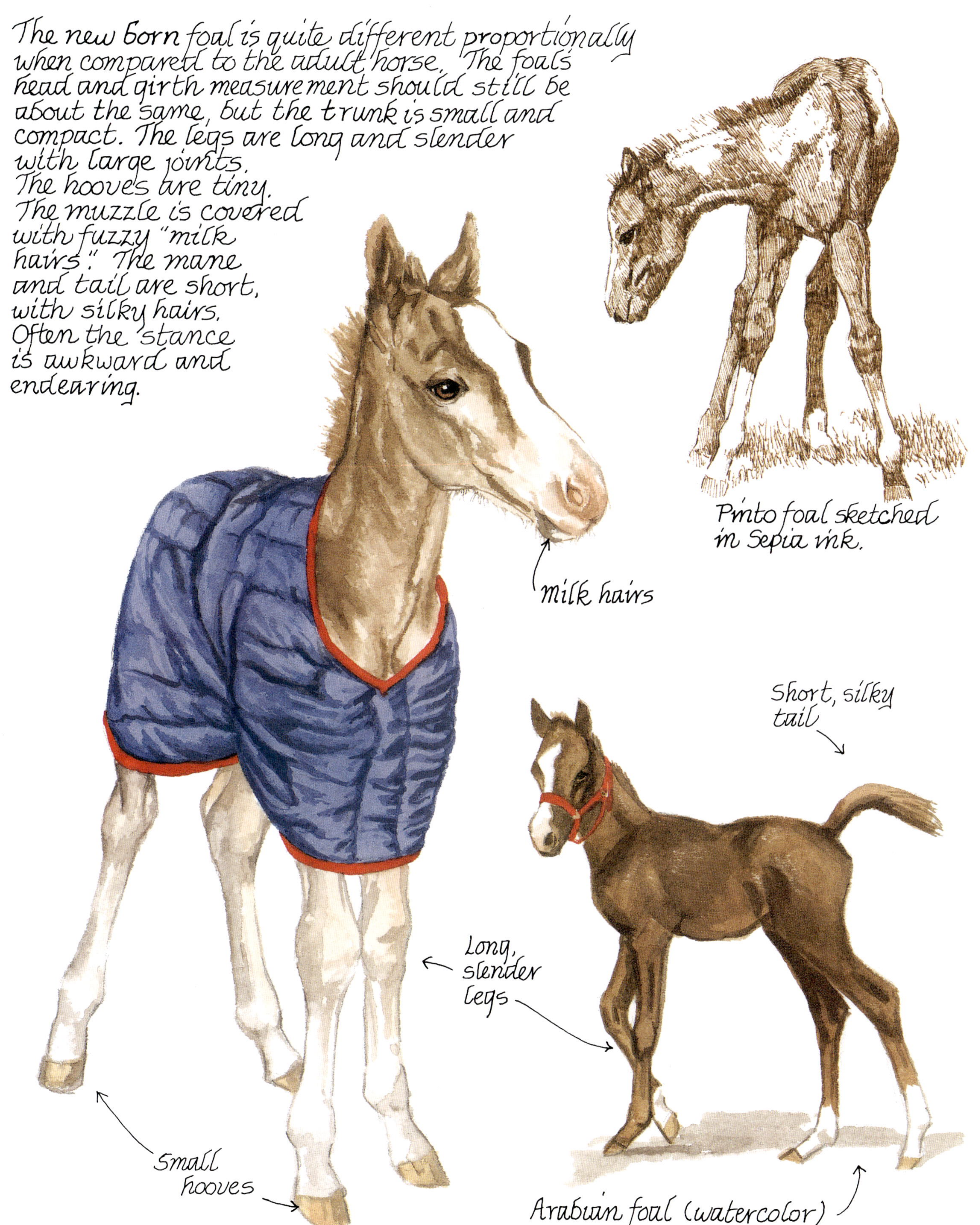

Pinto foal sketched in Sepia ink.

Arabian foal (watercolor)

Common Breeds and Colors

Thoroughbred (right)

Thoroughbreds are known for their speed. They are descended from an early cross of imported Arabian stallions and English sporting mares.

Arabian (below)

The Arabian is the oldest and purest of the modern breeds. Its beauty, stamina, and graceful movements make it a wonderful art subject.

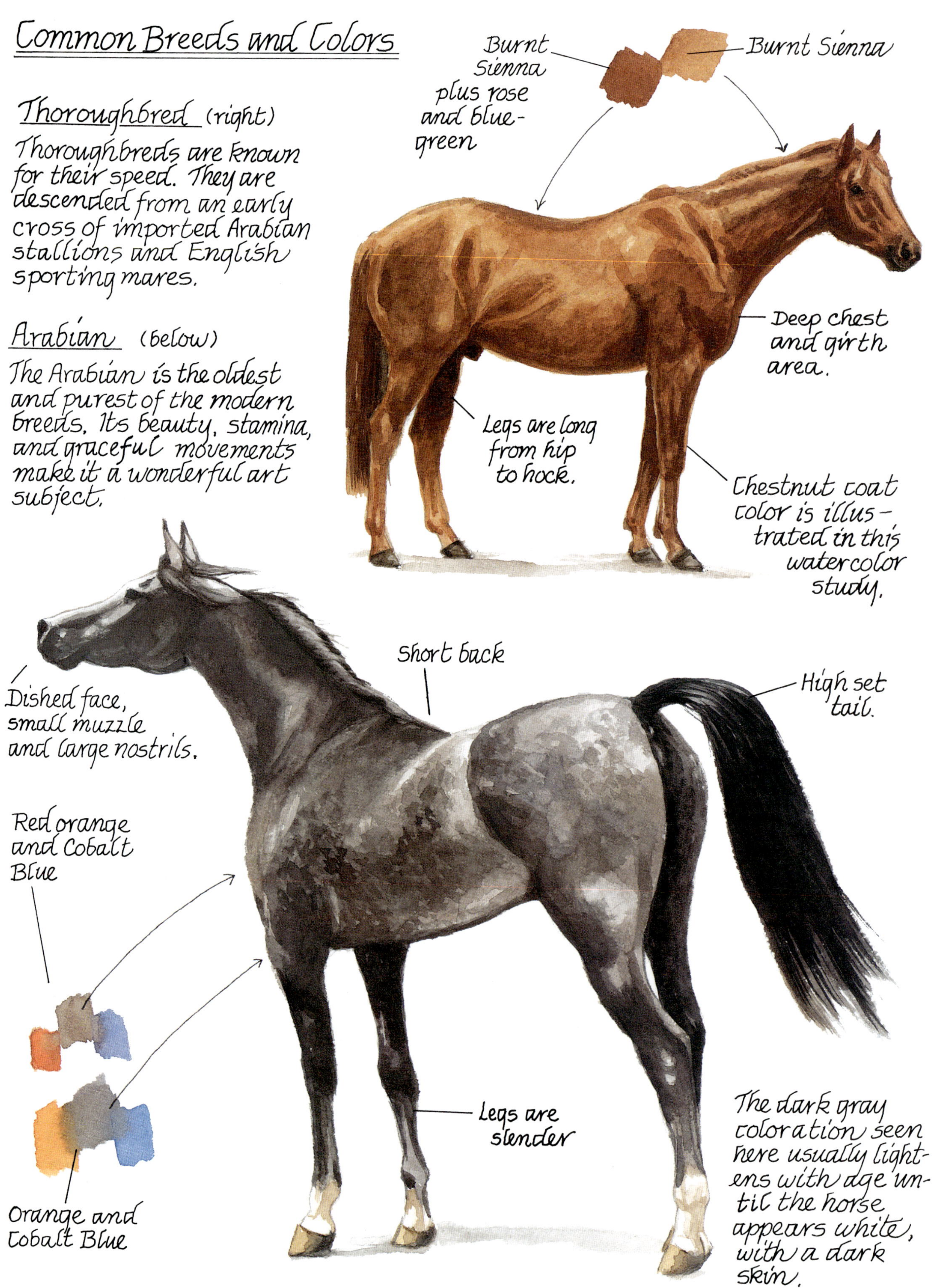

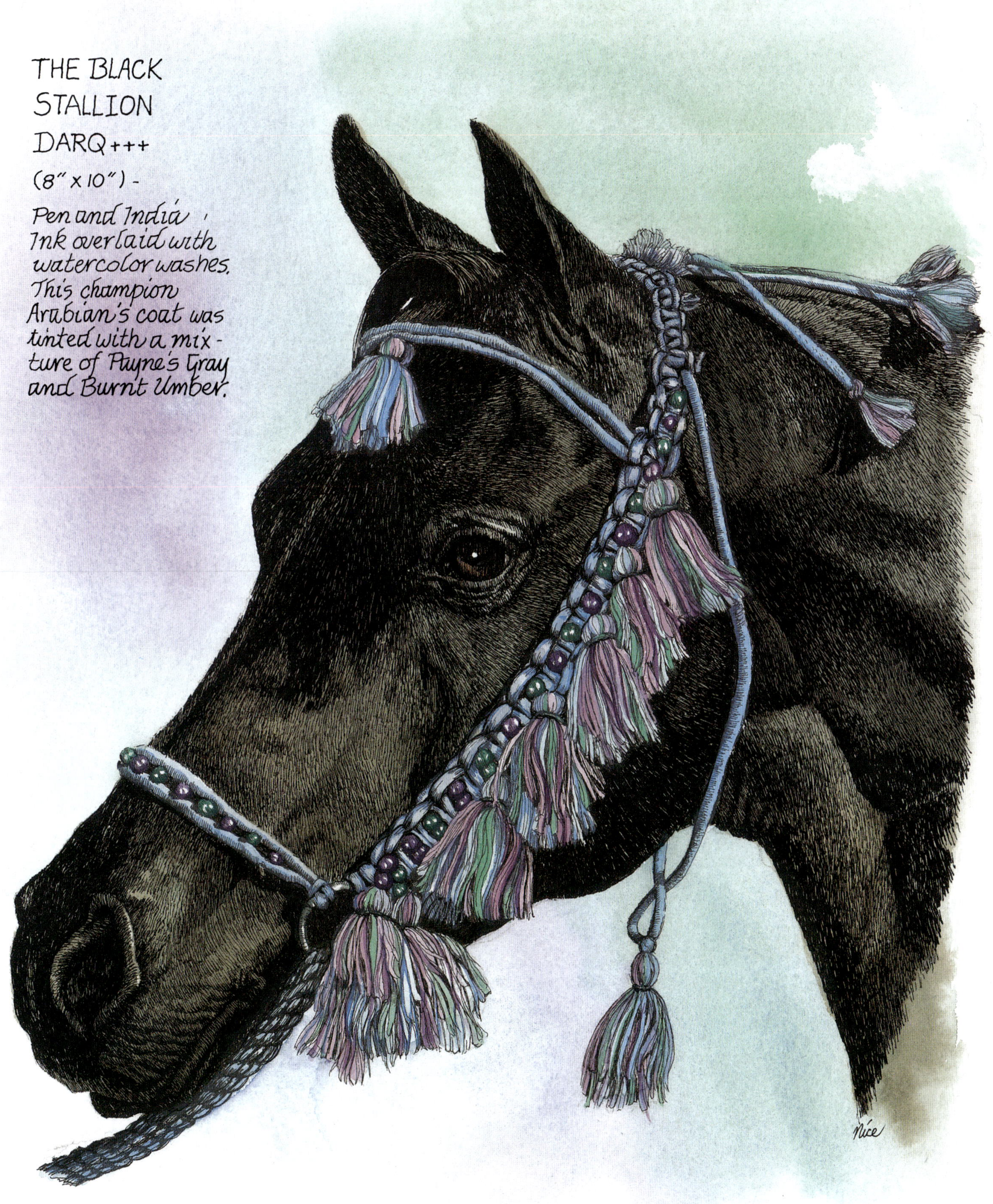

THE BLACK STALLION DARQ+++ (8" x 10") - Pen and India Ink overlaid with watercolor washes. This champion Arabian's coat was tinted with a mixture of Payne's Gray and Burnt Umber.

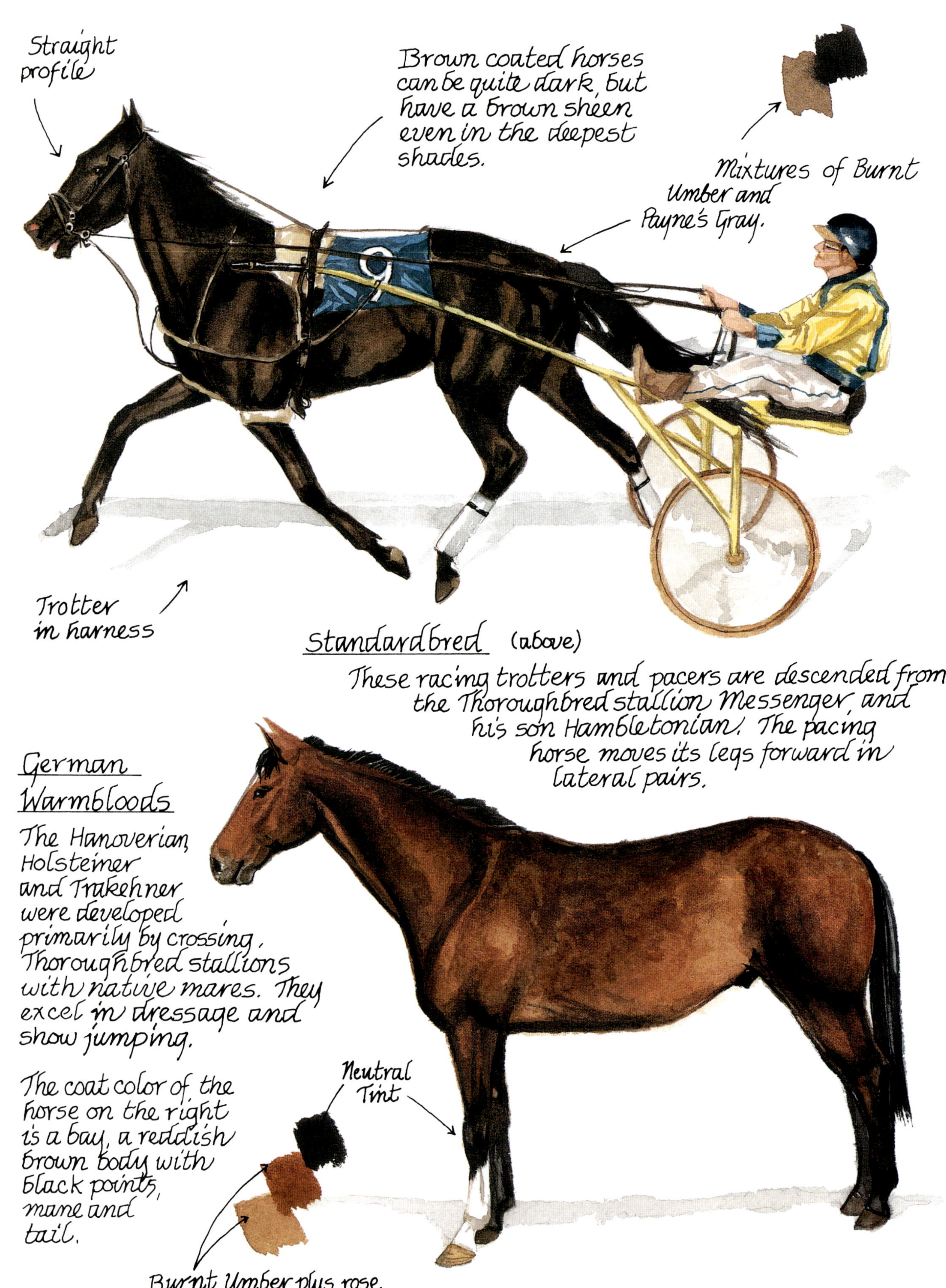
Straight profile
Brown coated horses can be quite dark, but have a brown sheen even in the deepest shades.
Mixtures of Burnt Umber and Payne's Gray.
9
Trotter in harness
Standardbred (above)
These racing trotters and pacers are descended from the Thoroughbred stallion Messenger, and his son Hambletonian. The pacing horse moves its legs forward in lateral pairs.
German Warmbloods
The Hanoverian, Holsteiner and Trakehner were developed primarily by crossing Thoroughbred stallions with native mares. They excel in dressage and show jumping.
The coat color of the horse on the right is a bay, a reddish brown body with black points, mane and tail.
Neutral Tint
Burnt Umber plus rose

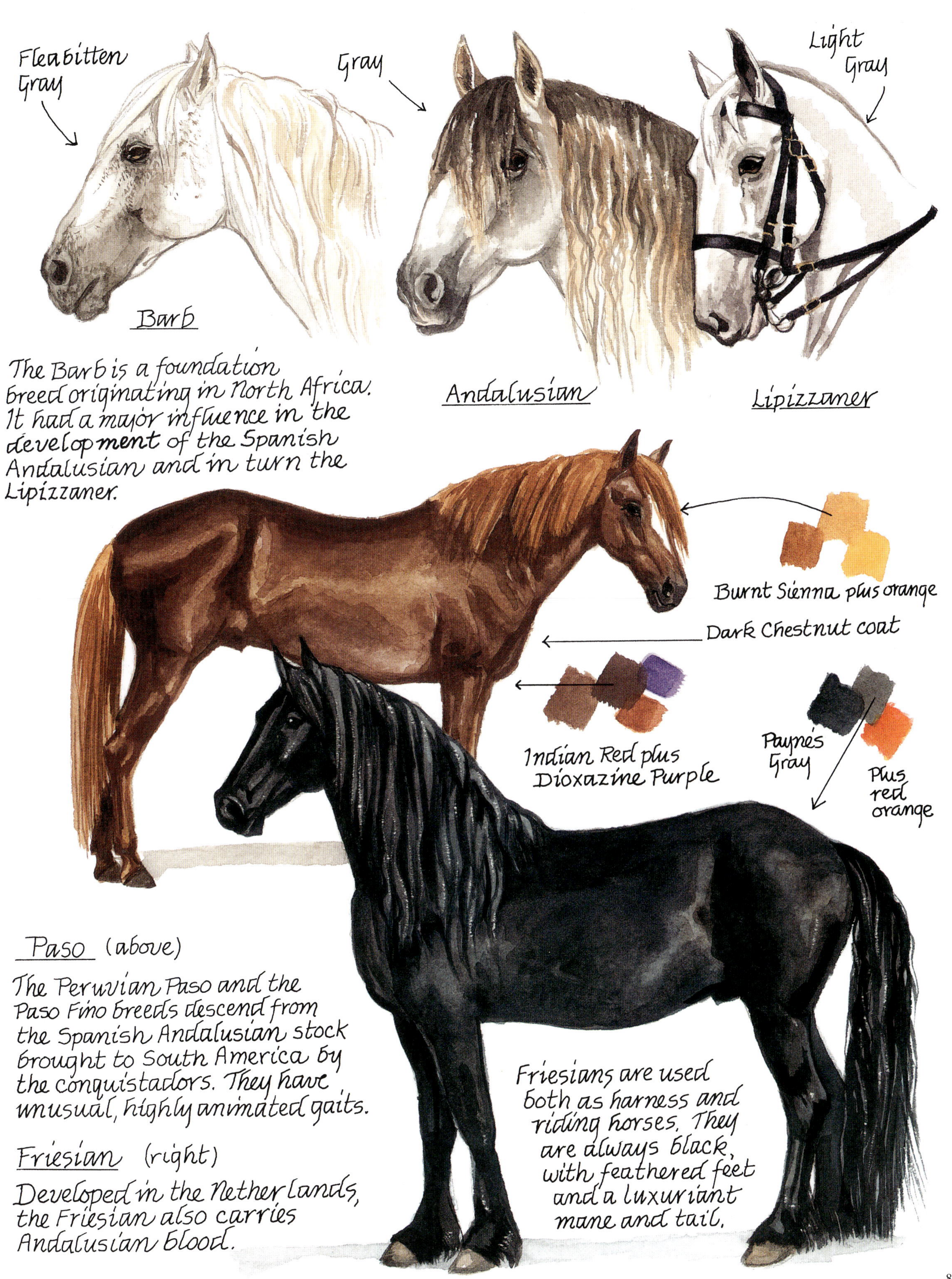

Fleabitten Gray
Gray
Light Gray
Barb
Andalusian
Lipizzaner
The Barb is a foundation breed originating in North Africa. It had a major influence in the development of the Spanish Andalusian and in turn the Lipizzaner.
Burnt Sienna plus orange
Dark Chestnut coat
Indian Red plus Dioxazine Purple
Payne's Gray
Plus red orange
Paso (above)
The Peruvian Paso and the Paso Fino breeds descend from the Spanish Andalusian stock brought to South America by the conquistadors. They have unusual, highly animated gaits.
Friesian (right)
Developed in the Netherlands, the Friesian also carries Andalusian blood.
Friesians are used both as harness and riding horses. They are always black, with feathered feet and a luxuriant mane and tail.

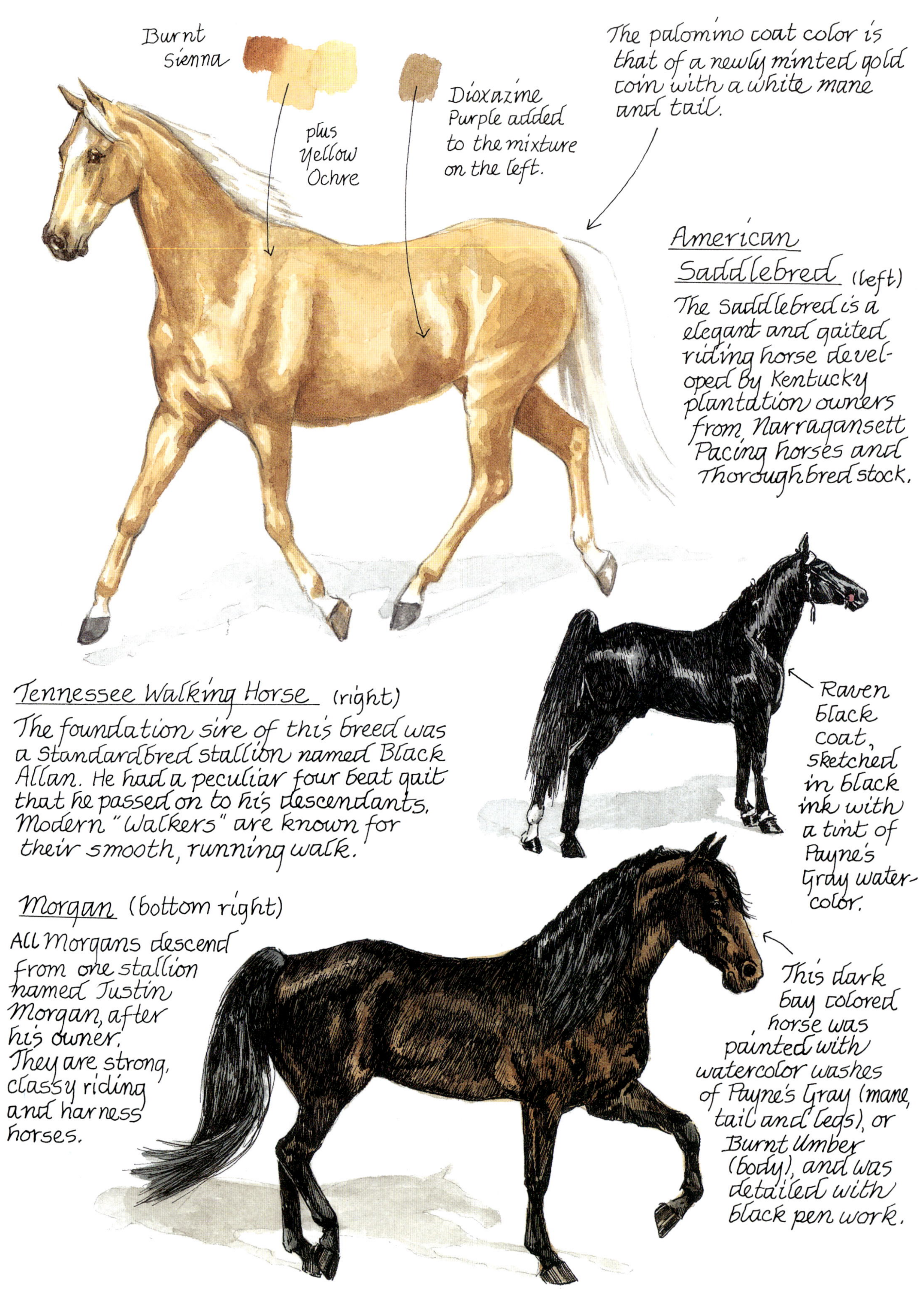
Burnt Sienna
plus Yellow Ochre
Dioxazine Purple added to the mixture on the left.
The palomino coat color is that of a newly minted gold coin with a white mane and tail.
American Saddlebred (left)
The Saddlebred is a elegant and gaited riding horse developed by Kentucky plantation owners from Narragansett Pacing horses and Thoroughbred stock.
Tennessee Walking Horse (right)
The foundation sire of this breed was a Standardbred stallion named Black Allan. He had a peculiar four beat gait that he passed on to his descendants. Modern "Walkers" are known for their smooth, running walk.
Raven black coat, sketched in black ink with a tint of Payne's Gray watercolor.
Morgan (bottom right)
All Morgans descend from one stallion named Justin Morgan, after his owner. They are strong, classy riding and harness horses.
This dark bay colored horse was painted with watercolor washes of Payne's Gray (mane, tail and legs), or Burnt Umber (body), and was detailed with black pen work.

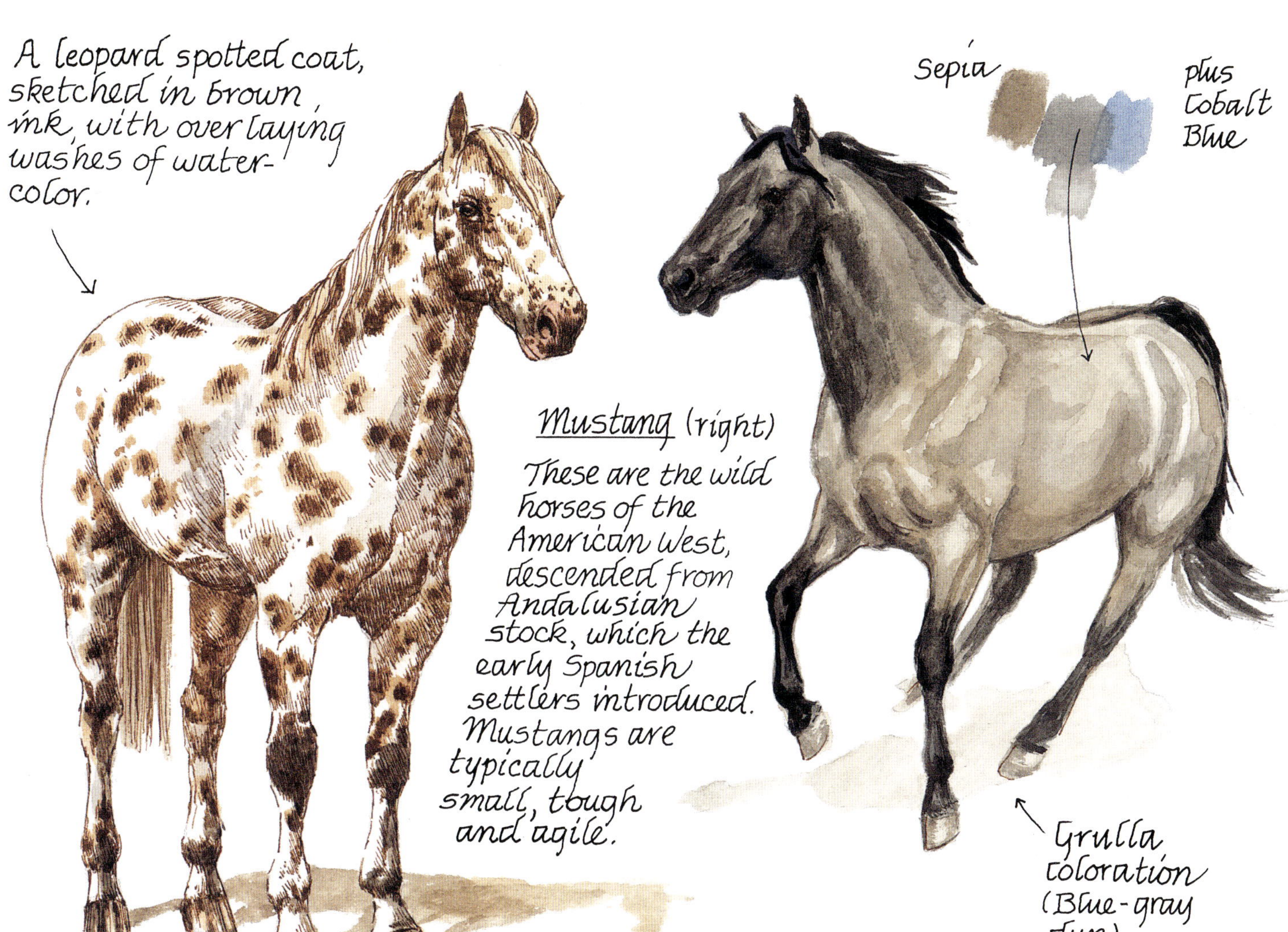

Appaloosa (above)

These spotted horses also carry the blood of wild Spanish Andalusian stock. The Nez Percé, a Native American people living in north-east Oregon in the eighteenth century, developed the breed. Appaloosas are noted for their white rump "blankets", spots, striped hooves and mottled skin.

Buckskin dun.

The body is a bright gold, similar to a palomino, but with black points. There is often a dark spine stripe.

Quarter Horse (left)

These are the horses that were developed to work the cattle herds of the old west. They were a mix of Mustang blood and English stock. Today's Quarter Horses are multi-purpose mounts which are strong, agile and fast over short distances.

The Draft Horse and Mule

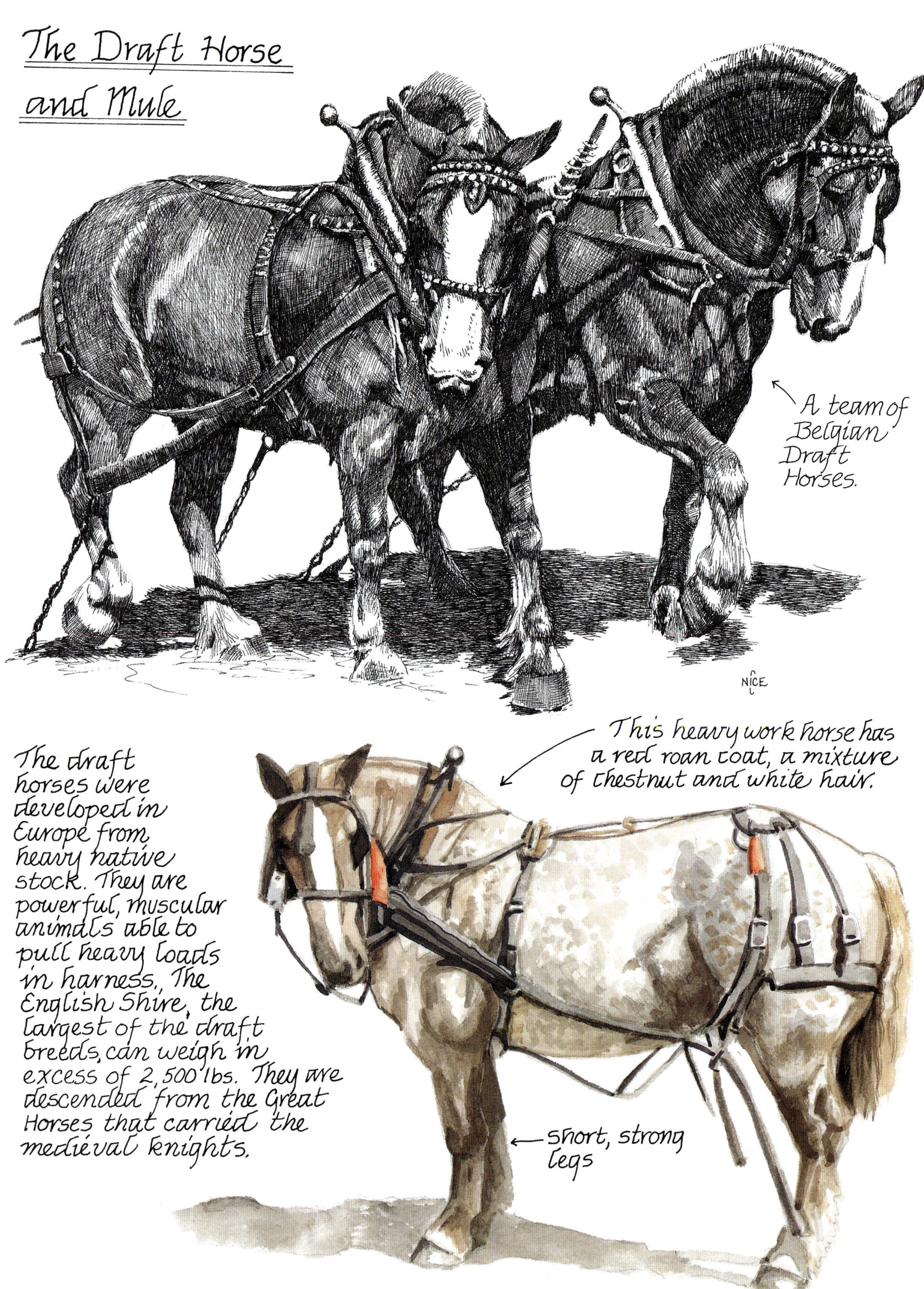

The draft horses were developed in Europe from heavy native stock. They are powerful, muscular animals able to pull heavy loads in harness. The English Shire, the largest of the draft breeds, can weigh in excess of 2,500 lbs. They are descended from the Great Horses that carried the medieval knights.

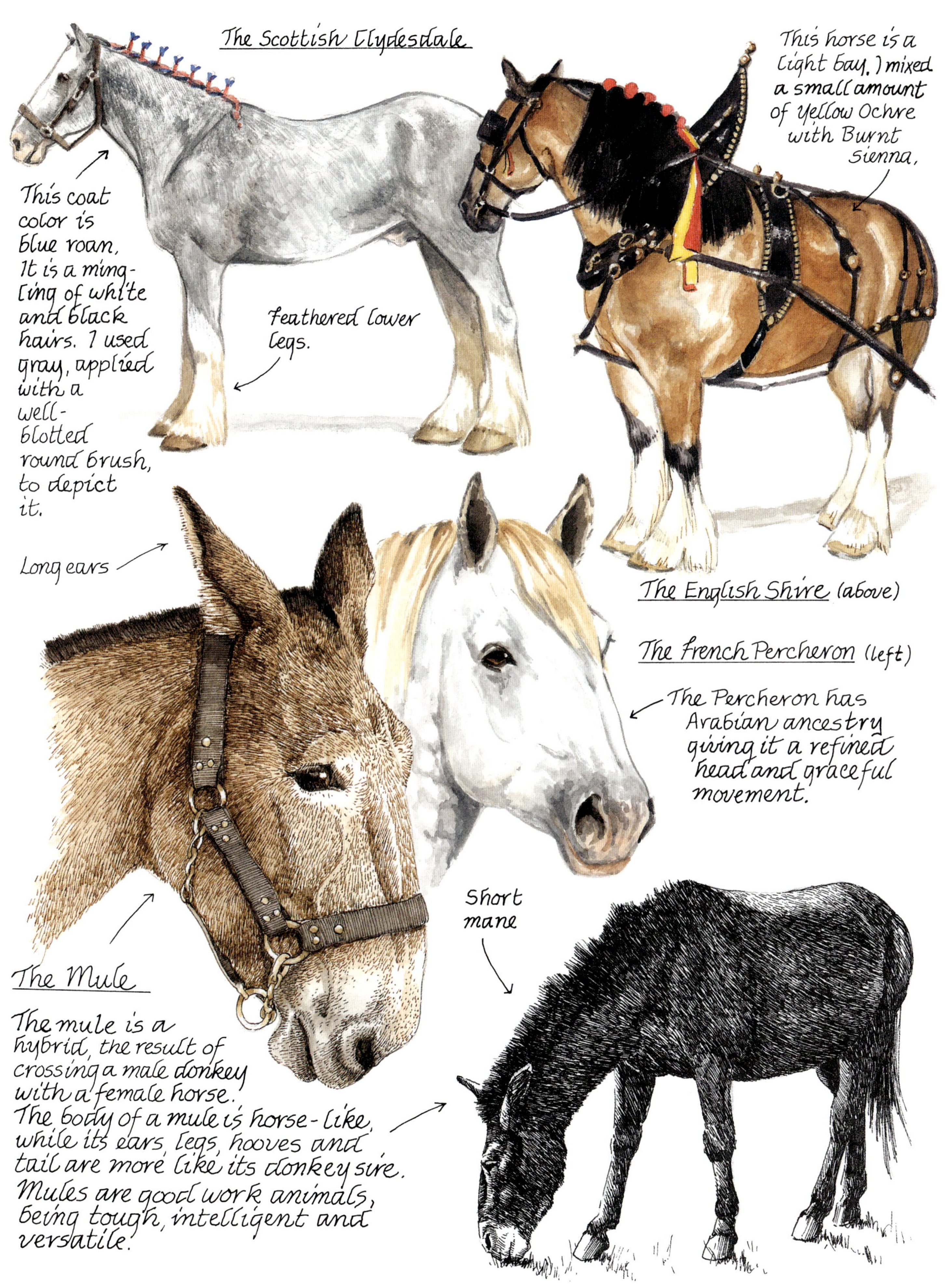
The Scottish Clydesdale
This horse is a light bay. I mixed a small amount of Yellow Ochre with Burnt Sienna.
This coat color is blue roan. It is a mingling of white and black hairs. I used gray, applied with a well-blotted round brush, to depict it.
Feathered lower legs.
Long ears
The English Shire (above)
The French Percheron (left)
The Percheron has Arabian ancestry giving it a refined head and graceful movement.
Short mane
The Mule
The mule is a hybrid, the result of crossing a male donkey with a female horse. The body of a mule is horse-like, while its ears, legs, hooves and tail are more like its donkey sire. Mules are good work animals, being tough, intelligent and versatile.

Portraying the Pony

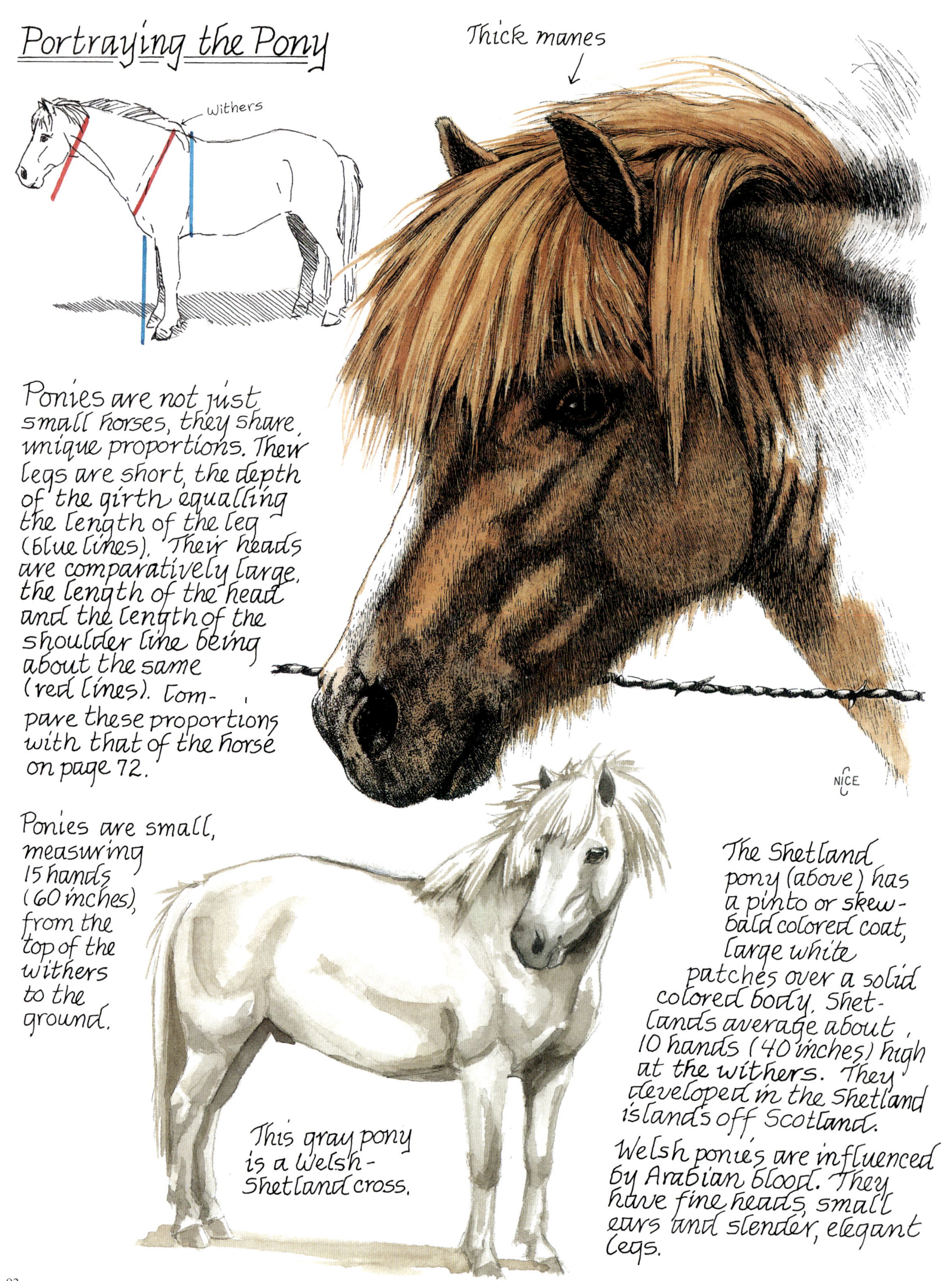

Ponies are not just small horses, they share unique proportions. Their legs are short, the depth of the girth equalling the length of the leg (blue lines). Their heads are comparatively large, the length of the head and the length of the shoulder line being about the same (red lines). Compare these proportions with that of the horse on page 72.

Ponies are small, measuring 15 hands (60 inches), from the top of the withers to the ground.

The Shetland pony (above) has a pinto or skewbald colored coat, large white patches over a solid colored body. Shetlands average about 10 hands (40 inches) high at the withers. They developed in the Shetland islands off Scotland.

This gray pony is a Welsh-Shetland cross.

Welsh ponies are influenced by Arabian blood. They have fine heads, small ears and slender, elegant legs.

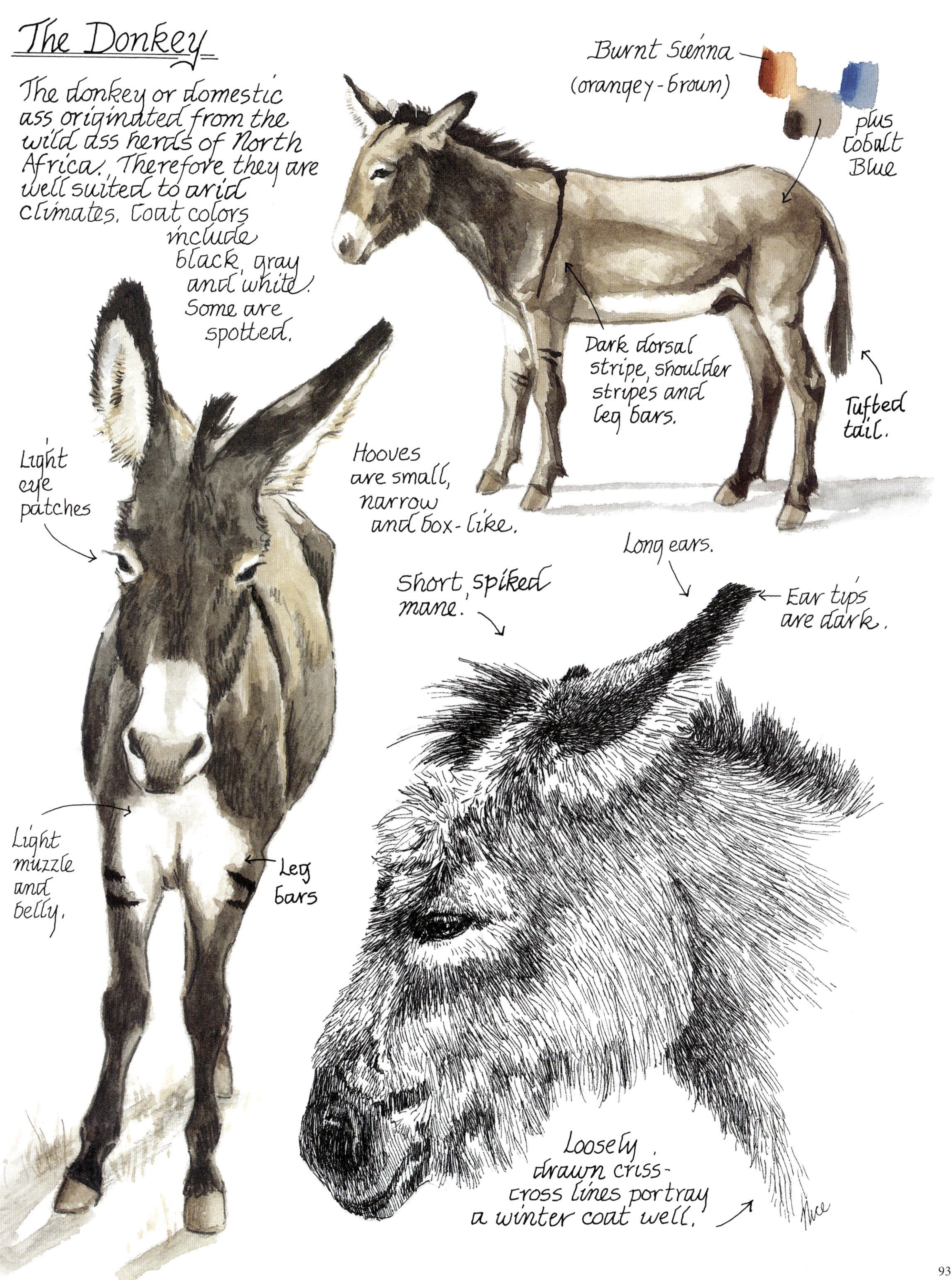
The Donkey
The donkey or domestic ass originated from the wild ass herds of North Africa. Therefore they are well suited to arid climates. Coat colors include black, gray and white. Some are spotted.
Burnt Sienna (orangey-brown)
plus Cobalt Blue
Dark dorsal stripe, shoulder stripes and leg bars.
Tufted tail.
Hooves are small, narrow and box-like.
Light eye patches
Light muzzle and belly.
Leg bars
Long ears.
Short, spiked mane.
Ear tips are dark.
Loosely drawn criss-cross lines portray a winter coat well.

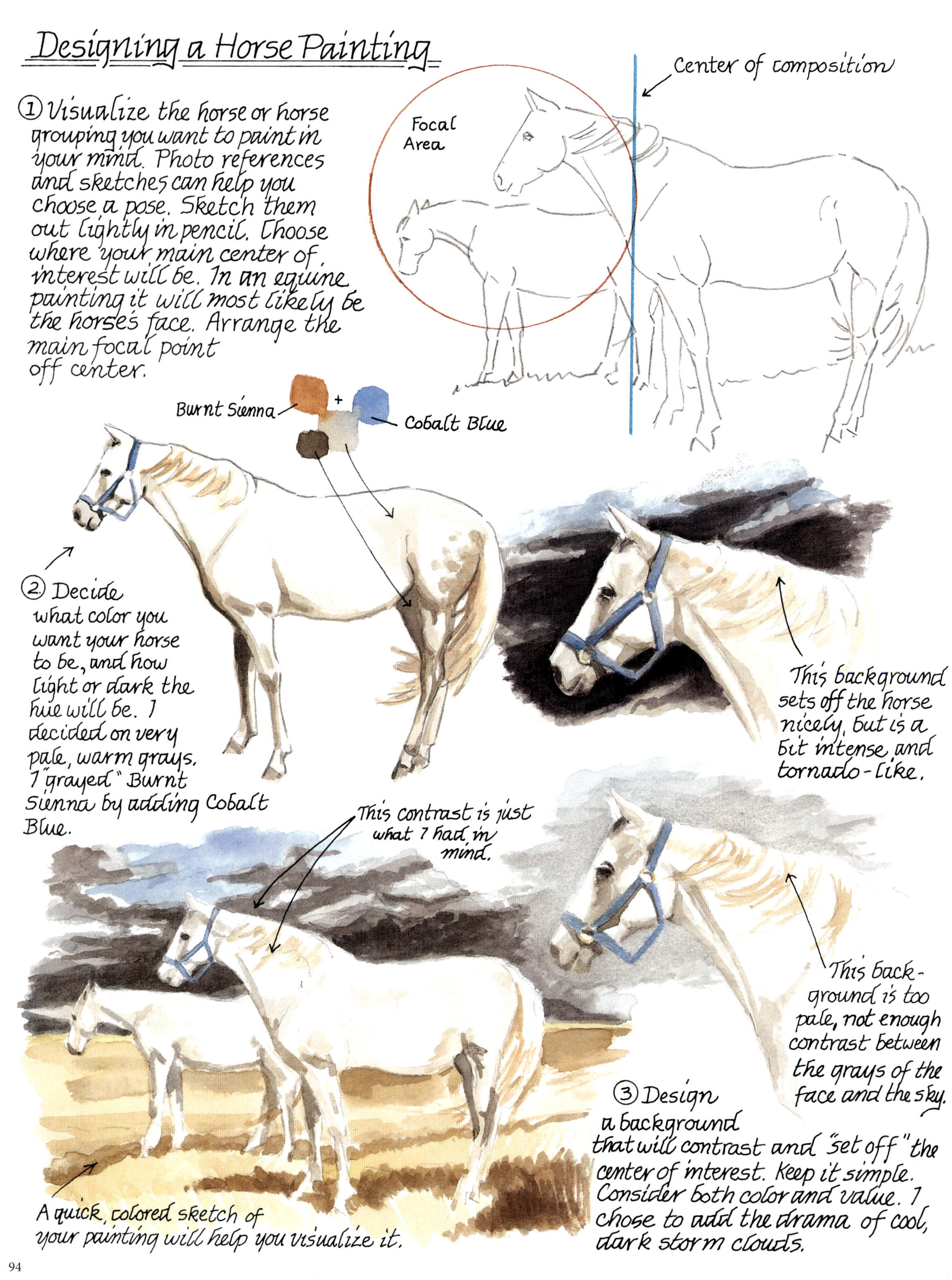
Designing a Horse Painting
Center of composition
Focal Area
① Visualize the horse or horse grouping you want to paint in your mind. Photo references and sketches can help you choose a pose. Sketch them out lightly in pencil. Choose where your main center of interest will be. In an equine painting it will most likely be the horse's face. Arrange the main focal point off center.
Burnt Sienna
+
Cobalt Blue
② Decide what color you want your horse to be, and how light or dark the hue will be. I decided on very pale, warm grays. I "grayed" Burnt Sienna by adding Cobalt Blue.
This background sets off the horse nicely, but is a bit intense and tornado-like.
This contrast is just what I had in mind.
This back-ground is too pale, not enough contrast between the grays of the face and the sky.
③ Design a background that will contrast and "set off" the center of interest. Keep it simple. Consider both color and value. I chose to add the drama of cool, dark storm clouds.
A quick, colored sketch of your painting will help you visualize it.

The sky is a Cobalt Blue / Phthalo. Blue mix, applied to a moist paper.

Dry edges form hard edged white clouds.

Soft edges can be formed by blotting the moist paint with a crumpled tissue.

The clouds were created using layered glazes.

Adding the halter brought the bright sky blue down where it could call attention to the main subject's face.

Neutral Tint plus Cobalt Blue.

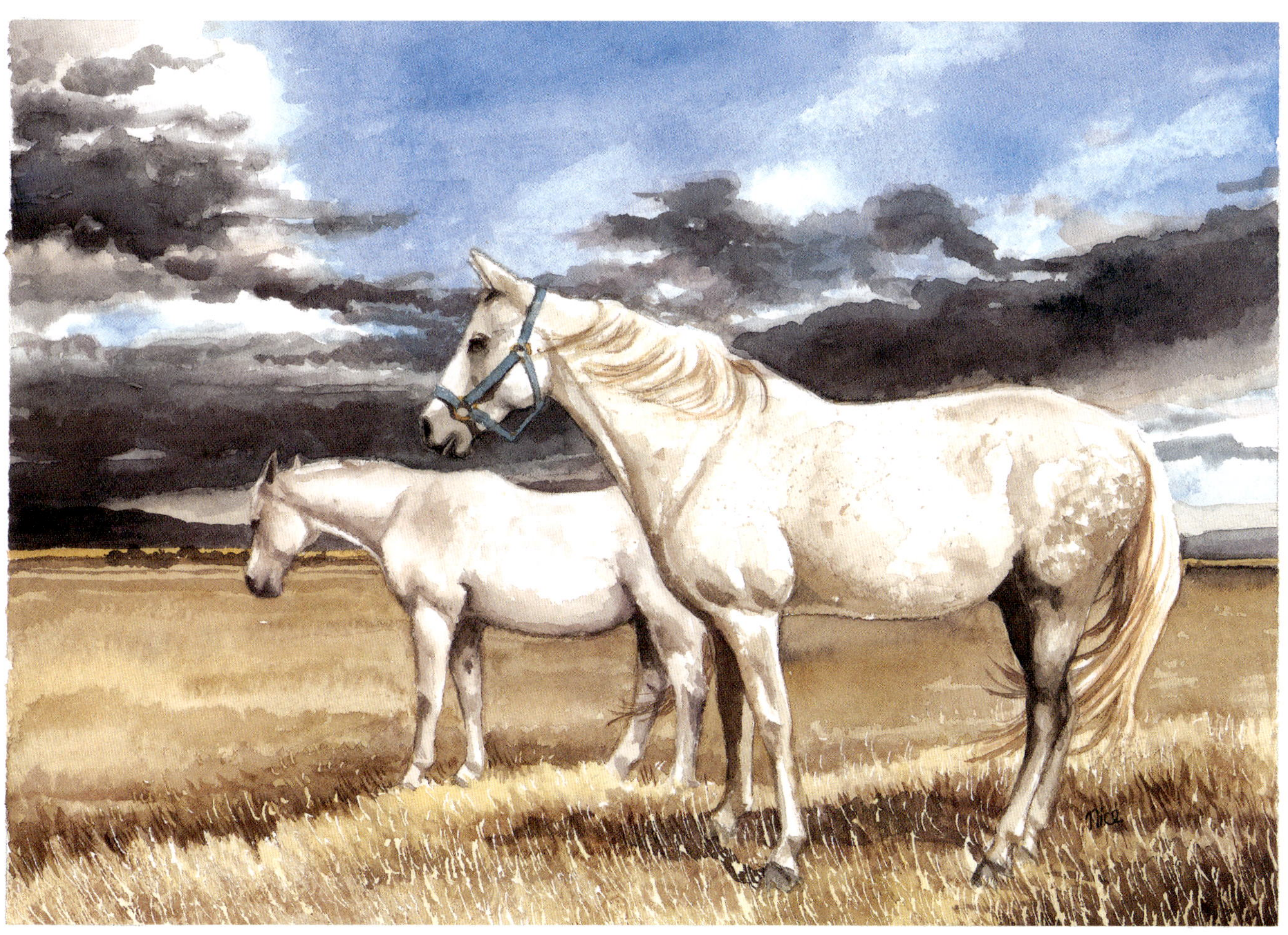

Mares Before the Storm — 8" x 10" (20.5 x 25.5 cm) - Watercolor.

The grass colors are mixtures of Yellow Ochre, Burnt Sienna and Dioxazine Violet.

The deep grass shadows help balance the dark of the clouds.

masking fluid used here.

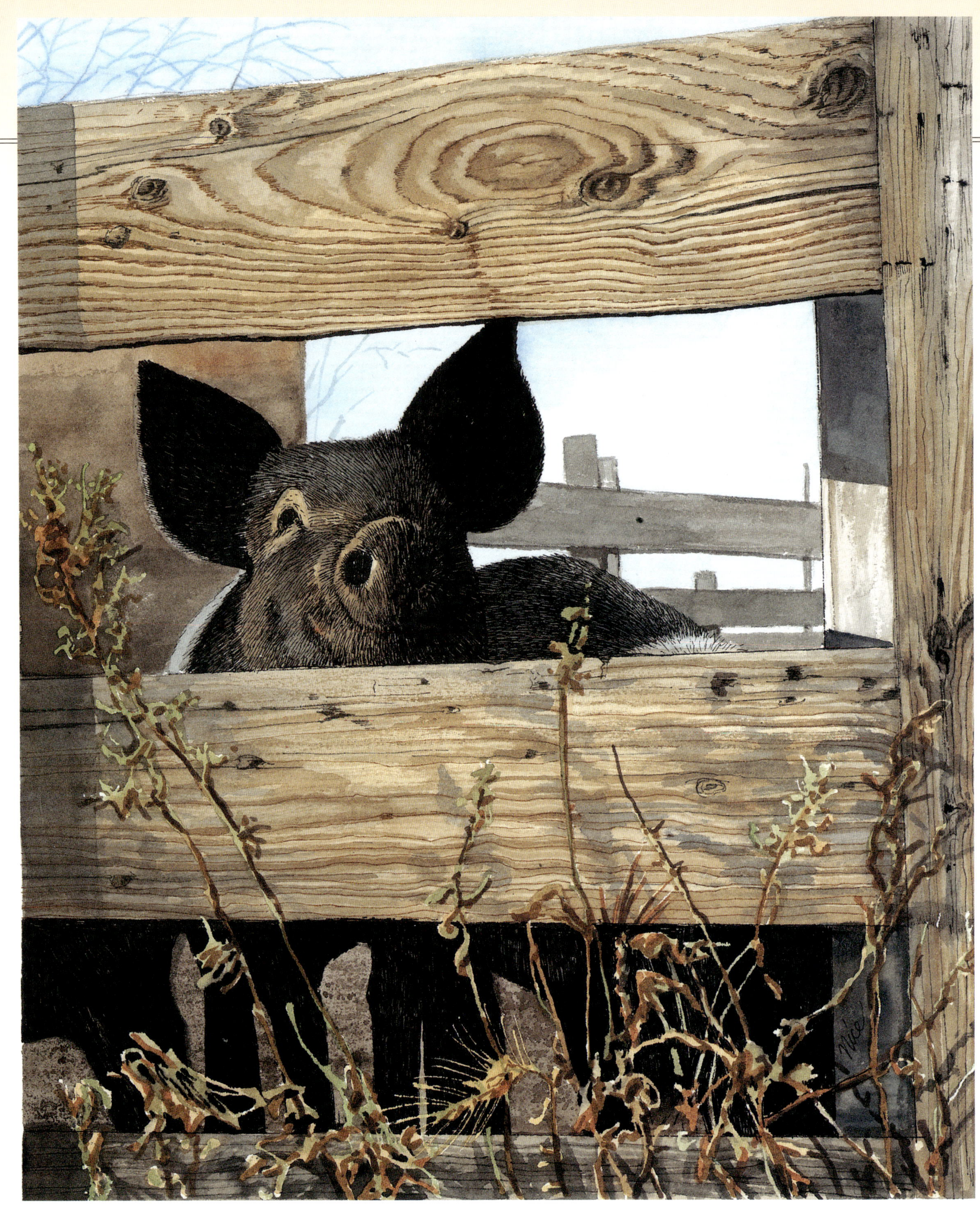

A PIG'S EYE VIEW 8" x 10" (20.5cm x 25.5cm) The Hampshire pig is in pen, ink and watercolor wash, while the background is all watercolor. Pen and brown ink applied to a wet surface is used to create the grainy texture of the wooden boards.

ANIMALS OF THE *field* AND *farm*

5

HOW DOES A CITY KID become familiar with farm animals? I was lucky enough to have a girlfriend whose grandfather owned a ranch in eastern Oregon. I spent many summer weeks at that working ranch, where the draft horses still pulled the hay rake, and the cattle, sheep and pigs weren't petting zoo animals, but livestock. My girlfriend's cousins, who raised calves and lambs to show at the fair, helped with the summer haying on the ranch. It was those country kids who taught me to see farm animals in a whole new light. Through their eyes, I began to notice how the animals were built and the muscle structures that rippled under their hides. My young artist eyes picked up on the color and texture of their coats. Although I have always loved animals, I believe that those many weeks spent on the ranch helped me develop a greater understanding and appreciation for farm animals. In the end, it wasn't just the livestock that enriched my life; I ended up marrying one of my girlfriend's country cousins.

If you were a city kid too and have never been lucky enough to get acquainted with a cow, sheep, pig or goat, this chapter will help you take a closer look at their build and perhaps a glimpse of their personality. Farm animals are a nostalgic subject that transports both the artist and the art viewer back to a time when life was slower paced and wonderfully earthy. The deer at the end of this chapter speak of peace, grace, and a touch of untamed beauty as they glide through the edges of the pasture at dawn. So come, grab your sketchbook and take a trip to the country with me.

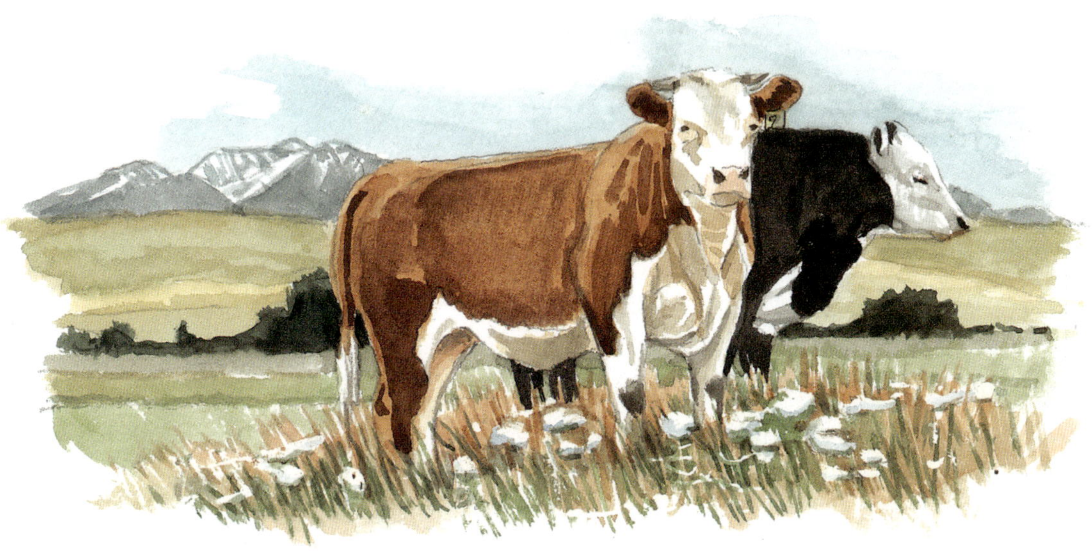

Cattle

As you can see from the preliminary drawings on the right, cattle have very box-like trunks when seen in profile. The heads are triangular. Note that the top line is much straighter across from head to tail, than that of a horse.

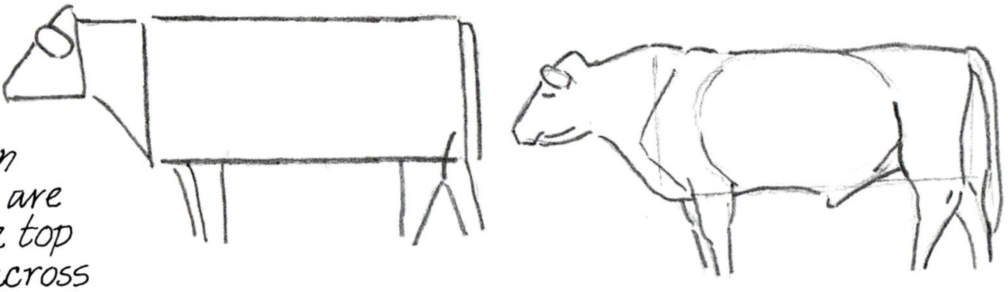

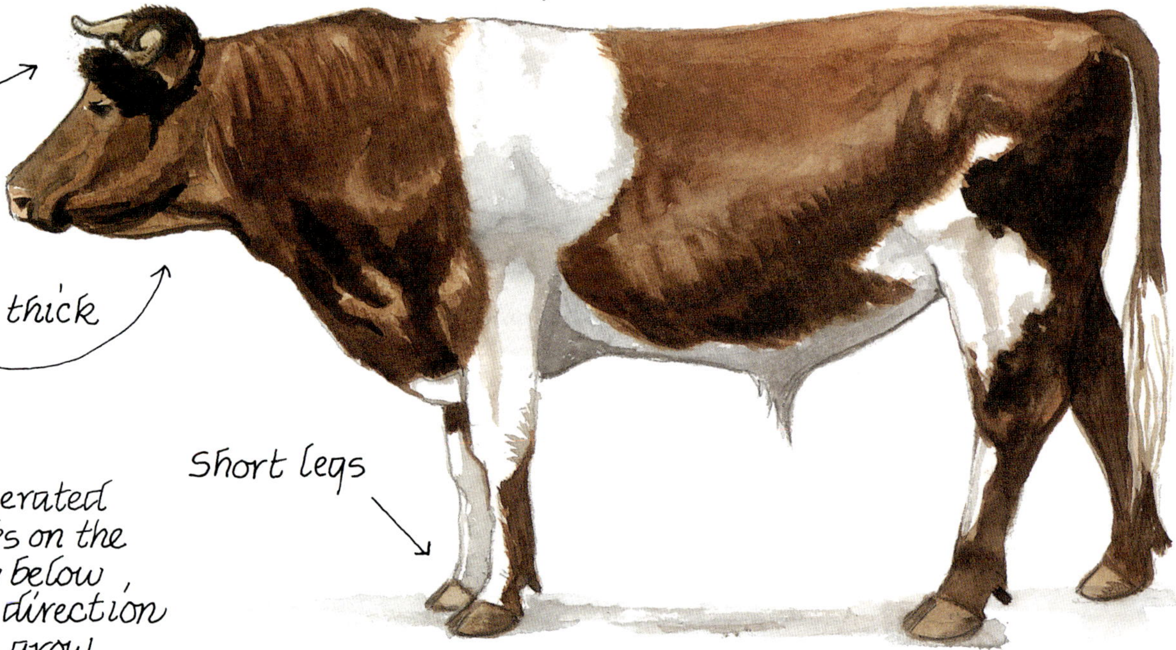

Thick girth

High set tail.

High poll

Horns curve inward and upward

Short, thick neck

Short legs

The exaggerated hair marks on the dairy cow below, show the direction the hairs grow.

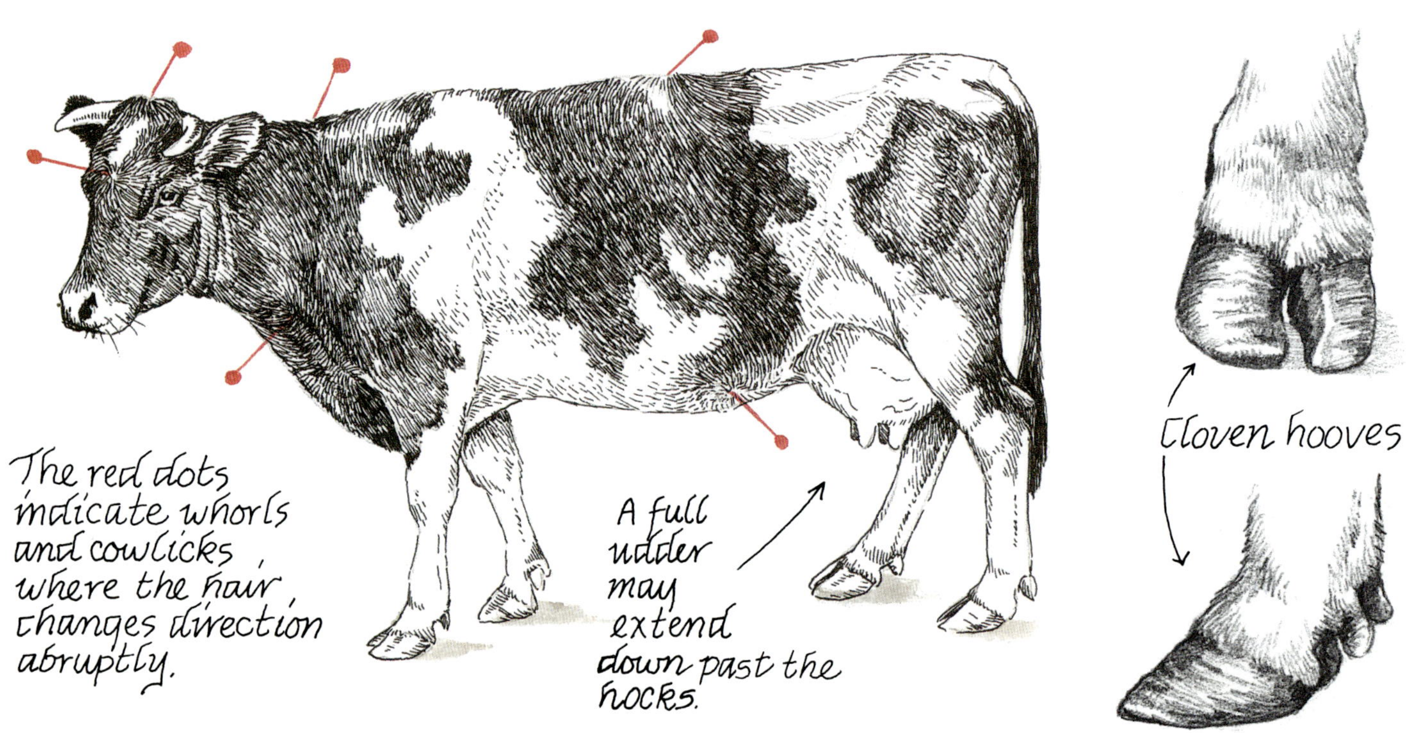

Animals seen at a distance are represented by simplified shapes, and toned down values and colors. ⟶

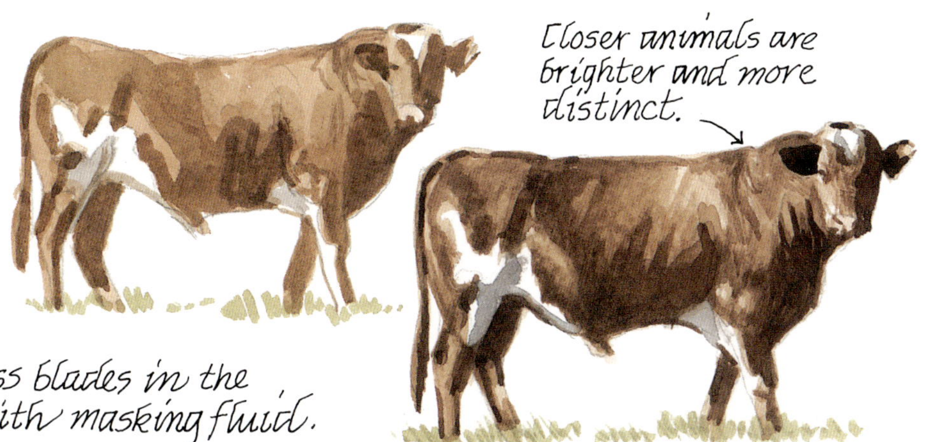

The Hereford calf seen below was blocked in with watercolor washes and detailed with colored pencil.
The Queen Anne's lace and grass blades in the foreground were protected with masking fluid.

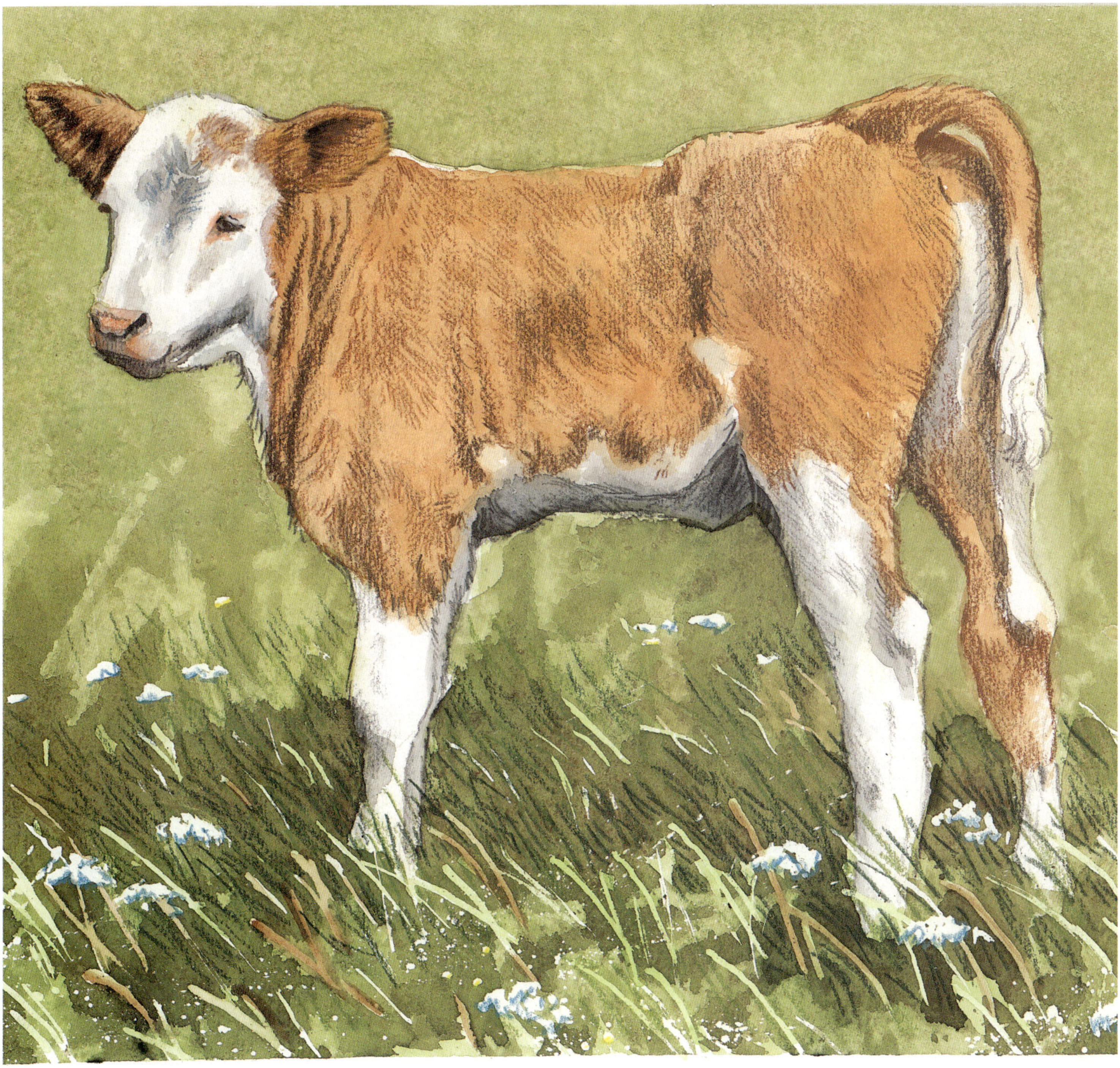

A Collection of Cow Studies

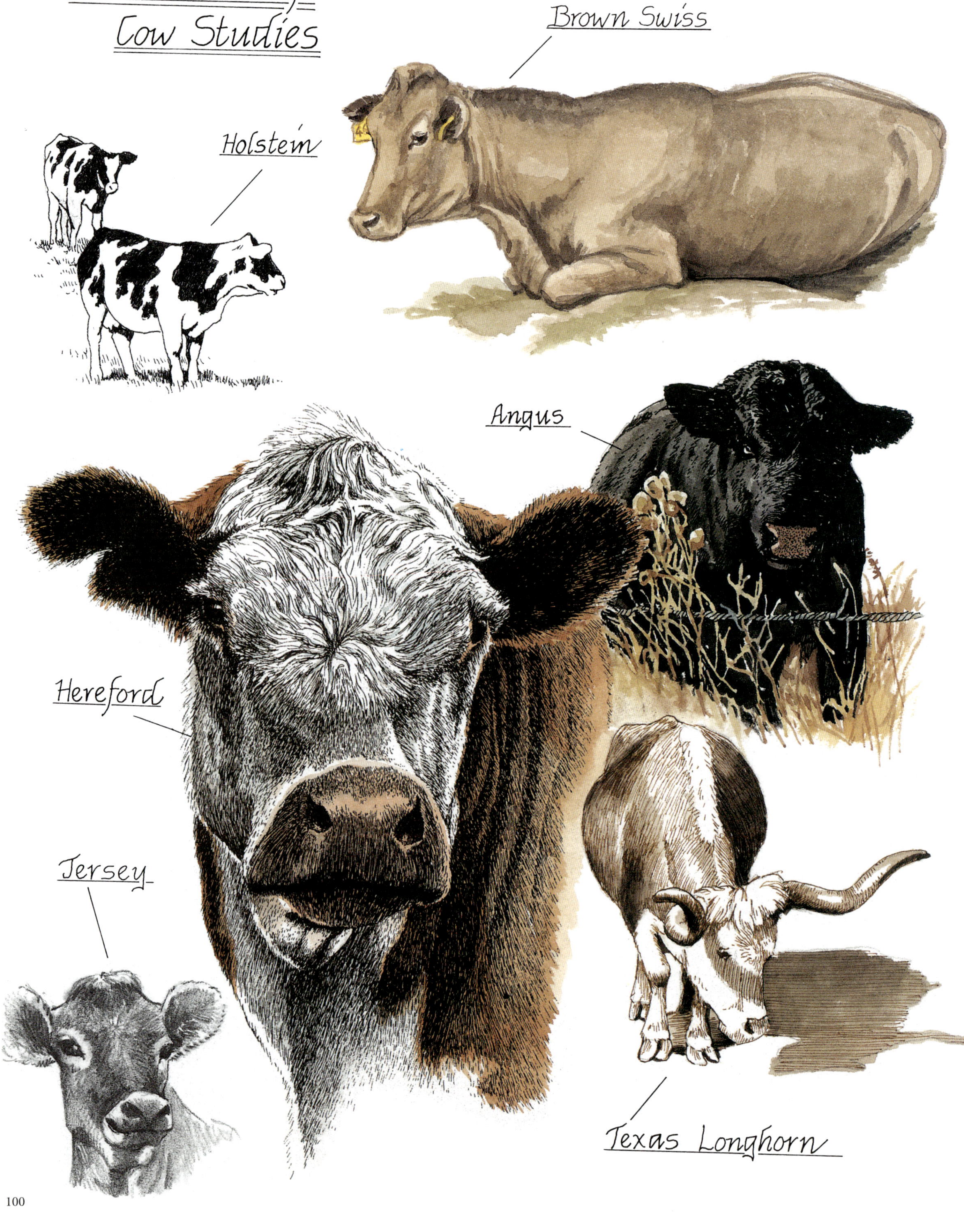

Brown Swiss

Holstein

Angus

Hereford

Jersey

Texas Longhorn

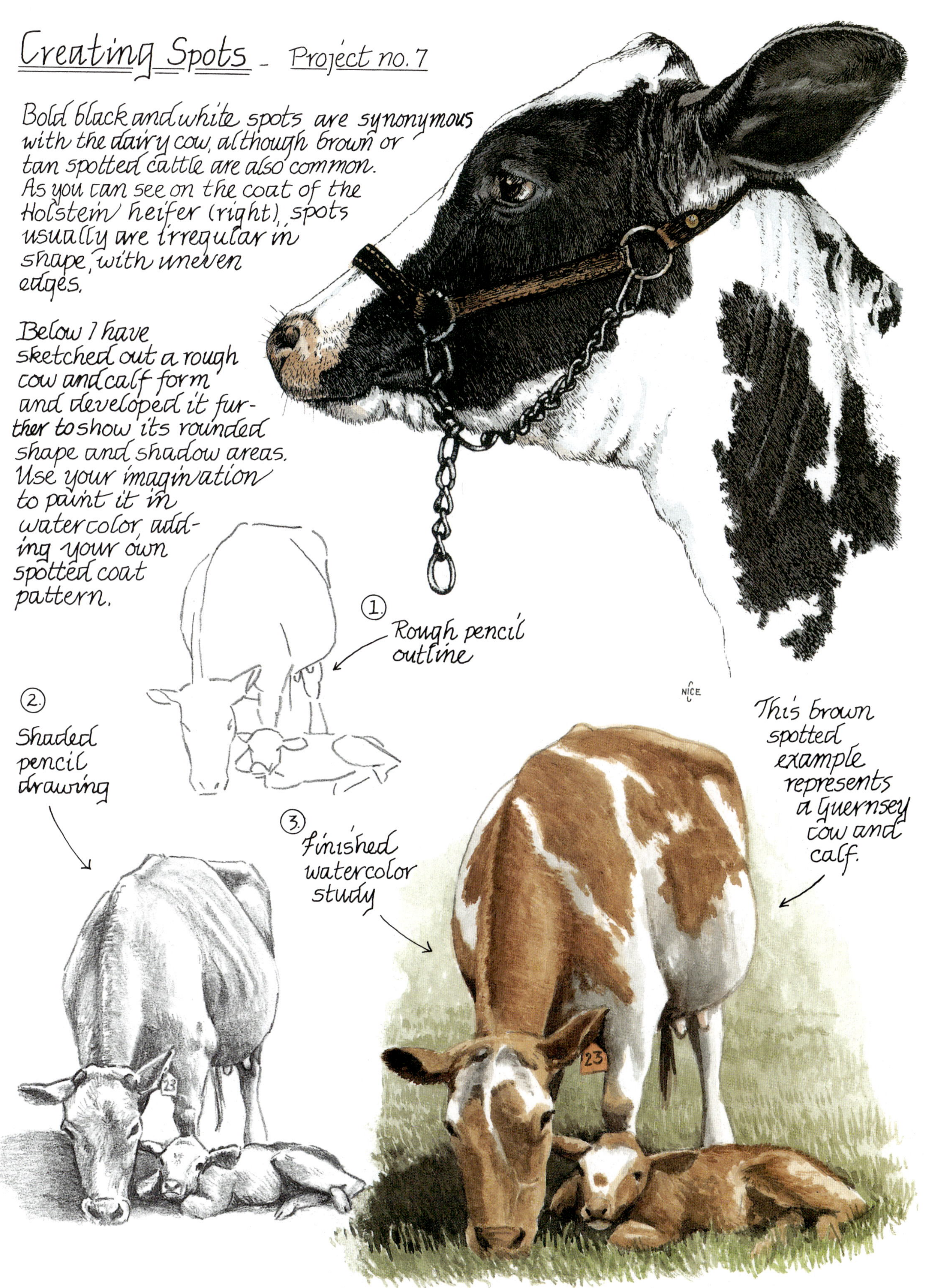
Creating Spots - Project no. 7
Bold black and white spots are synonymous with the dairy cow, although brown or tan spotted cattle are also common. As you can see on the coat of the Holstein heifer (right), spots usually are irregular in shape, with uneven edges.
Below I have sketched out a rough cow and calf form and developed it further to show its rounded shape and shadow areas. Use your imagination to paint it in watercolor, adding your own spotted coat pattern.
1. Rough pencil outline
2. Shaded pencil drawing
3. Finished watercolor study
This brown spotted example represents a Guernsey cow and calf.
NICE
23
23

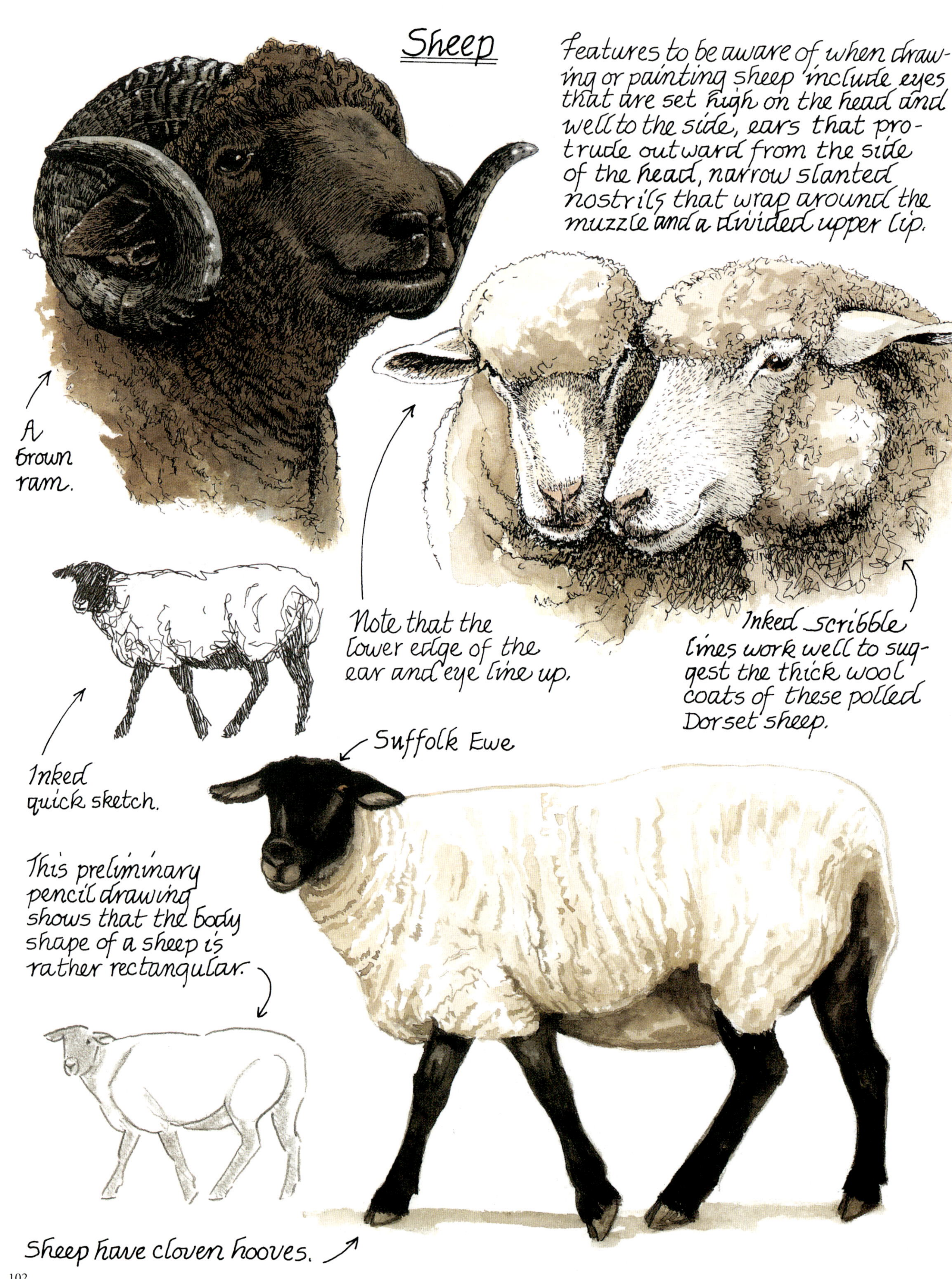
Sheep
Features to be aware of when drawing or painting sheep include eyes that are set high on the head and well to the side, ears that protrude outward from the side of the head, narrow slanted nostrils that wrap around the muzzle and a divided upper lip.
A brown ram.
Note that the lower edge of the ear and eye line up.
Inked scribble lines work well to suggest the thick wool coats of these polled Dorset sheep.
Inked quick sketch.
Suffolk Ewe
This preliminary pencil drawing shows that the body shape of a sheep is rather rectangular.
Sheep have cloven hooves.

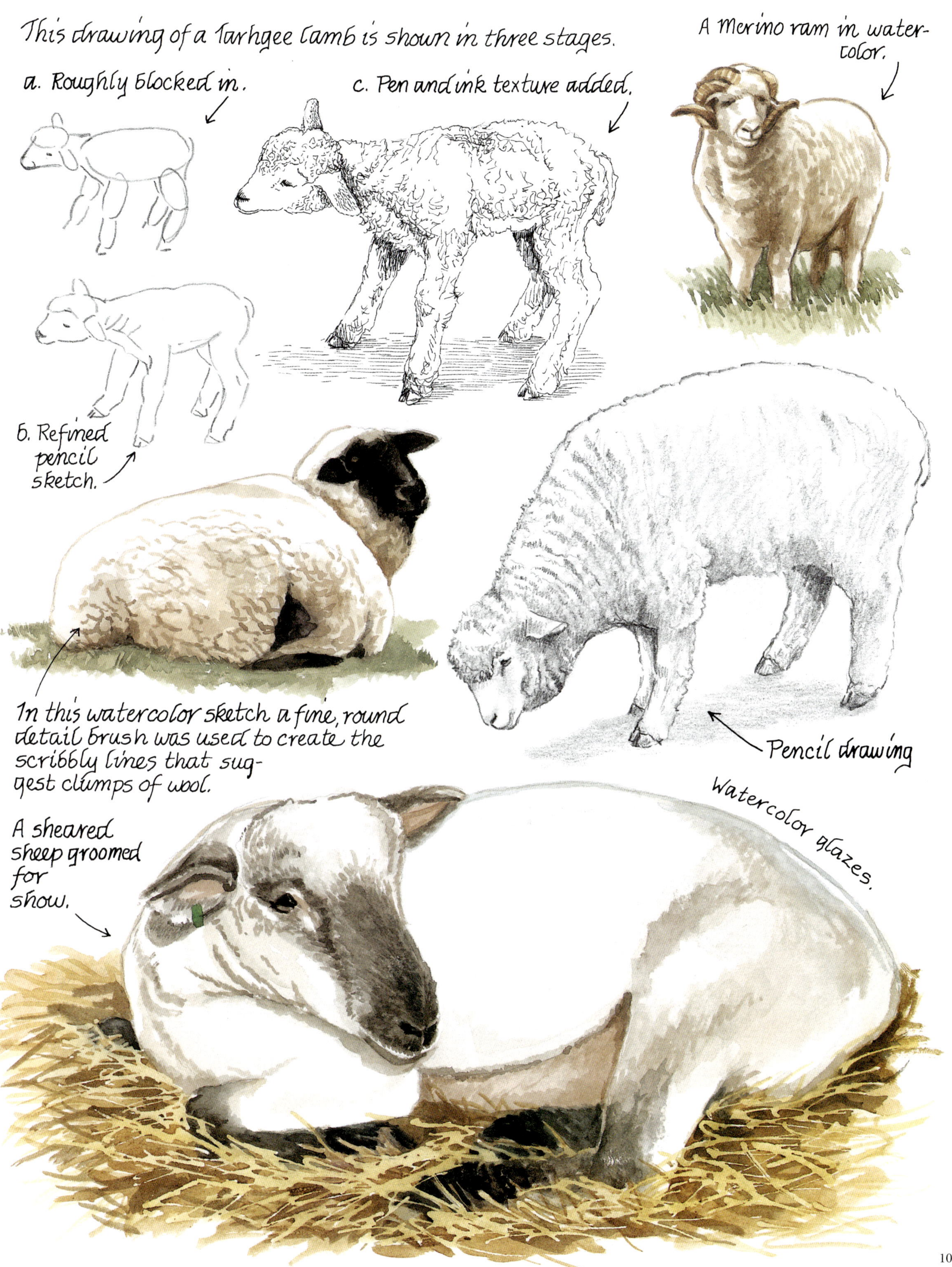
This drawing of a Tarhgee Lamb is shown in three stages.
a. Roughly blocked in.
b. Refined pencil sketch.
c. Pen and ink texture added.
A Merino ram in watercolor.
In this watercolor sketch a fine, round detail brush was used to create the scribbly lines that suggest clumps of wool.
Pencil drawing
A sheared sheep groomed for show.
Watercolor glazes.

Goats

Goats are the jesters of the farm yard, their comical poses providing great sketching material.

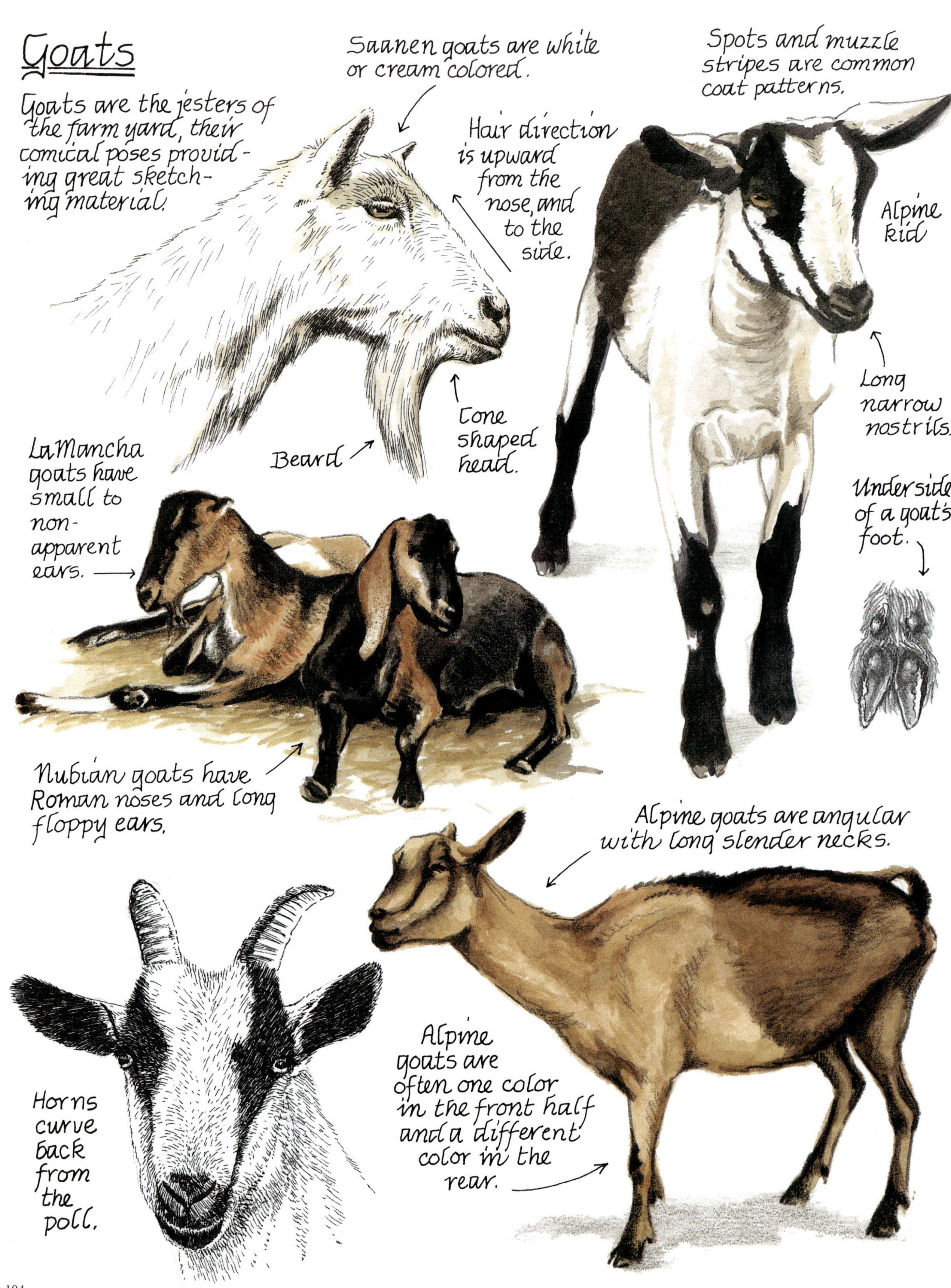

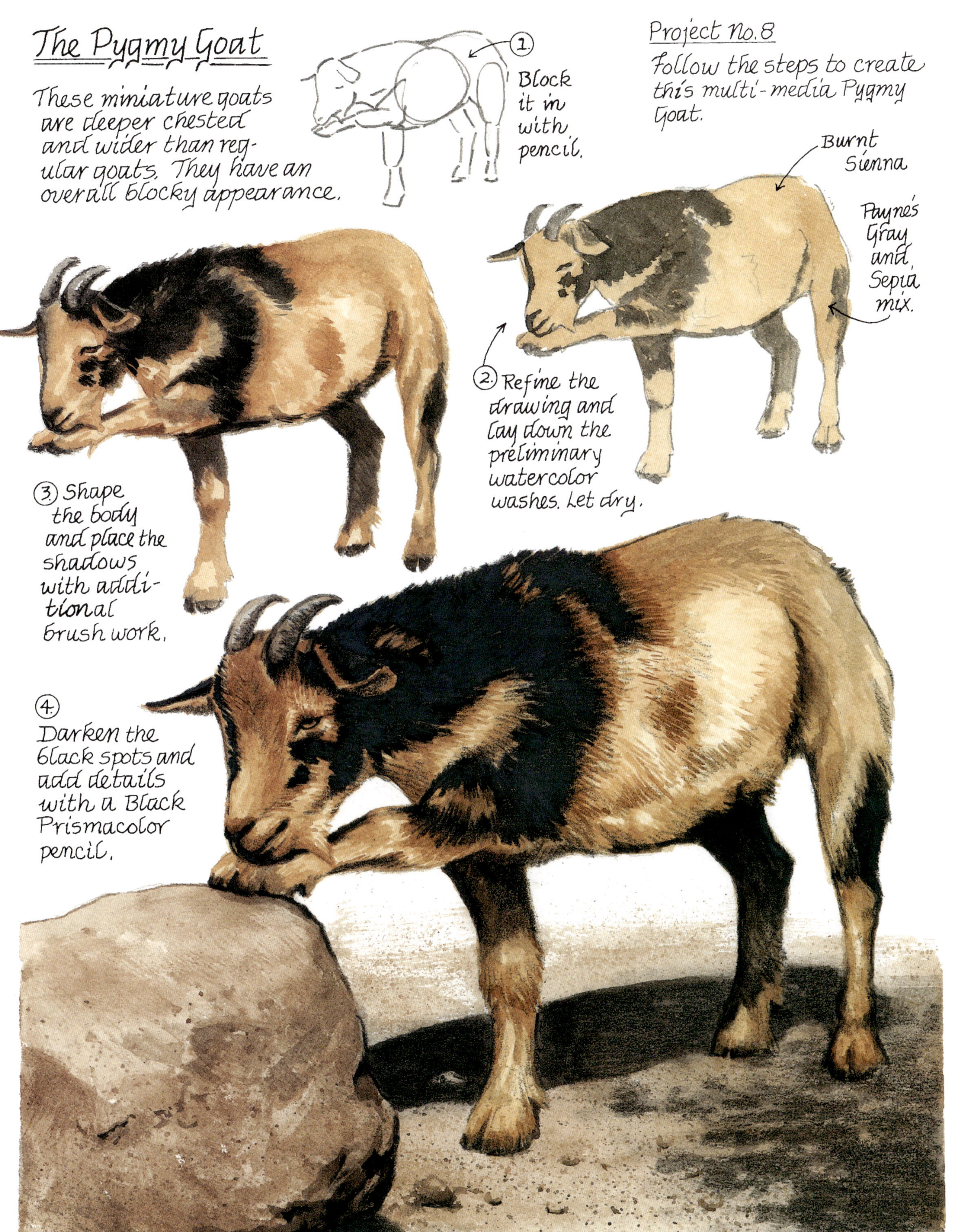
The Pygmy Goat
These miniature goats are deeper chested and wider than regular goats. They have an overall blocky appearance.
① Block it in with pencil.
Project No. 8
Follow the steps to create this multi-media Pygmy Goat.
Burnt Sienna
Payne's Gray and Sepia mix.
② Refine the drawing and lay down the preliminary watercolor washes. Let dry.
③ Shape the body and place the shadows with additional brush work.
④ Darken the black spots and add details with a Black Prismacolor pencil.

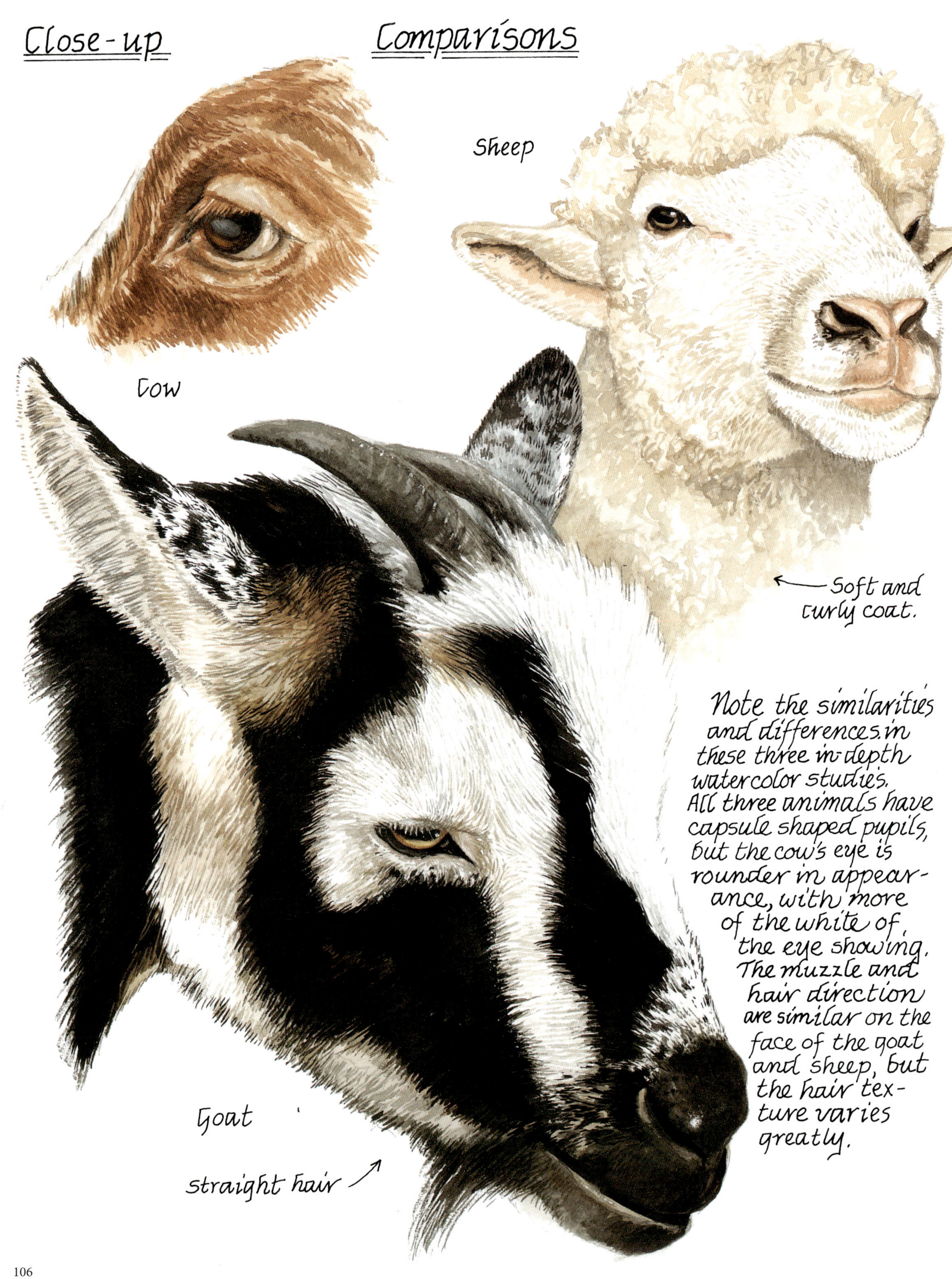
Close-up Comparisons
Sheep
Cow
Soft and curly coat.
Note the similarities and differences in these three in-depth watercolor studies. All three animals have capsule shaped pupils, but the cow's eye is rounder in appearance, with more of the white of the eye showing. The muzzle and hair direction are similar on the face of the goat and sheep, but the hair texture varies greatly.
Goat
straight hair

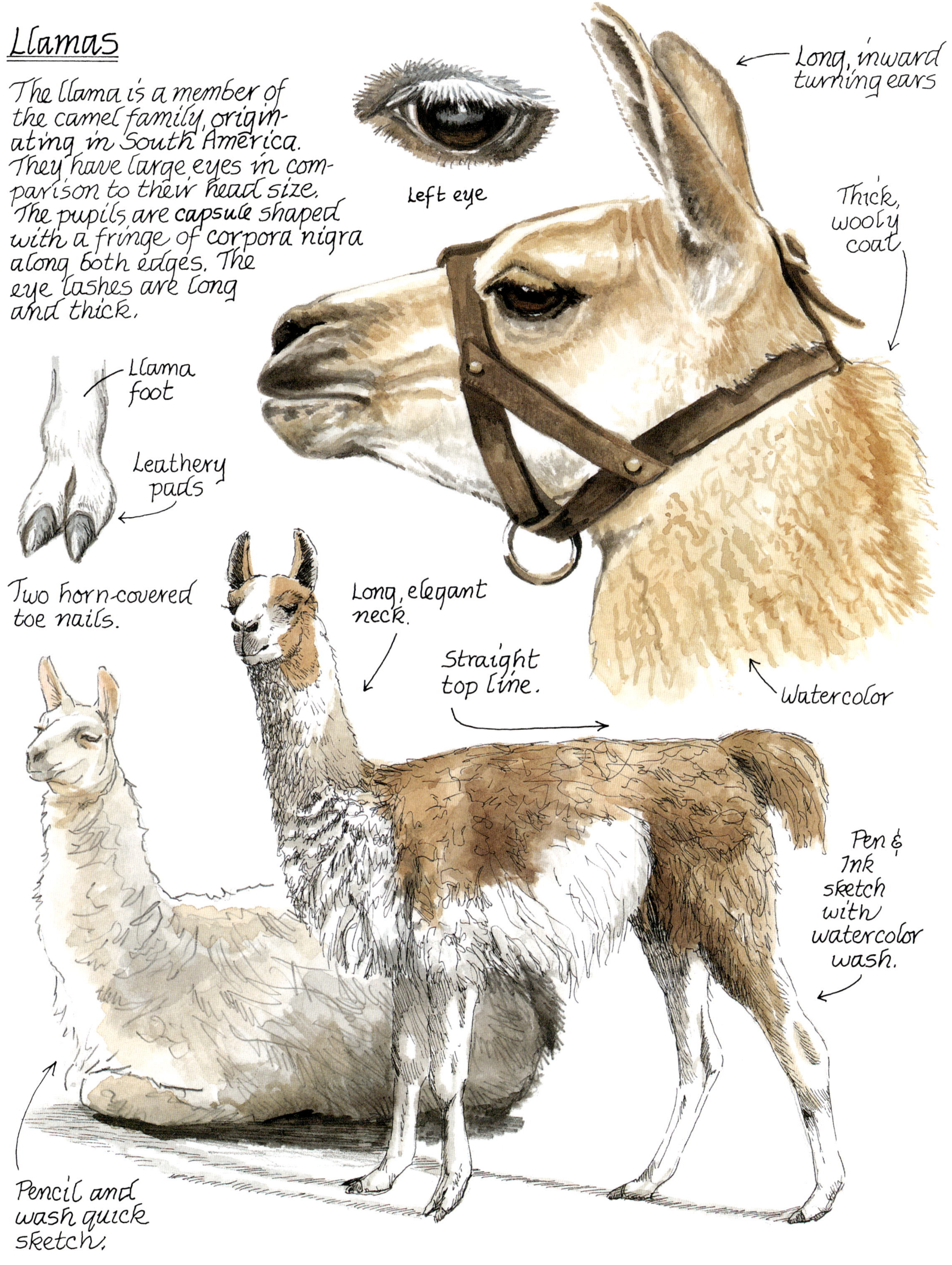
Llamas
The llama is a member of the camel family, originating in South America. They have large eyes in comparison to their head size. The pupils are capsule shaped with a fringe of corpora nigra along both edges. The eye lashes are long and thick.
Left eye
Long, inward turning ears
Thick, wooly coat
Llama foot
Leathery pads
Two horn-covered toe nails.
Long, elegant neck.
Straight top line.
Watercolor
Pen & Ink sketch with watercolor wash.
Pencil and wash quick sketch.

Pigs

Swine, with their comical flat snouts, large fan-like ears, rounded backs, short legs and curly tails are the most unique of the farm yard animals.

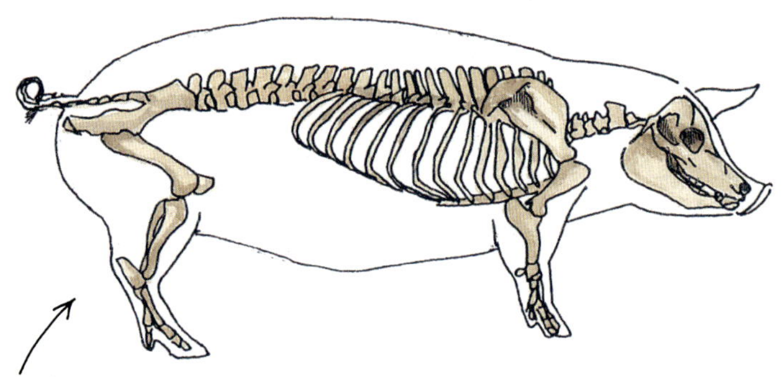

Pig skeleton. Note how long the body is compared to its height.

1. Ovals work well to rough in the rounded shape of the pig's body.

2. This is the refined version of sketch no. 1. The green line indicates the length of the pig from tail tip to snout. The vertical marks show the width of the head. The length equals four heads.

Curled tail.

Convex back

Big ears

Short legs.

A young Yorkshire Pig.

Large, flat snout.

Cloven feet

Large dew claw

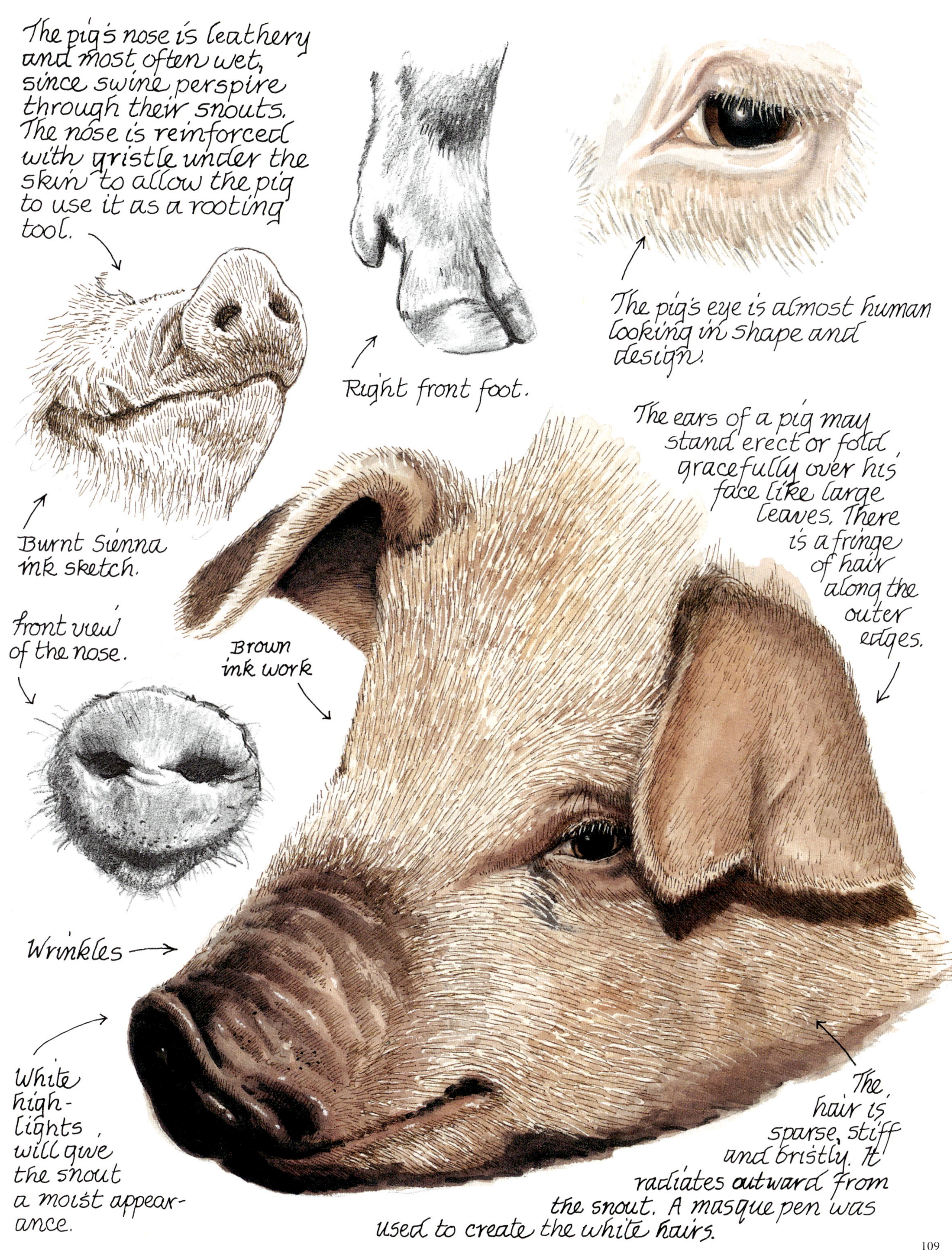
The pig's nose is leathery and most often wet, since swine perspire through their snouts. The nose is reinforced with gristle under the skin to allow the pig to use it as a rooting tool.
Right front foot.
The pig's eye is almost human looking in shape and design.
Burnt Sienna ink sketch.
The ears of a pig may stand erect or fold gracefully over his face like large leaves. There is a fringe of hair along the outer edges.
Front view of the nose.
Brown ink work
Wrinkles
White high-lights will give the snout a moist appear-ance.
The hair is sparse, stiff and bristly. It radiates outward from the snout. A masque pen was used to create the white hairs.

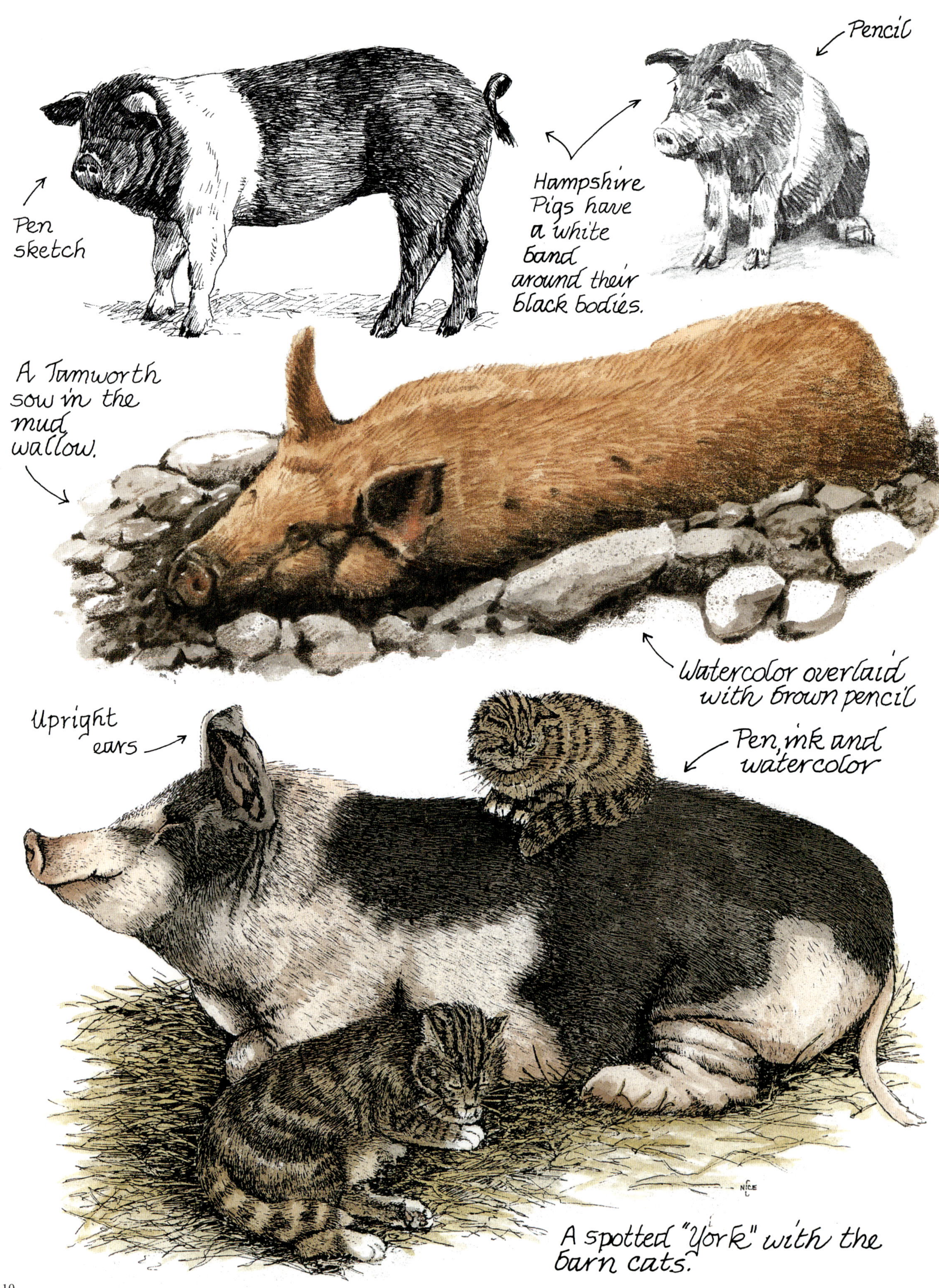
Pencil
Pen sketch
Hampshire Pigs have a white band around their black bodies.
A Tamworth sow in the mud wallow.
Watercolor overlaid with brown pencil
Upright ears
Pen, ink and watercolor
A spotted "York" with the barn cats.

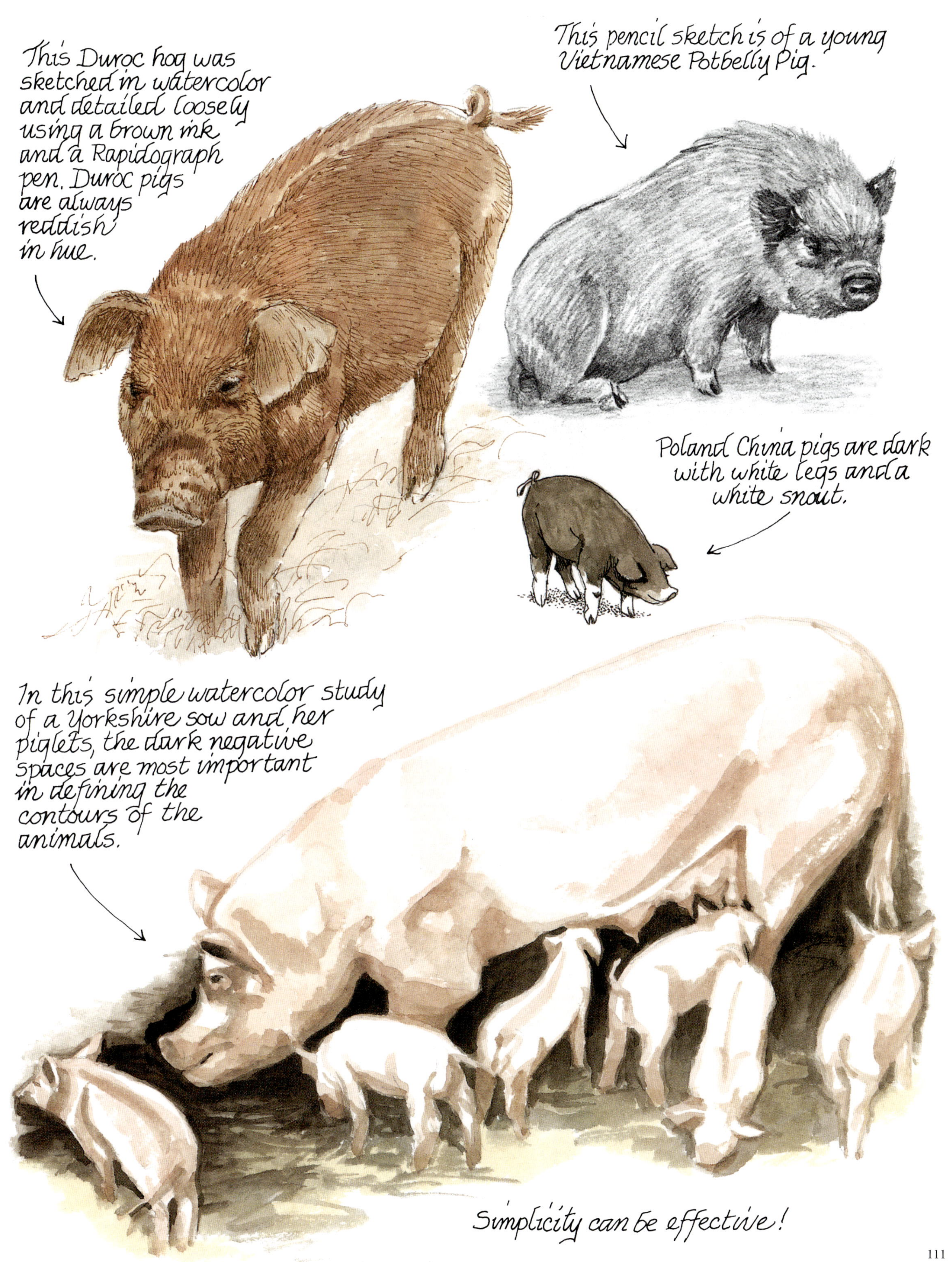
This Duroc hog was sketched in watercolor and detailed loosely using a brown ink and a Rapidograph pen. Duroc pigs are always reddish in hue.
This pencil sketch is of a young Vietnamese Potbelly Pig.
Poland China pigs are dark with white legs and a white snout.
In this simple watercolor study of a Yorkshire sow and her piglets, the dark negative spaces are most important in defining the contours of the animals.
Simplicity can be effective!

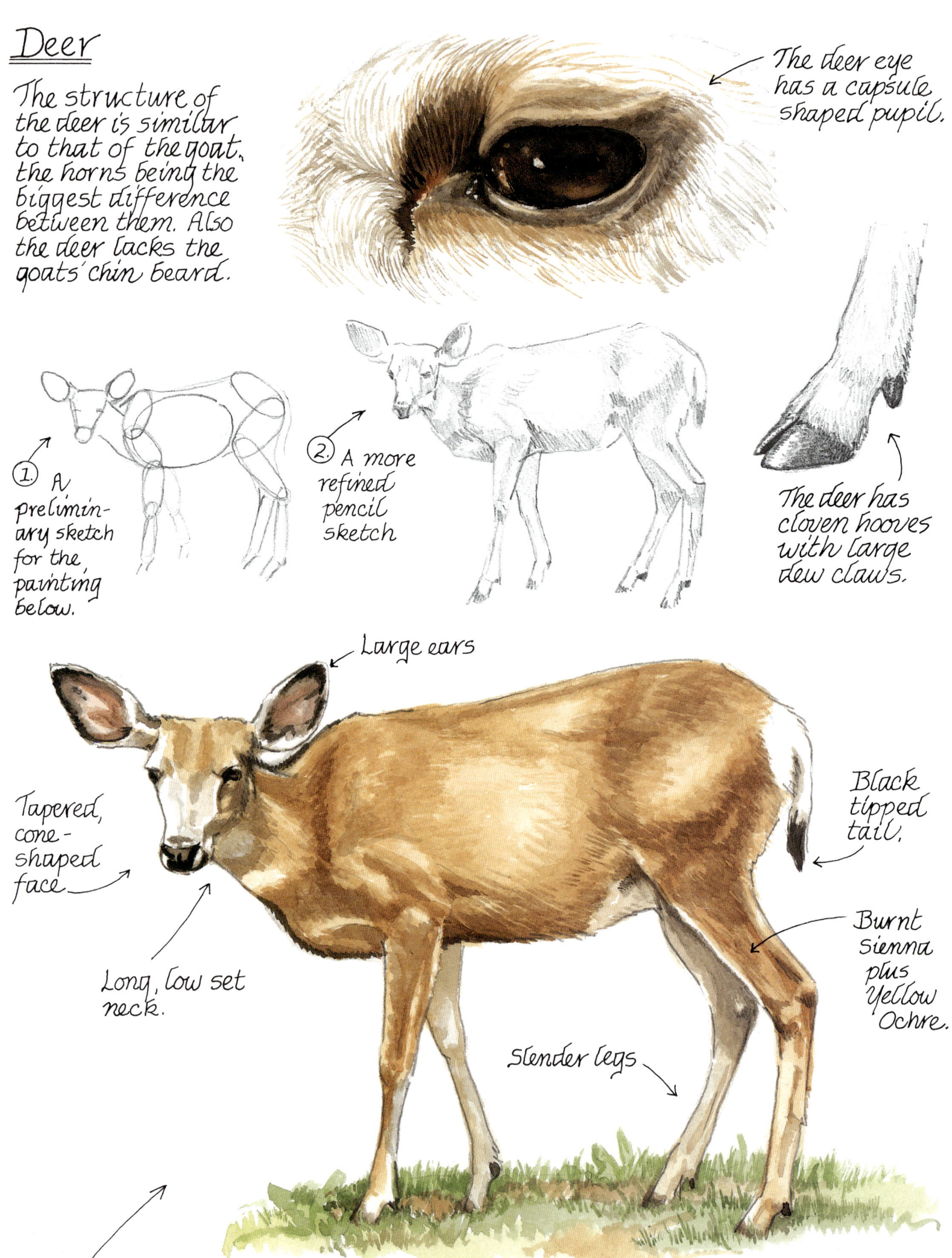

A watercolor study of a Mule Deer.

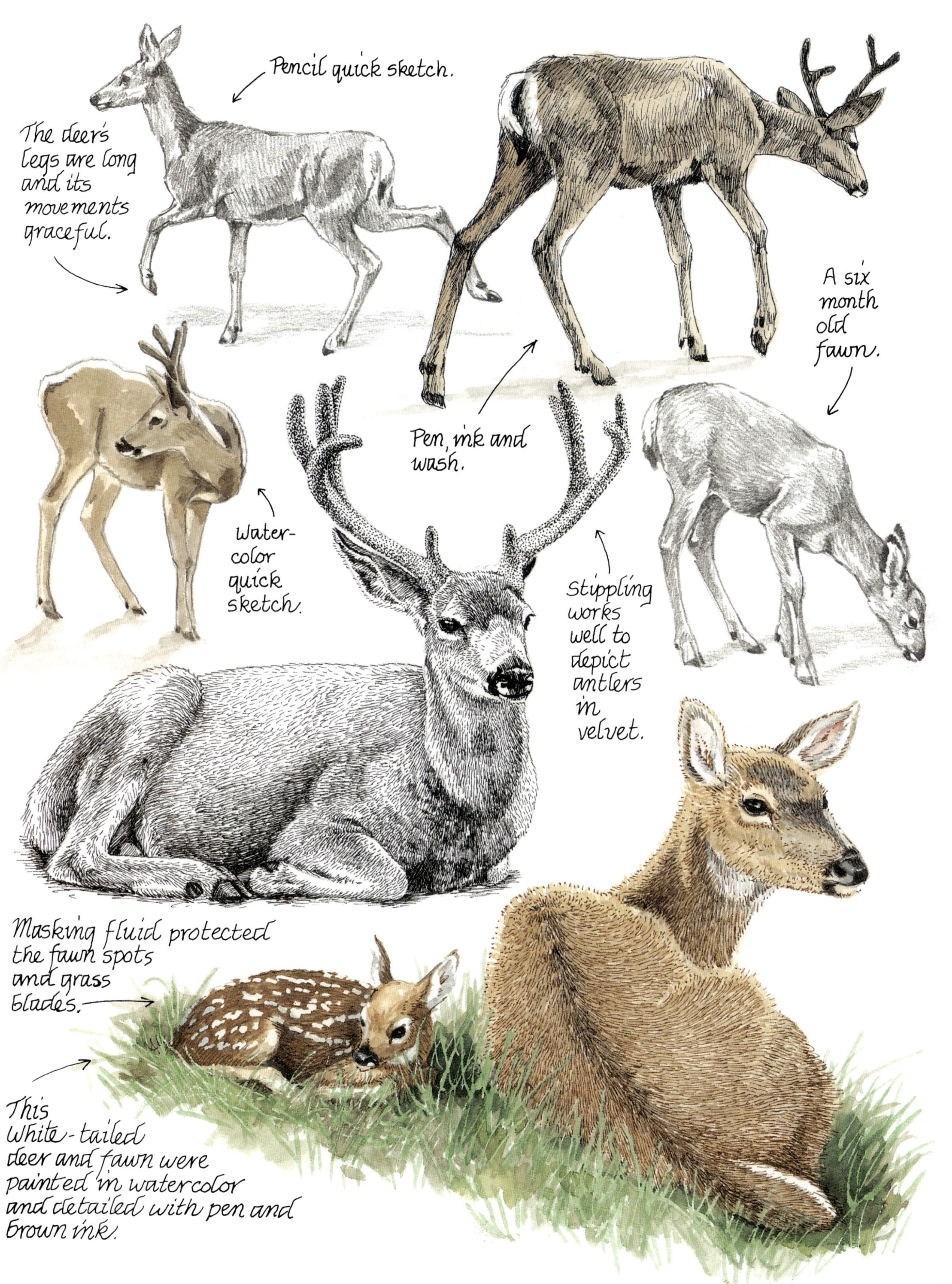
Pencil quick sketch.
The deer's legs are long and its movements graceful.
A six month old fawn.
Pen, ink and wash.
Water-color quick sketch.
Stippling works well to depict antlers in velvet.
Masking fluid protected the fawn spots and grass blades.
This White-tailed deer and fawn were painted in watercolor and detailed with pen and brown ink.

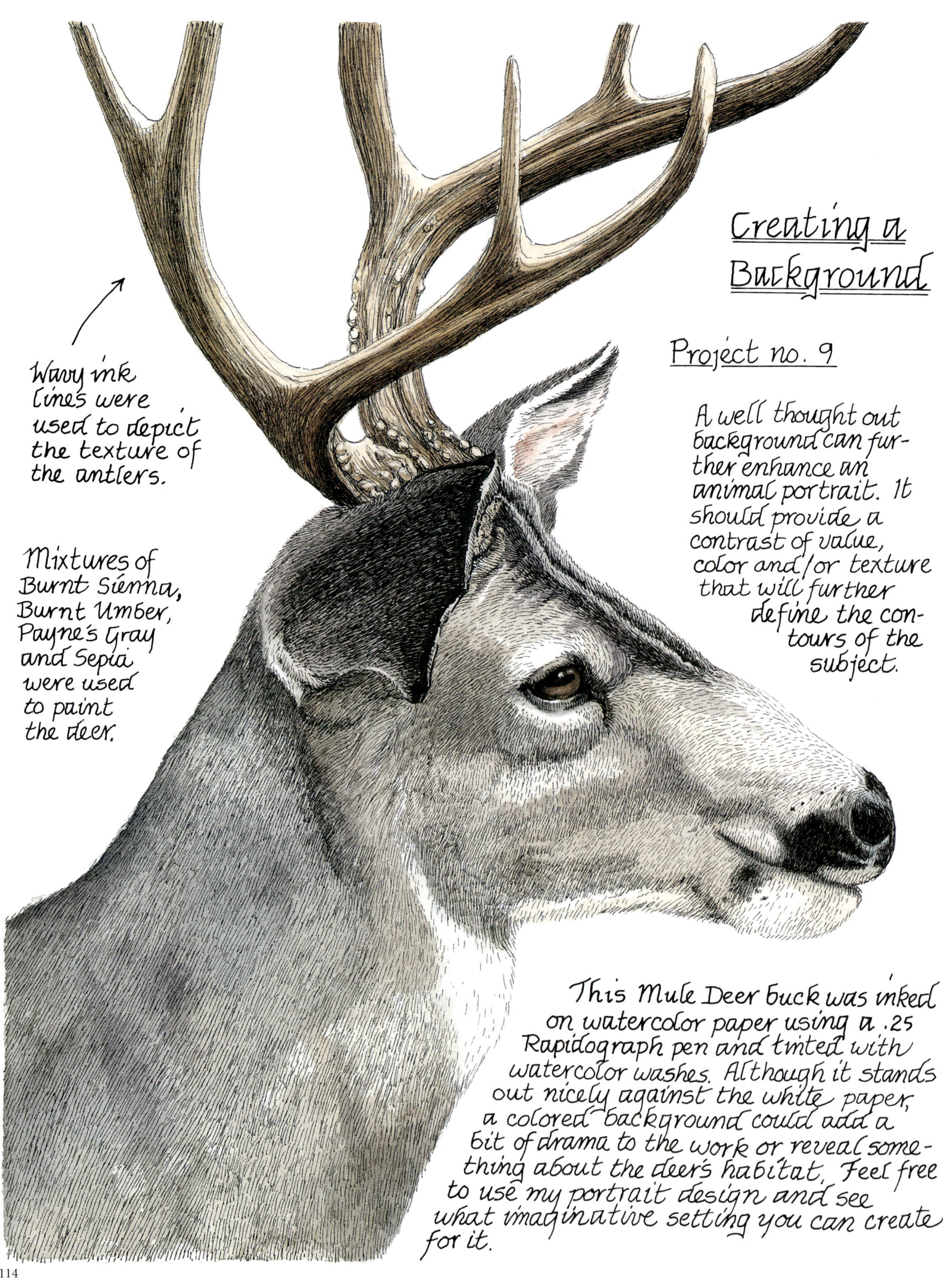
Creating a Background
Project no. 9
A well thought out background can further enhance an animal portrait. It should provide a contrast of value, color and/or texture that will further define the contours of the subject.
Wavy ink lines were used to depict the texture of the antlers.
Mixtures of Burnt Sienna, Burnt Umber, Payne's Gray and Sepia were used to paint the deer.
This Mule Deer buck was inked on watercolor paper using a .25 Rapidograph pen and tinted with watercolor washes. Although it stands out nicely against the white paper, a colored background could add a bit of drama to the work or reveal something about the deer's habitat. Feel free to use my portrait design and see what imaginative setting you can create for it.

A background should be either lighter or darker than the subject. Contrast is the key to creating a background that "pops" the subject forward. →

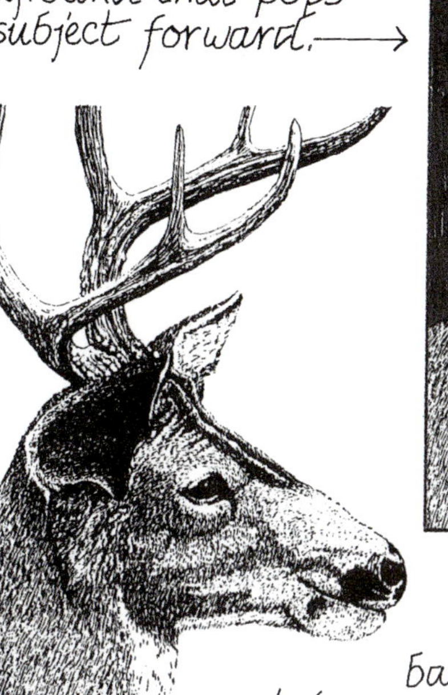

This background is less striking. It competes with the subject in both value and texture. However, the darker stippling around the neck and face provides some definition.

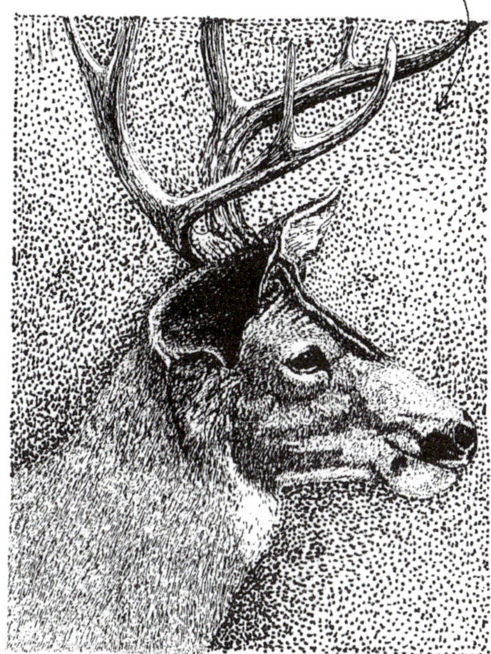

Complementary colors provide great contrast for a background, but keep in mind that background hues should be muted to maintain the look of distance. See the paintings below.

This background is too busy!

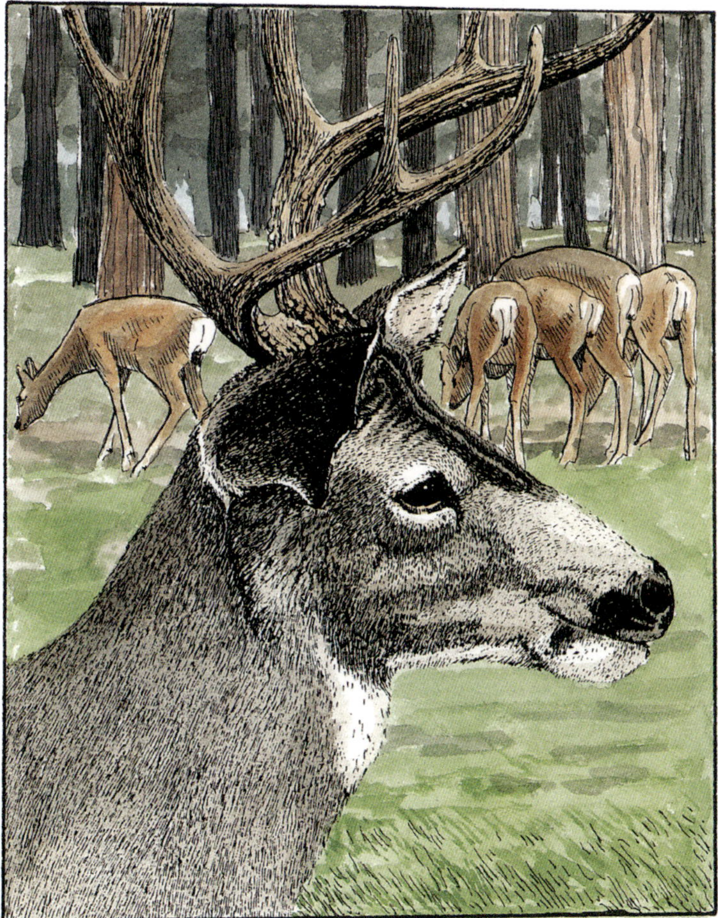

Better!

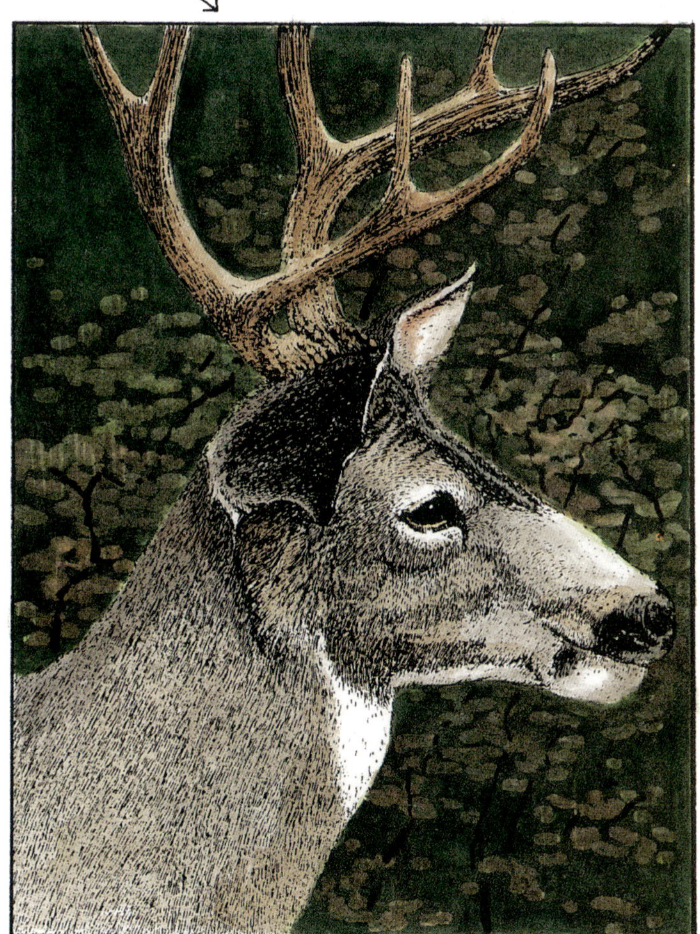

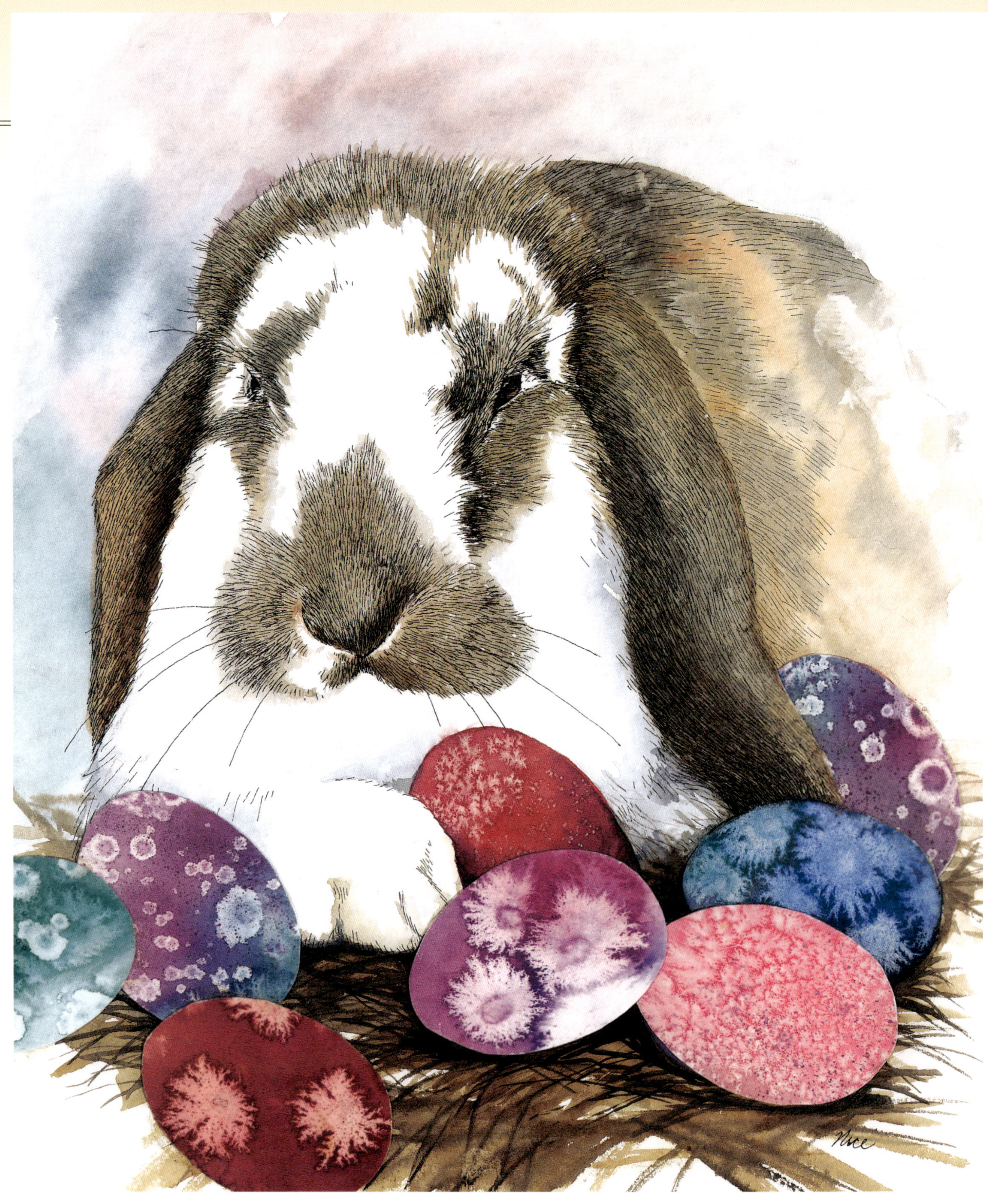

LOP-EARED RABBIT 8½" x 11" (21.7cm x 27.9cm) Collage with watercolor, pen and ink.

SKETCHING THE *small* AND *furry* CREATURES

6

THE WHIMSICAL COLLAGE PAINTING of a lop-eared rabbit on the facing page sets the mood for this chapter. The calico rabbit, detailed in pen and ink and tinted with watercolor washes, is intently guarding a clutch of brightly decorated eggs. The eggs, which were cut out and glued onto the rabbit painting, are painted with vivid watercolor washes, textured with salt, alcohol, and water drops. This painting combines the innocent wonder of childhood, the cuteness of a small furry animal, and the fun of artistic experimentation.

Like many children, one of the first pets I had was a hamster. How I loved that little fellow! I tried to draw him from life, when he would hold still. On the next few pages we'll take a closer look at the cute little creatures that share the lives of children and the young at heart. Just for fun I've thrown in some inventive ways of depicting them and a few adventurous backgrounds.

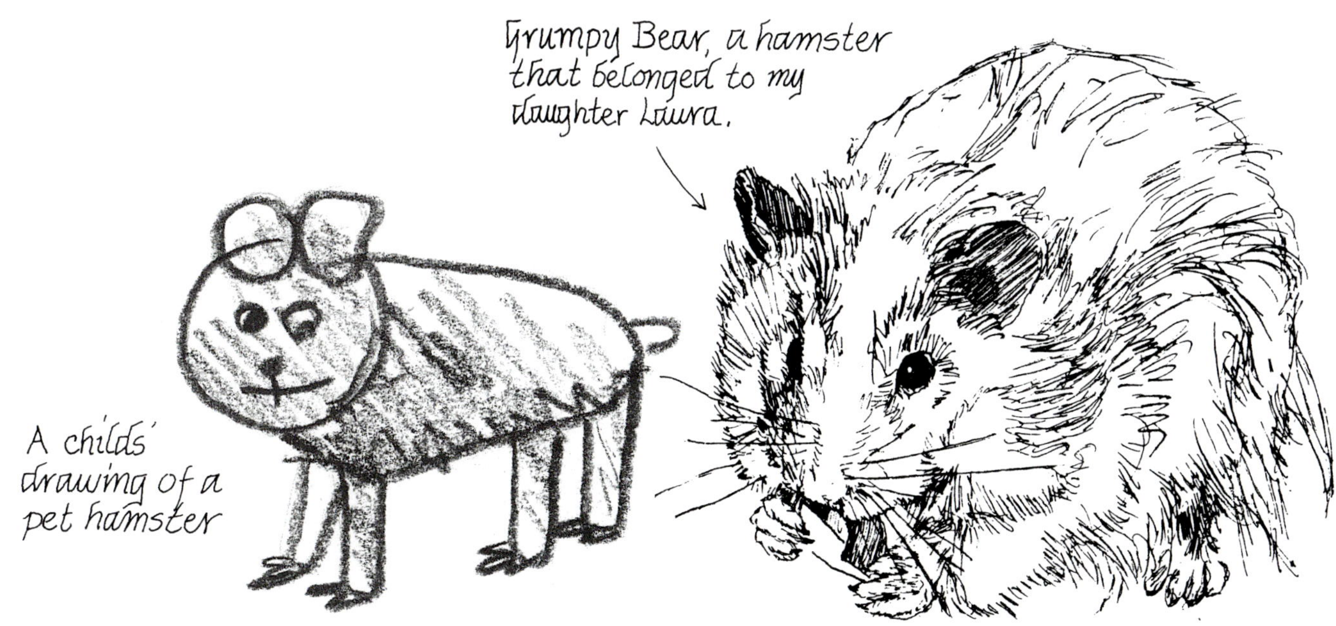

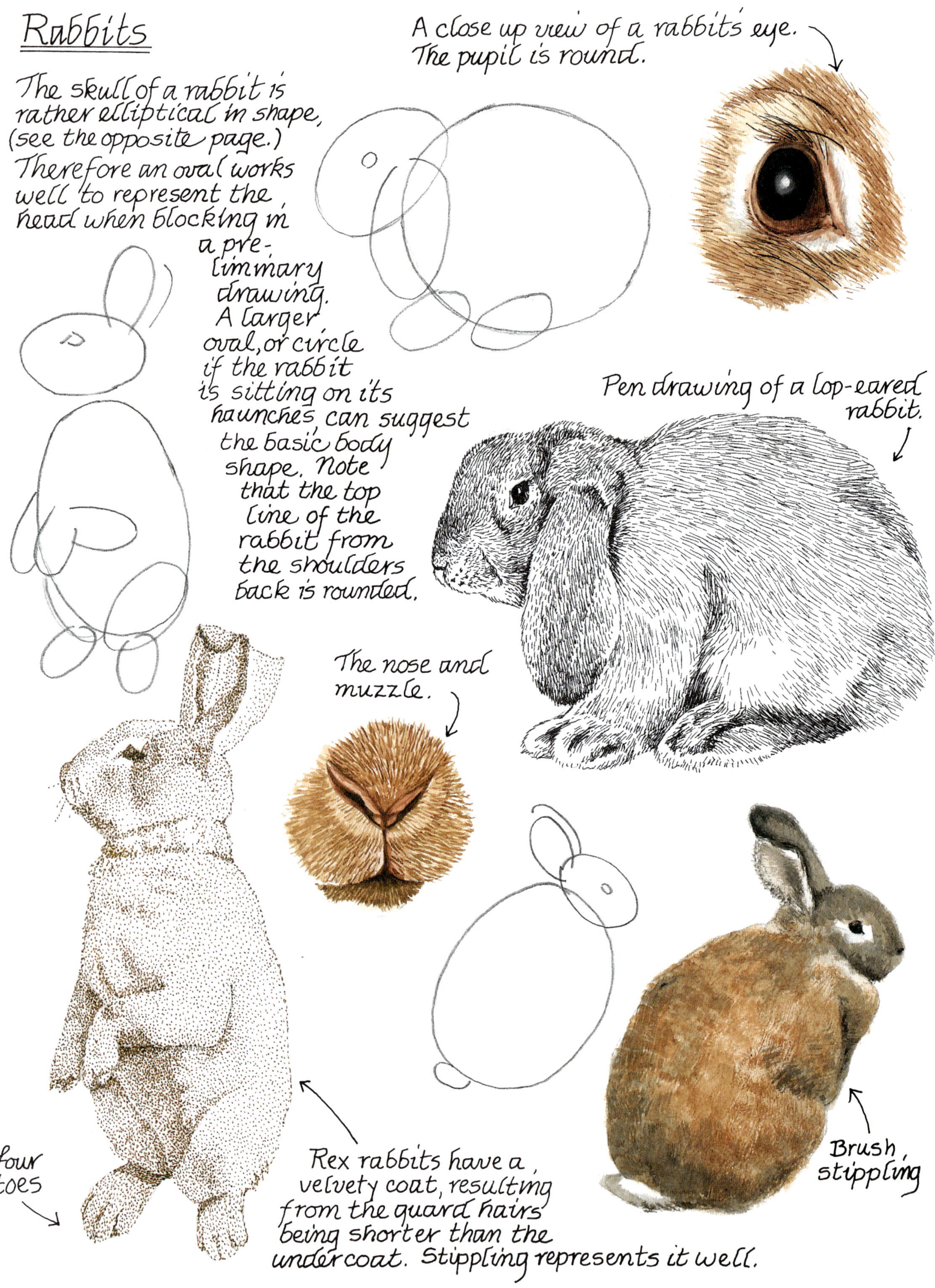
Rabbits
The skull of a rabbit is rather elliptical in shape, (see the opposite page.) Therefore an oval works well to represent the head when blocking in a preliminary drawing. A larger oval, or circle if the rabbit is sitting on its haunches, can suggest the basic body shape. Note that the top line of the rabbit from the shoulders back is rounded.
A close up view of a rabbit's eye. The pupil is round.
Pen drawing of a lop-eared rabbit.
The nose and muzzle.
four toes
Rex rabbits have a velvety coat, resulting from the guard hairs being shorter than the undercoat. Stippling represents it well.
Brush stippling

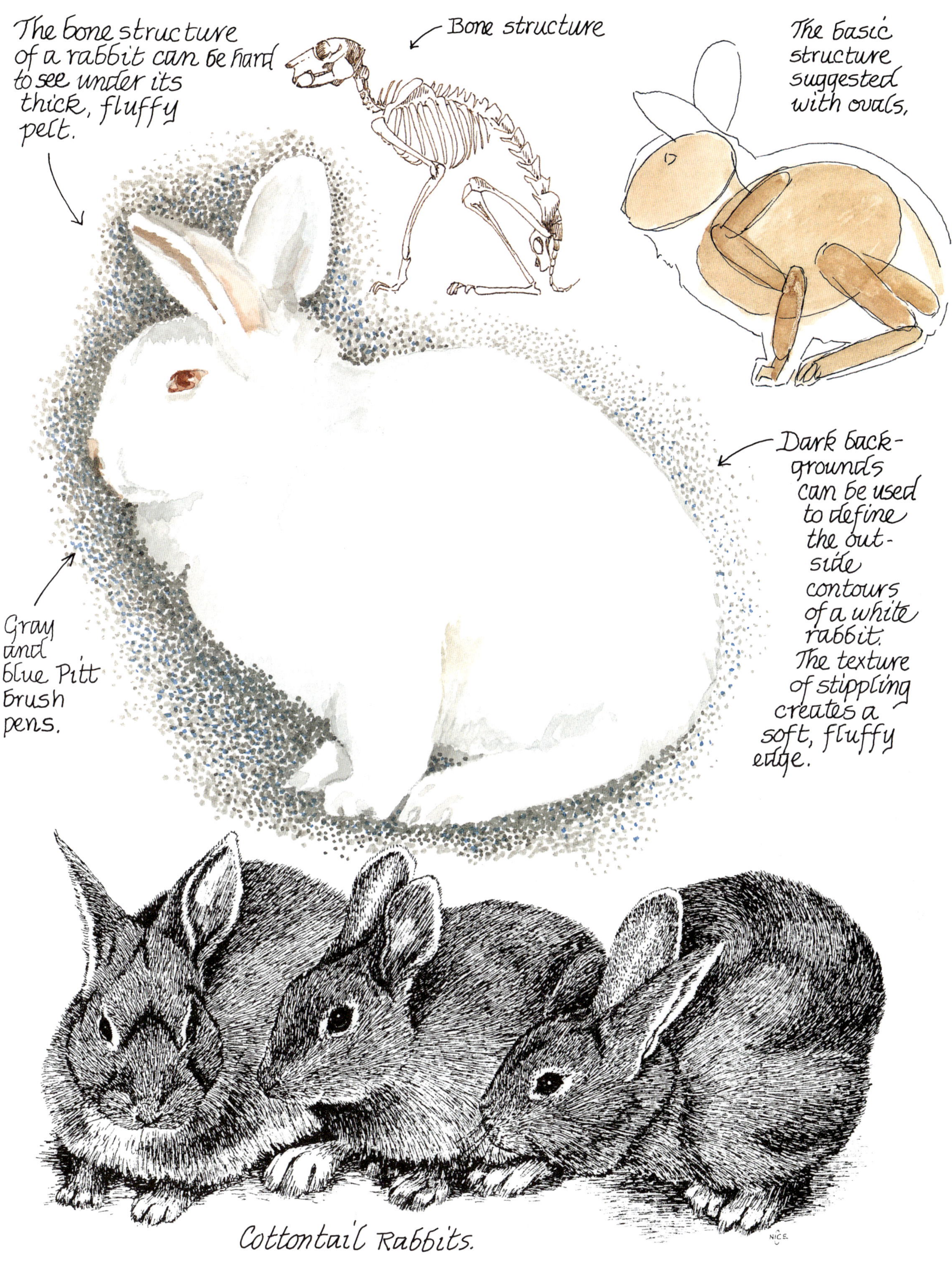
The bone structure of a rabbit can be hard to see under its thick, fluffy pelt.
Bone structure
The basic structure suggested with ovals.
Dark backgrounds can be used to define the outside contours of a white rabbit. The texture of stippling creates a soft, fluffy edge.
Gray and blue Pitt brush pens.
Cottontail Rabbits.
NICE

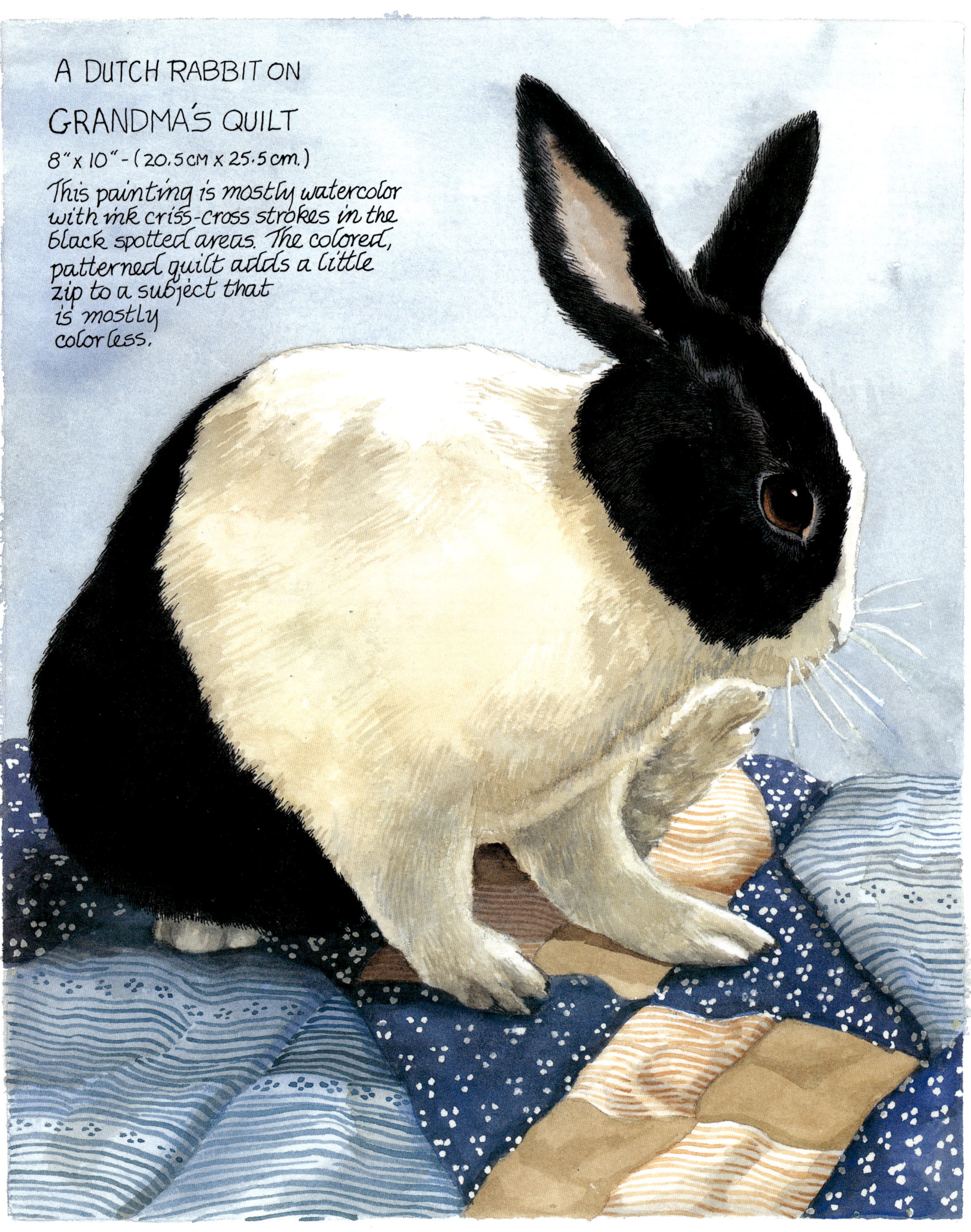
A DUTCH RABBIT ON
GRANDMA'S QUILT
8" x 10" - (20.5 CM x 25.5 cm.)
This painting is mostly watercolor with ink criss-cross strokes in the black spotted areas. The colored, patterned quilt adds a little zip to a subject that is mostly colorless.

Sponge Texturing

Project no. 10

Use a small, moist sea sponge to stamp on the fluffy texture of a rabbit's coat.

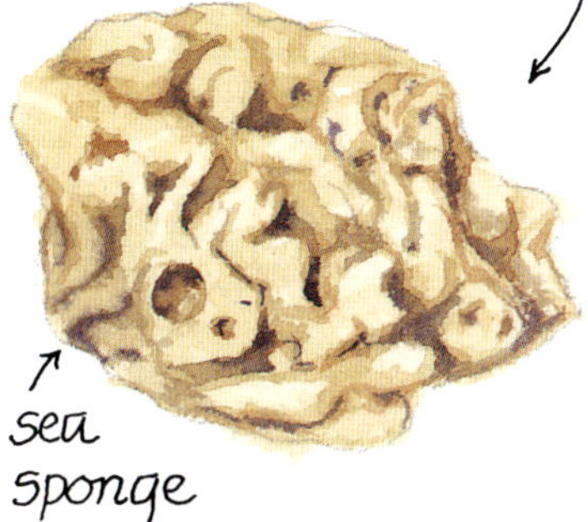
sea sponge

① Sketch a rabbit onto watercolor paper. Make it large enough to maneuver a sponge in.

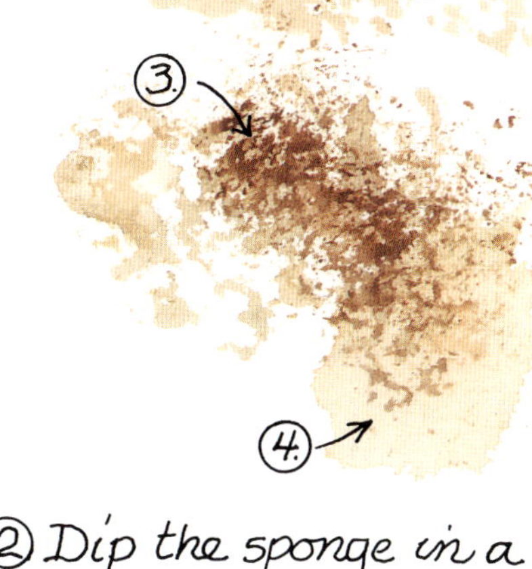

② Dip the sponge in a pale wash of color and tap it over the dry surface of the rabbit. Leave white areas unstamped. Let it dry.

③ Sponge a darker tone into the shadow areas.

④ Glaze the colored fur areas of the rabbit with a pale wash of the first color stamped on.

⑤. Use brush stippling to fill in areas that were difficult to sponge.

⑥ The smooth areas of the rabbit are painted in using a small round brush. This includes the inner ears and eyes.

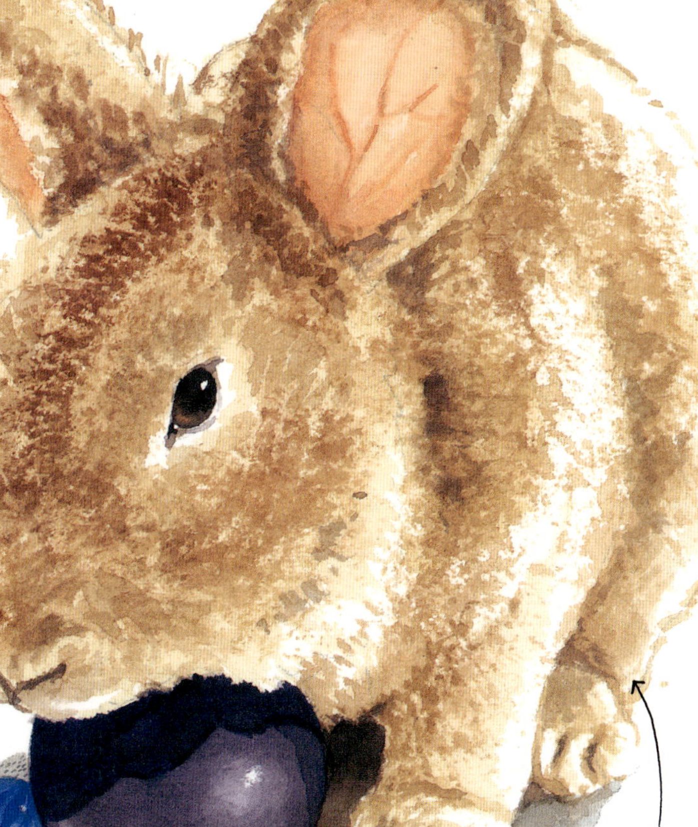

The ball and marbles, were added to the painting for a bit more color and interest. They call attention to the eye which is of a similar shape and value, and help the viewer focus on the head. The toys also add a sense of playfulness to the composition.

Burnt Sienna plus Yellow Ochre

Ferrets

These peppy little pets are in the same family as minks, weasels and otters. The domesticated ferret has a long, slender body and short legs. The top-line of the back is rounded when the animal is standing in a hunched position or scampering about. The coat is sleekly furred, the natural color being shades of brown. Albinos are also common.

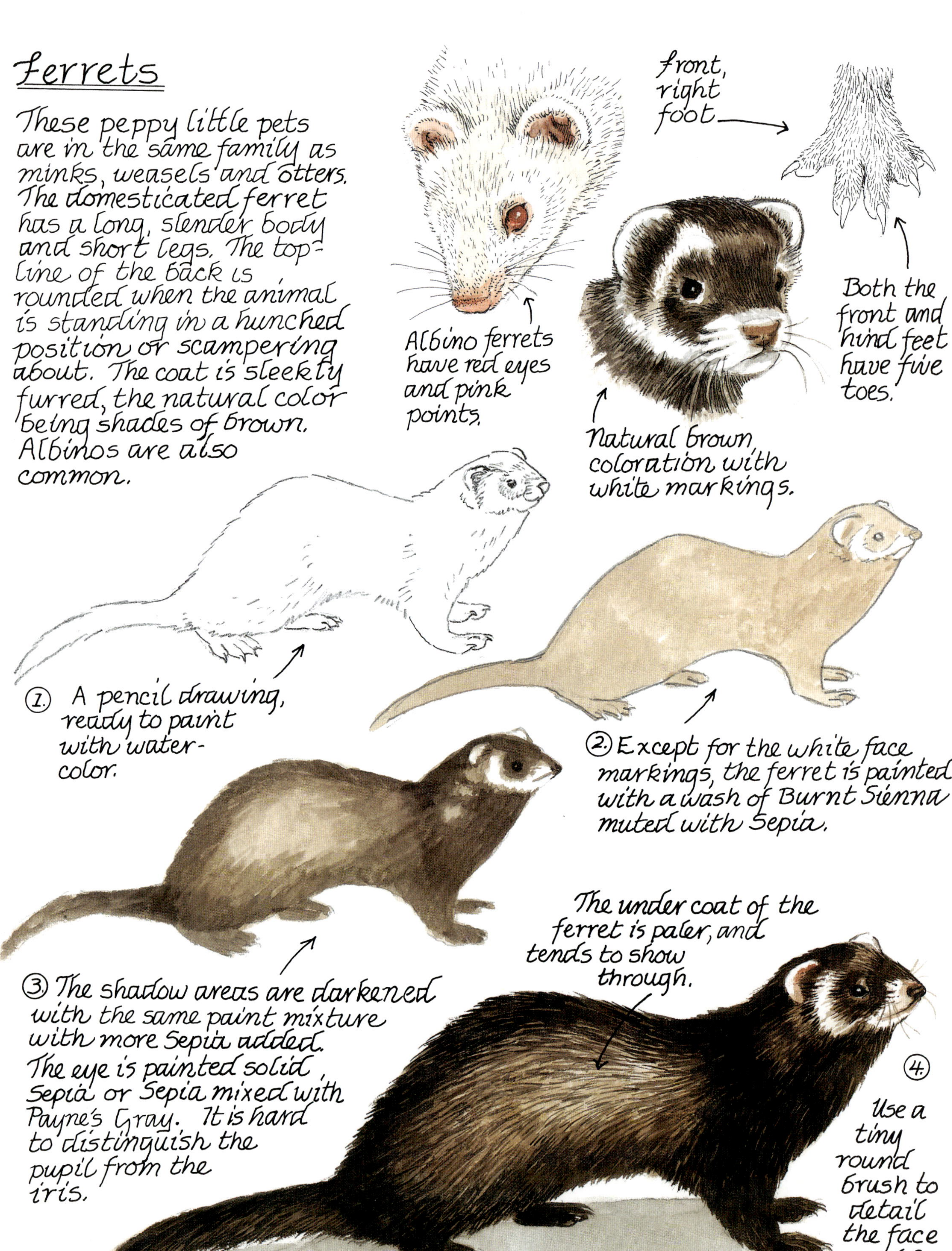

The Guinea Pig Group

Guinea pigs and chinchillas both belong to the same sub-group within the rodent family (caviomorphs). They are fairly easy to draw. The bodies, covered with a thick coat of hair, have an oval shape.

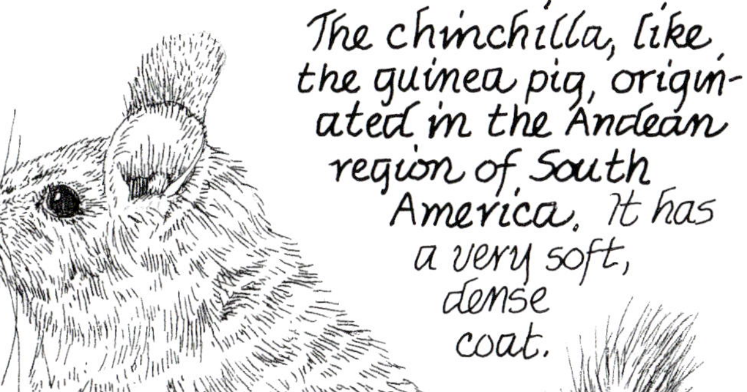

The chinchilla, like the guinea pig, originated in the Andean region of South America. It has a very soft, dense coat.

The guinea pig has a large head and no tail.

The chinchilla has a bushy tail. The standard color of the coat is a mottled gray.

The color of the guinea pig ranges from white, through numerous shades of brown, to black. Spotted coats are common. This guinea pig, painted in watercolor, is a tortoiseshell and white color.

The Abyssinian breed has a series of whorls and ridges over its coat, as the hair changes direction many times.

The Peruvian (angora) breed has a silky, long coat.

This is a smooth-coated guinea pig. Both watercolor and pen and colored inks were used to paint it.

Four toes on the front feet and three on the back feet.

Hamsters

Hamsters are friendly, inquisitive and intelligent. These cuddly little creatures have an excess of loose skin folds which makes them appear chubby, and ripples when they walk. As with the guinea pig, an elliptical form is a good way to begin drawing the rounded shape of the Hamster.

Side view of the basic hamster form.

Like most rodents, the hamster has a well rounded eye shape. The eye sits shallowly in the skull and protrudes. The pupil is round and hard to see against the dark iris.

Hamsters do have tails, but they are short nubbins which are usually hidden beneath the fur.

The dwarf Russian hamster has a dark dorsal stripe. One form turns white in the winter.

The more common Syrian or Golden Hamster comes in both a long haired and short haired version. The hamster has carrying pouches on the inside of its cheeks, stretching back to the shoulders. The Golden hamster below has his pouches half filled.

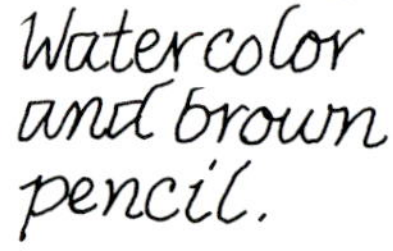

Watercolor and brown pencil.

Burnt Sienna ink strokes

Burnt Sienna wash

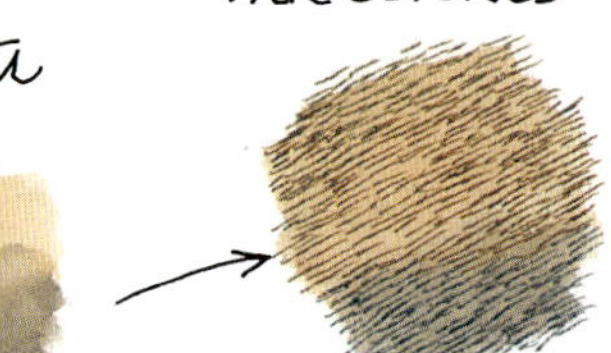

Sepia wash

Sepia ink strokes

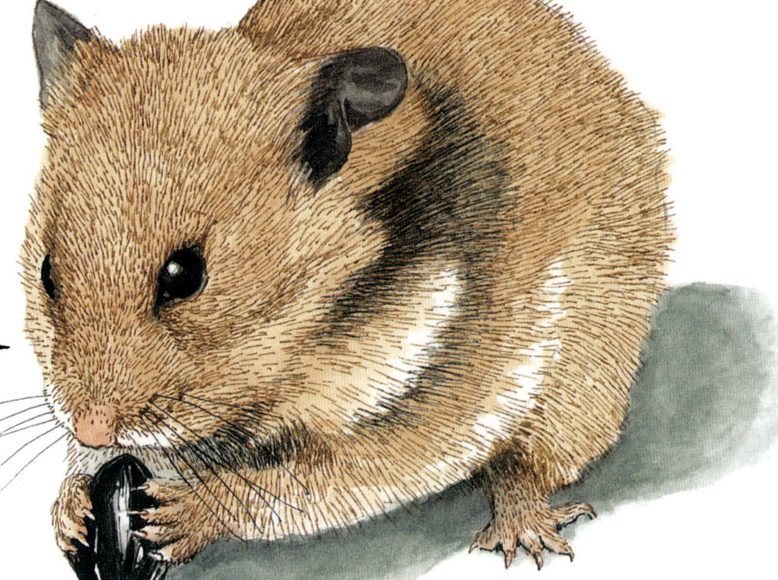

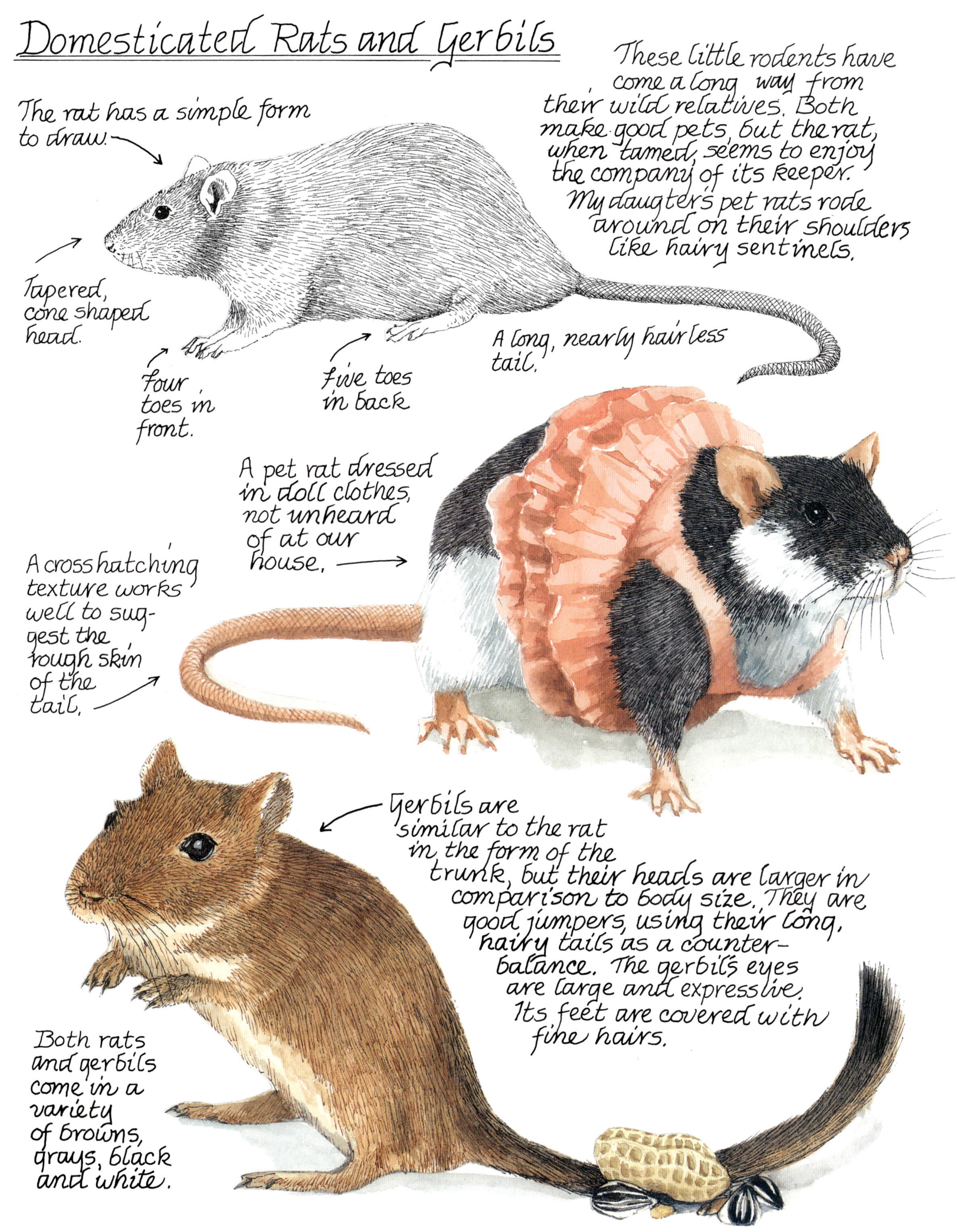
Domesticated Rats and Gerbils
These little rodents have come a long way from their wild relatives. Both make good pets, but the rat, when tamed, seems to enjoy the company of its keeper. My daugter's pet rats rode around on their shoulders like hairy sentinels.
The rat has a simple form to draw.
Tapered, cone shaped head.
four toes in front.
five toes in back
A long, nearly hairless tail.
A pet rat dressed in doll clothes, not unheard of at our house.
A crosshatching texture works well to suggest the rough skin of the tail.
Gerbils are similar to the rat in the form of the trunk, but their heads are larger in comparison to body size. They are good jumpers, using their long, hairy tails as a counter-balance. The gerbil's eyes are large and expressive. Its feet are covered with fine hairs.
Both rats and gerbils come in a variety of browns, grays, black and white.

Squirrels and Chipmunks

There are many people who consider these furry little rascals more of a pest than a pet, but they do make cute and willing sketching subjects.

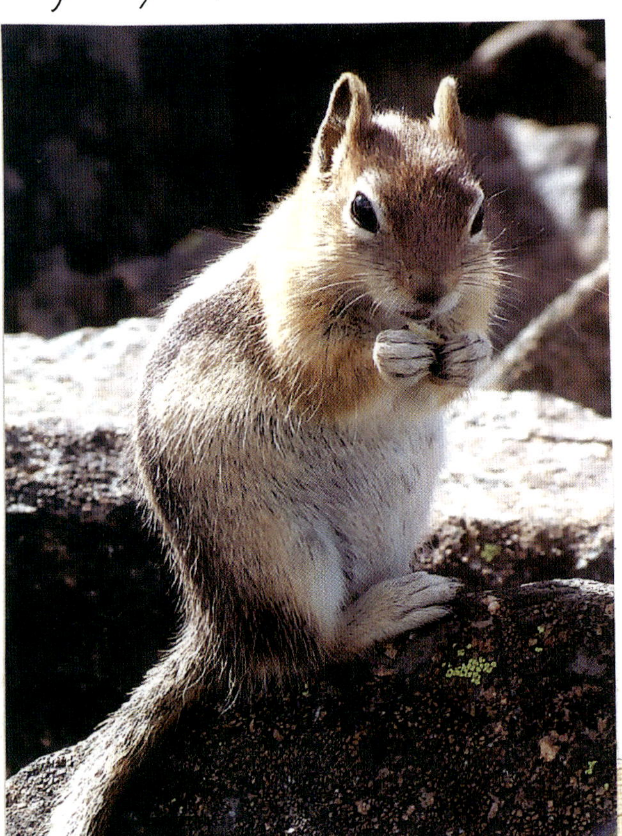

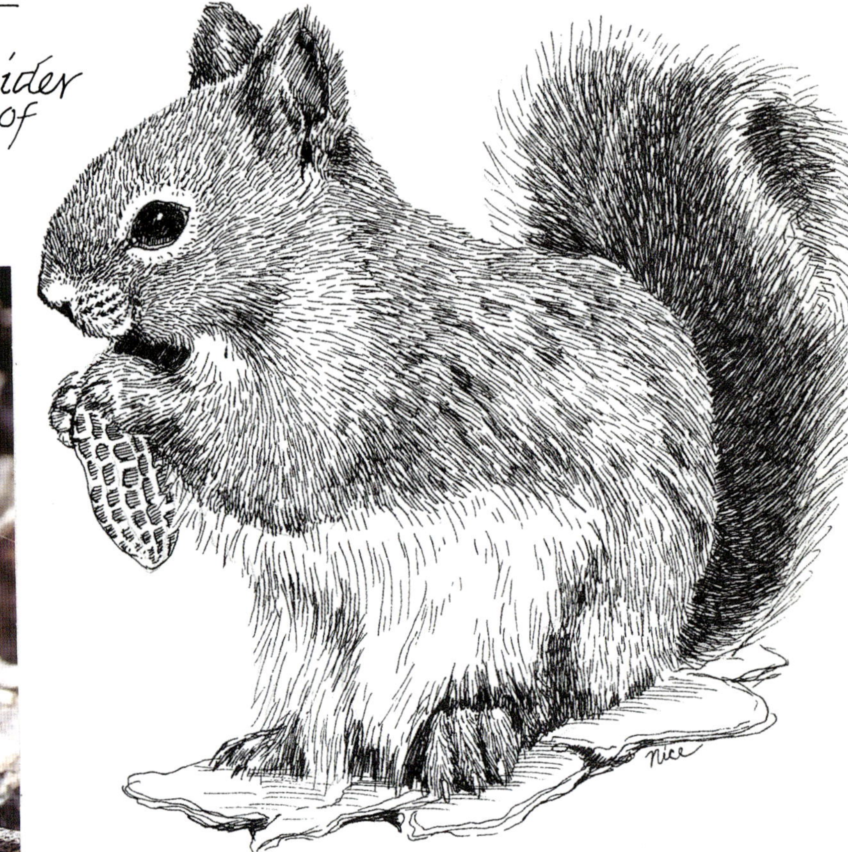

As you can see in these photos and the ink drawing above, it will only cost you peanuts to get these little guys to pose.

Project no. 11

Working from the photos on this page, or an original photograph or live sketch, create a squirrel or chipmunk painting. Choose a background that not only will set off your subject, but will reveal a little about its habitat.

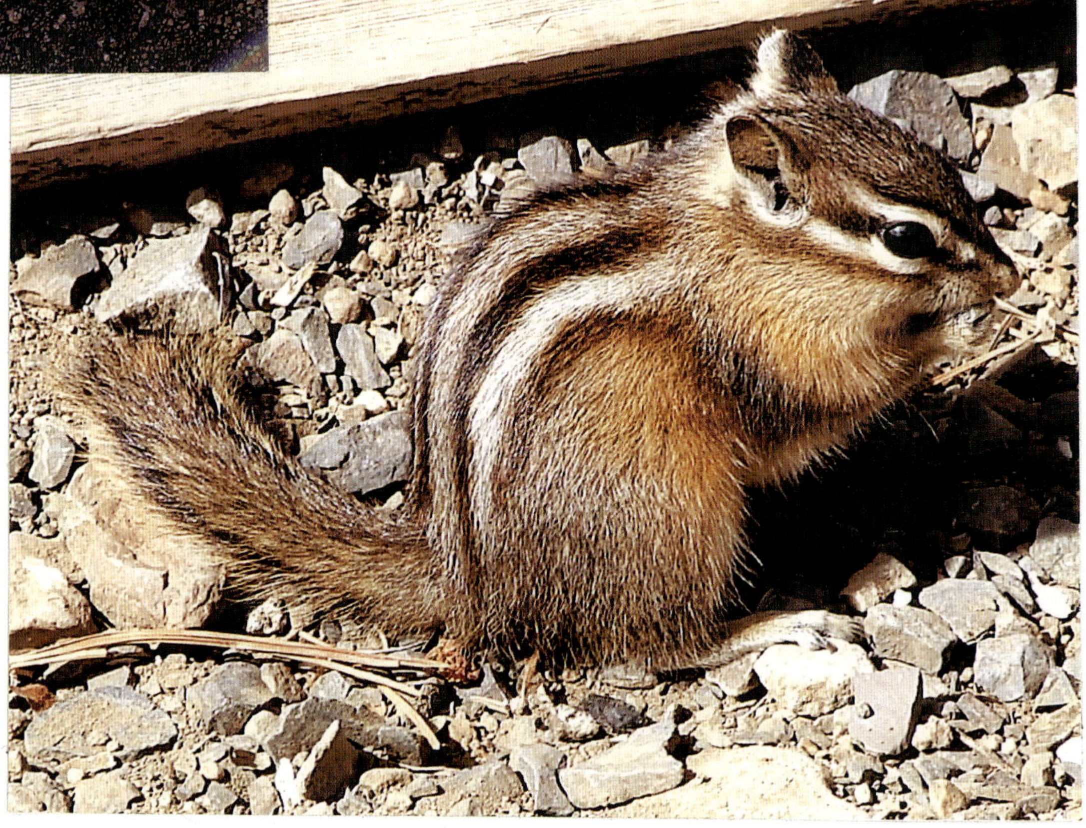

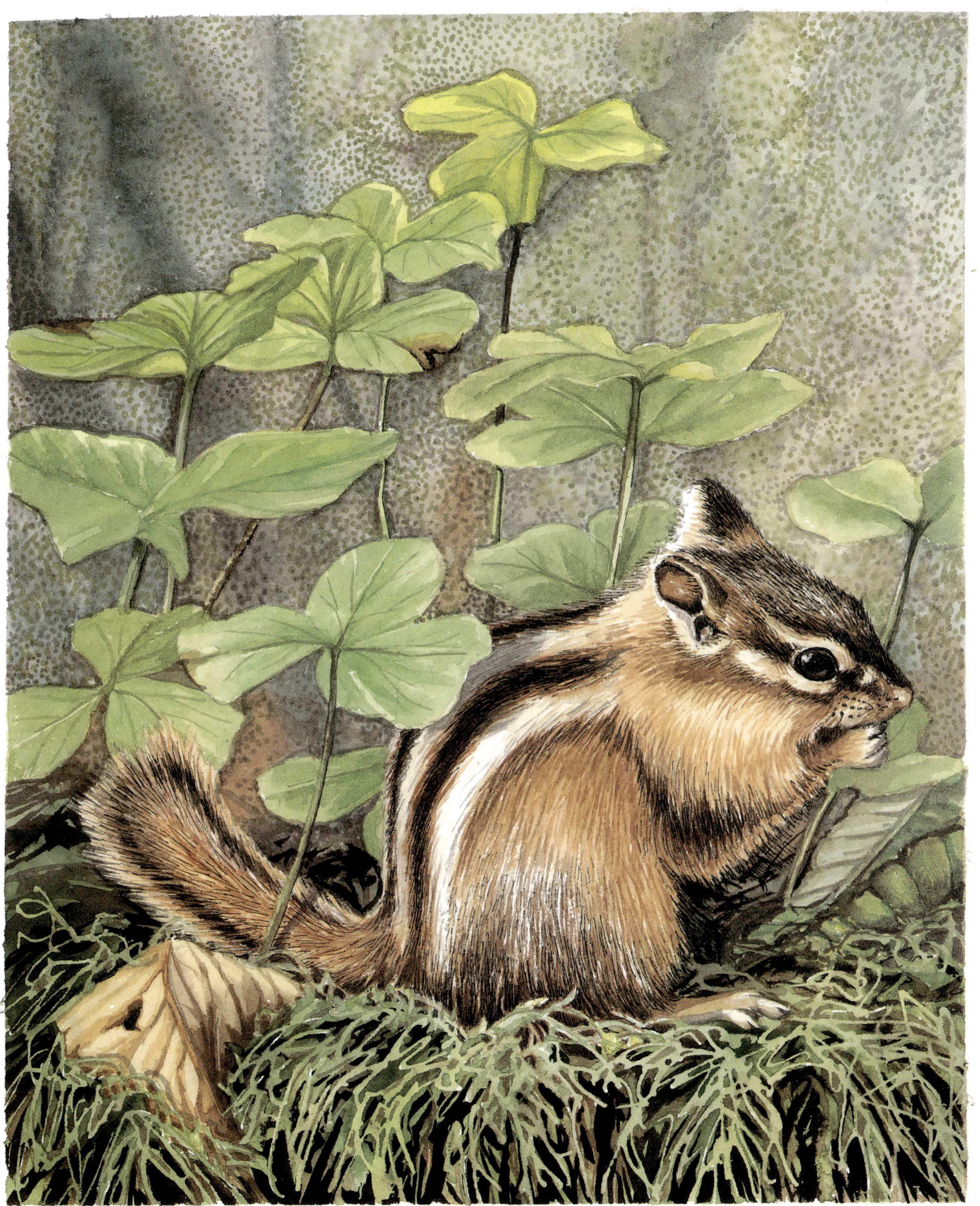

CHIPMUNK IN A WOOD SORREL PATCH 8" x 10" (20.5cm x 25.5cm) The chipmunk fur is depicted with layered washes applied with a fine round brush and finished with touches of pen and sepia ink. The green background works well to complement the reddish brown colors of the chipmunk's fur.

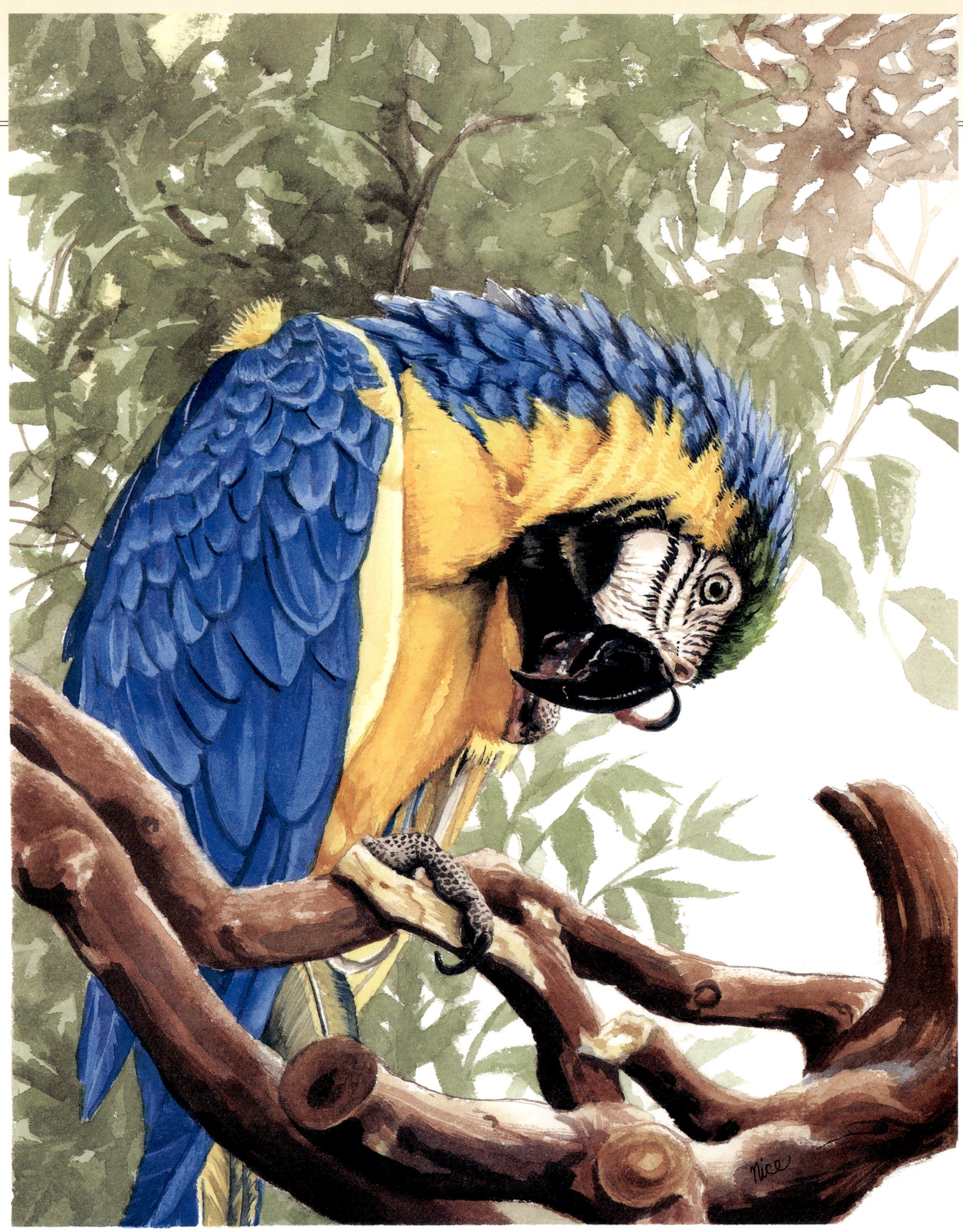

BLUE AND GOLD MACAW 9" x 12" (23cm x 30.5cm) Painted in watercolor.

familiar FOWL

7

THE LITTLE GREEN FELLOW seen below, sipping orange juice from the bottom of a glass, is my Gray Cheek Parakeet, Elfin Green. Like most members of the parrot family, he was intelligent, playful, and a bit of a rascal. He was often perched on my shoulder as I wrote and illustrated some of my first books. When Elfin got bored, down he came to investigate my pencils, pens, and brushes, strewing them about or dropping them over the side of the work table. Elfin could talk. His favorite phrase was "I bite," and then he would, followed by an evil chuckle. Elfin Green has passed on, but I dedicate this chapter to his memory. If you have a favorite pet bird or a fondness for farm fowls, the following pages will give you a closer look at feathers, bills, and bird feet, and how to depict them in a realistic manner.

Squirt out a palette of bright colors. While the geese are rather dignified in their coloration, the ducks may surprise you with a splash of blue or green. The chickens with their rose red combs and wattles will give your warm hues a workout. If you're ready to play with brilliant primary colors, paint a parrot. You don't have to own one to enjoy depicting their unbelievably bright plumage. The blue and gold macaw seen on the facing page was painted from a photograph at a petting zoo. Pet store parrots love attention, and with the permission of the owner, will make wonderful subjects to sketch and photograph. Who knows, some smooth talking parrot may convince you to bring it home as a colorful addition to your art studio. "Awk, Polly wants to paint!"

Drawing the Basic Bird

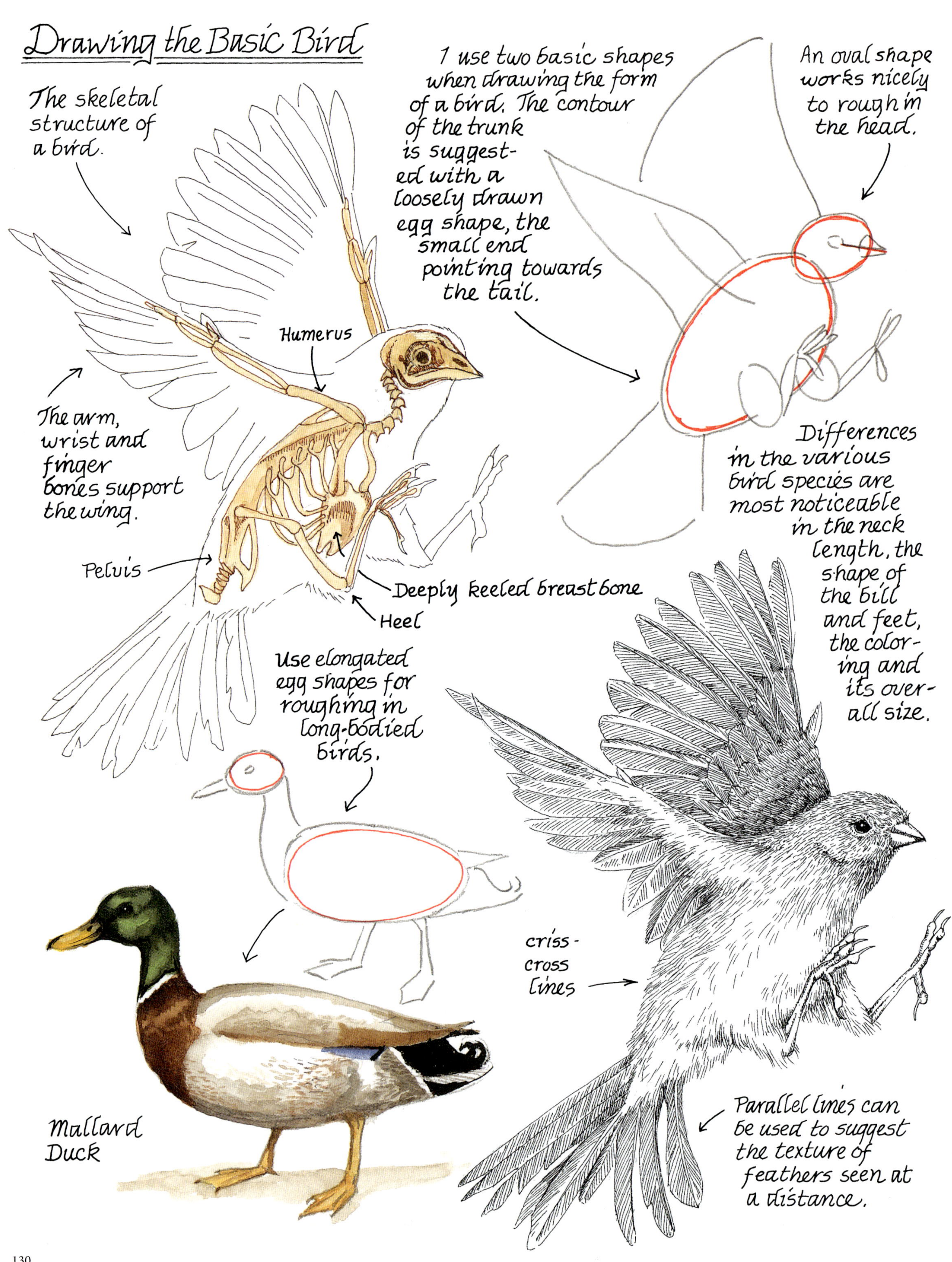

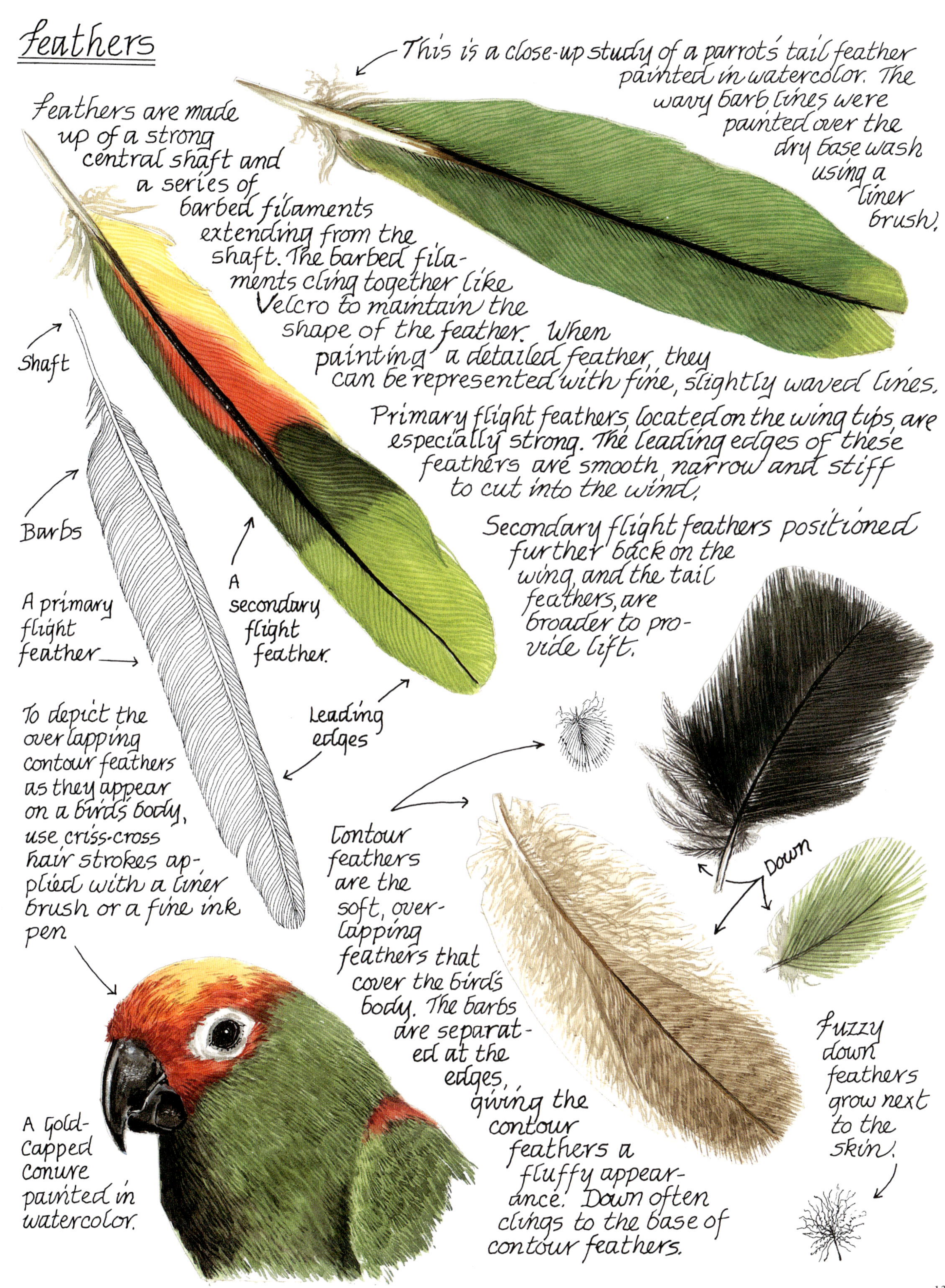
Feathers
This is a close-up study of a parrot's tail feather painted in watercolor. The wavy barb lines were painted over the dry base wash using a liner brush.
Feathers are made up of a strong central shaft and a series of barbed filaments extending from the shaft. The barbed filaments cling together like Velcro to maintain the shape of the feather. When painting a detailed feather, they can be represented with fine, slightly waved lines.
Primary flight feathers, located on the wing tips, are especially strong. The leading edges of these feathers are smooth, narrow and stiff to cut into the wind.
Secondary flight feathers positioned further back on the wing, and the tail feathers, are broader to provide lift.
Shaft
Barbs
A primary flight feather
A secondary flight feather.
Leading edges
To depict the overlapping contour feathers as they appear on a bird's body, use criss-cross hair strokes applied with a liner brush or a fine ink pen
Contour feathers are the soft, overlapping feathers that cover the bird's body. The barbs are separated at the edges, giving the contour feathers a fluffy appearance. Down often clings to the base of contour feathers.
Down
Fuzzy down feathers grow next to the skin.
A Gold-capped Conure painted in watercolor.

Ducks and Geese

The main difference in appearance between a duck and a goose is in the shape of the bill.

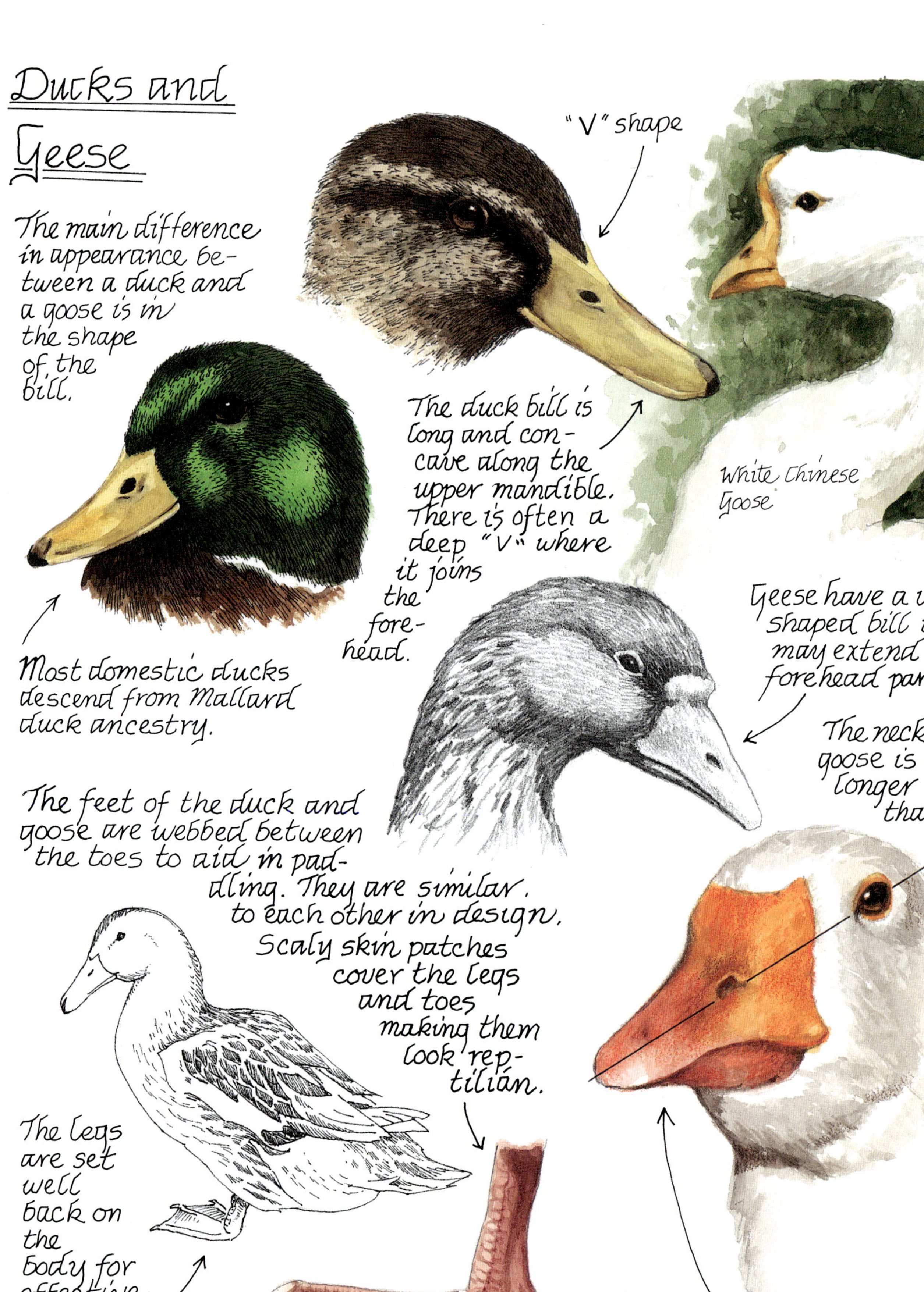

The duck bill is long and concave along the upper mandible. There is often a deep "V" where it joins the forehead.

Most domestic ducks descend from Mallard duck ancestry.

Geese have a wedge shaped bill that may extend up the forehead partway.

The neck of a goose is usually longer than that of a duck.

The feet of the duck and goose are webbed between the toes to aid in paddling. They are similar to each other in design. Scaly skin patches cover the legs and toes making them look reptilian.

The legs are set well back on the body for effective swimming propulsion.

Three forward facing toes.

Note how the tip of the bill, the nostril and the corner of the eye line up. Although it's not true of every duck and goose breed, it works as a guide in most cases.

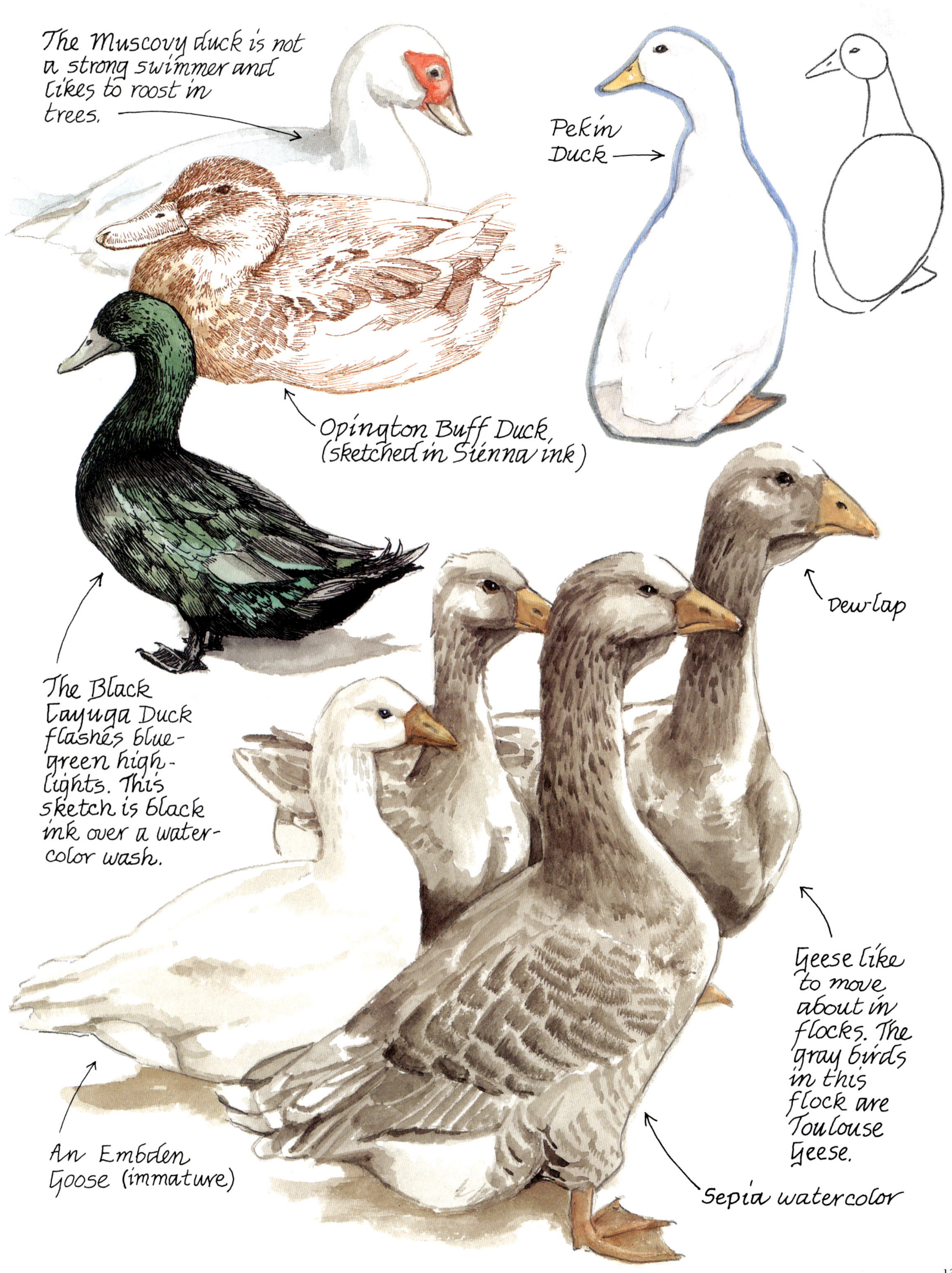
The Muscovy duck is not a strong swimmer and likes to roost in trees.
Pekin Duck
Opington Buff Duck, (sketched in Sienna ink)
Dewlap
The Black Cayuga Duck flashes blue-green highlights. This sketch is black ink over a watercolor wash.
Geese like to move about in flocks. The gray birds in this flock are Toulouse Geese.
An Embden Goose (immature)
Sepia watercolor

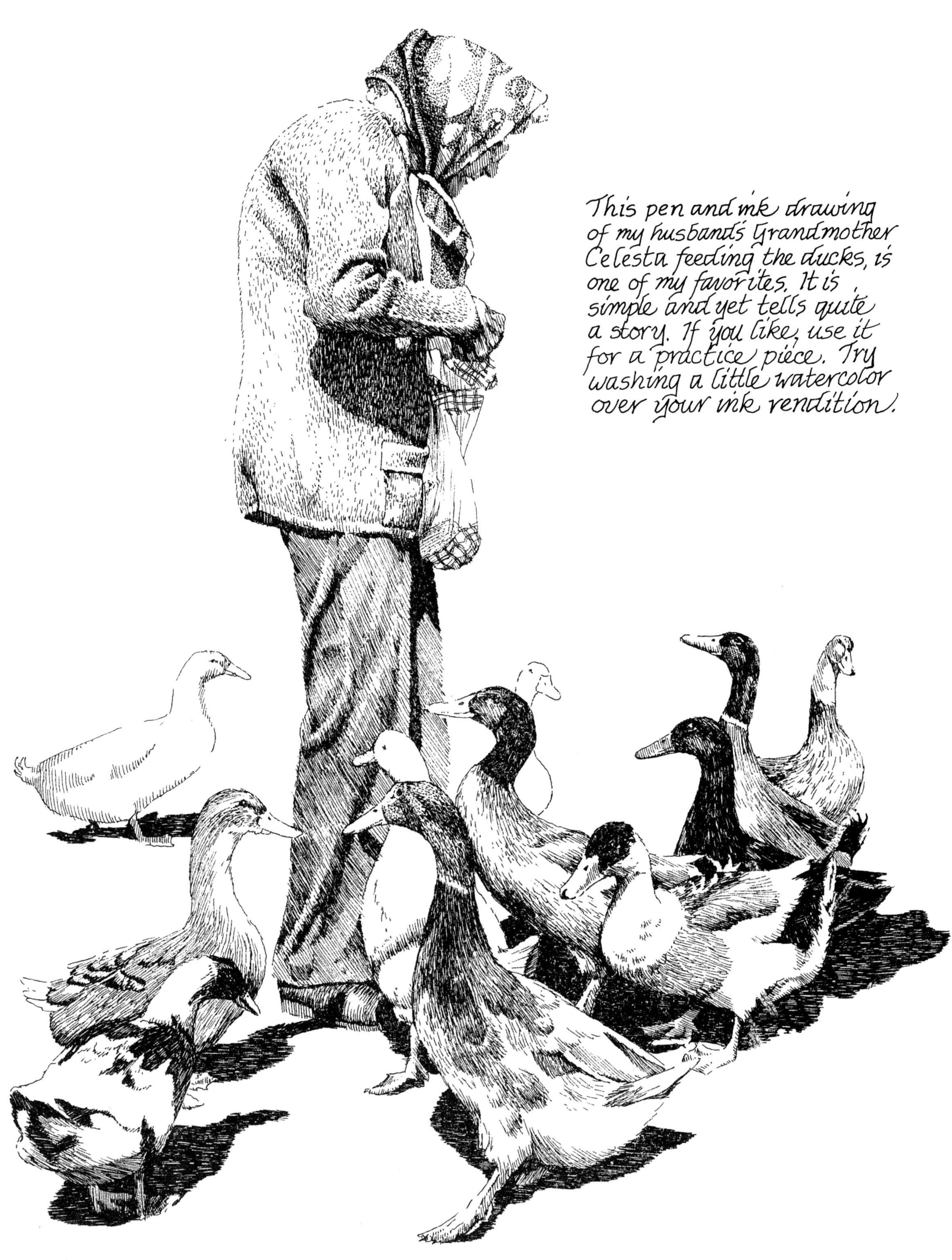

This pen and ink drawing of my husband's Grandmother Celesta feeding the ducks, is one of my favorites. It is simple and yet tells quite a story. If you like, use it for a practice piece. Try washing a little watercolor over your ink rendition.

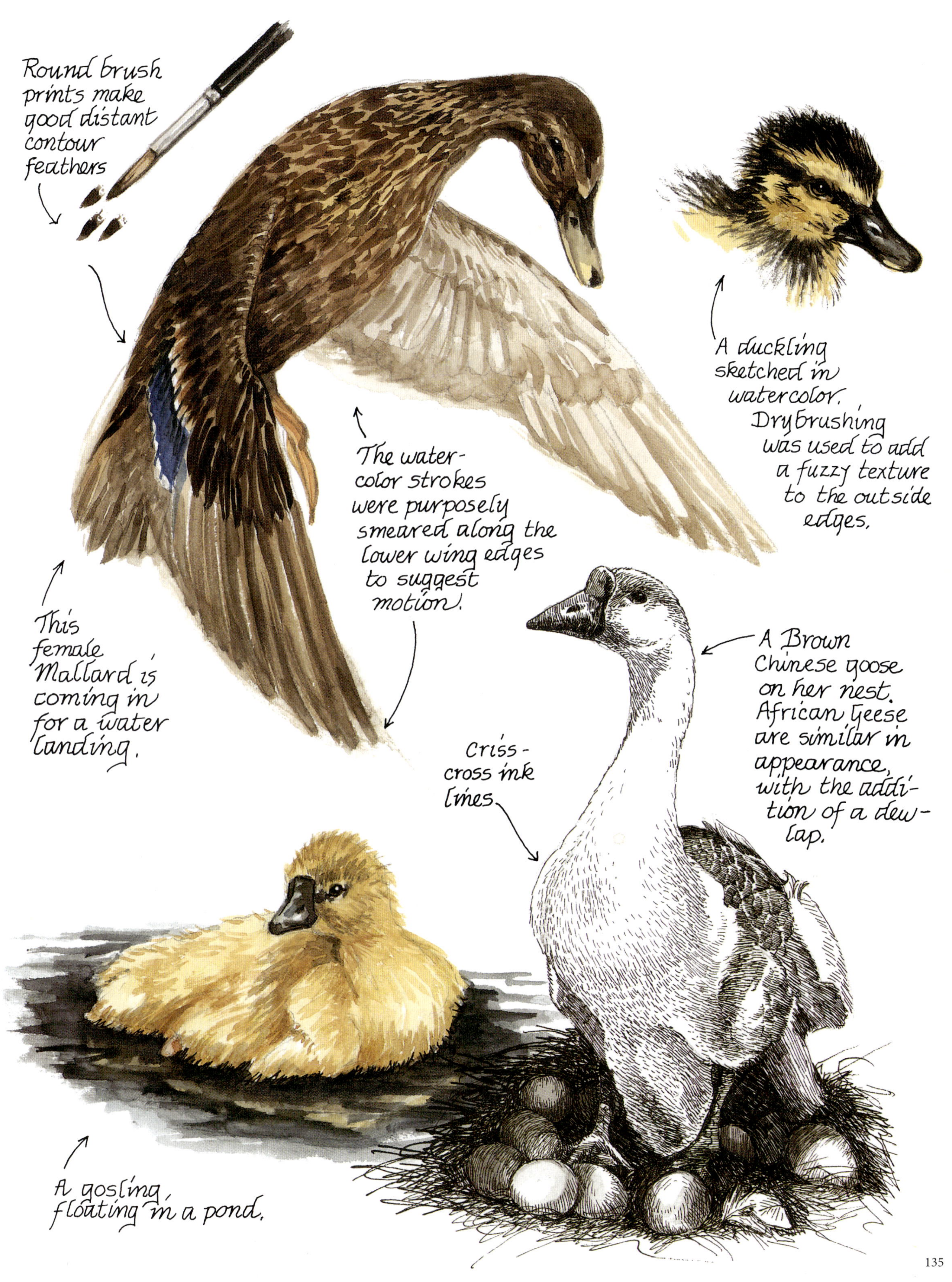
Round brush prints make good distant contour feathers
A duckling sketched in watercolor. Drybrushing was used to add a fuzzy texture to the outside edges.
The water-color strokes were purposely smeared along the lower wing edges to suggest motion.
This female Mallard is coming in for a water landing.
A Brown Chinese goose on her nest. African Geese are similar in appearance, with the addition of a dewlap.
Criss-cross ink lines
A gosling floating in a pond.

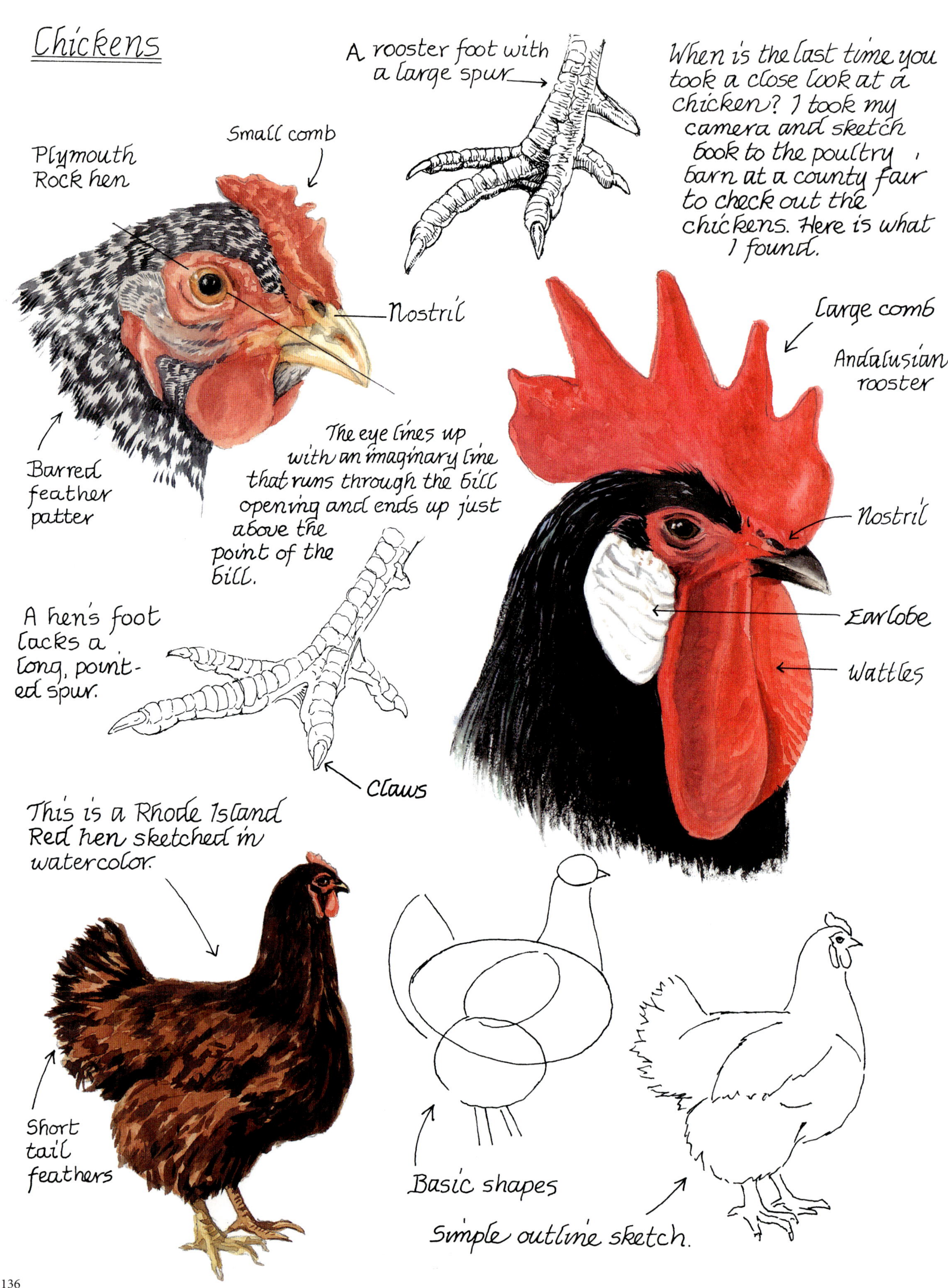
Chickens
A rooster foot with a large spur
When is the last time you took a close look at a chicken? I took my camera and sketch book to the poultry barn at a county fair to check out the chickens. Here is what I found.
Small comb
Plymouth Rock hen
Nostril
Barred feather patter
The eye lines up with an imaginary line that runs through the bill opening and ends up just above the point of the bill.
Large comb
Andalusian rooster
Nostril
Earlobe
Wattles
A hen's foot lacks a long, pointed spur.
Claws
This is a Rhode Island Red hen sketched in watercolor.
Short tail feathers
Basic shapes
Simple outline sketch.

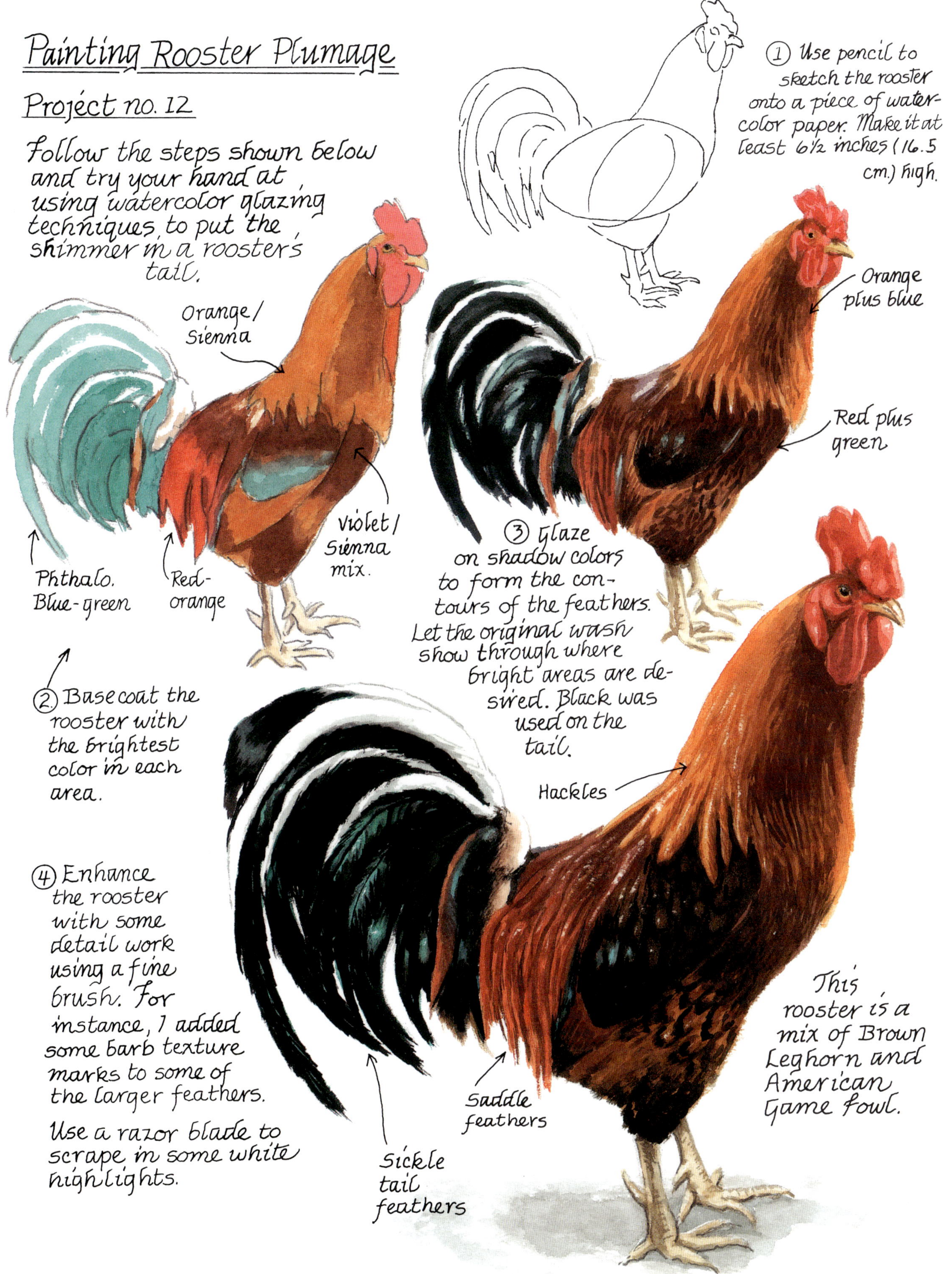
Painting Rooster Plumage
Project no. 12
Follow the steps shown below and try your hand at using watercolor glazing techniques to put the shimmer in a rooster's tail.
① Use pencil to sketch the rooster onto a piece of watercolor paper. Make it at least 6½ inches (16.5 cm.) high.
Orange/ Sienna
Violet/ Sienna mix.
Phthalo. Blue-green
Red-orange
② Basecoat the rooster with the brightest color in each area.
Orange plus blue
Red plus green
③ Glaze on shadow colors to form the contours of the feathers. Let the original wash show through where bright areas are desired. Black was used on the tail.
Hackles
④ Enhance the rooster with some detail work using a fine brush. For instance, I added some barb texture marks to some of the larger feathers.
Use a razor blade to scrape in some white highlights.
Saddle feathers
Sickle tail feathers
This rooster is a mix of Brown Leghorn and American Game fowl.

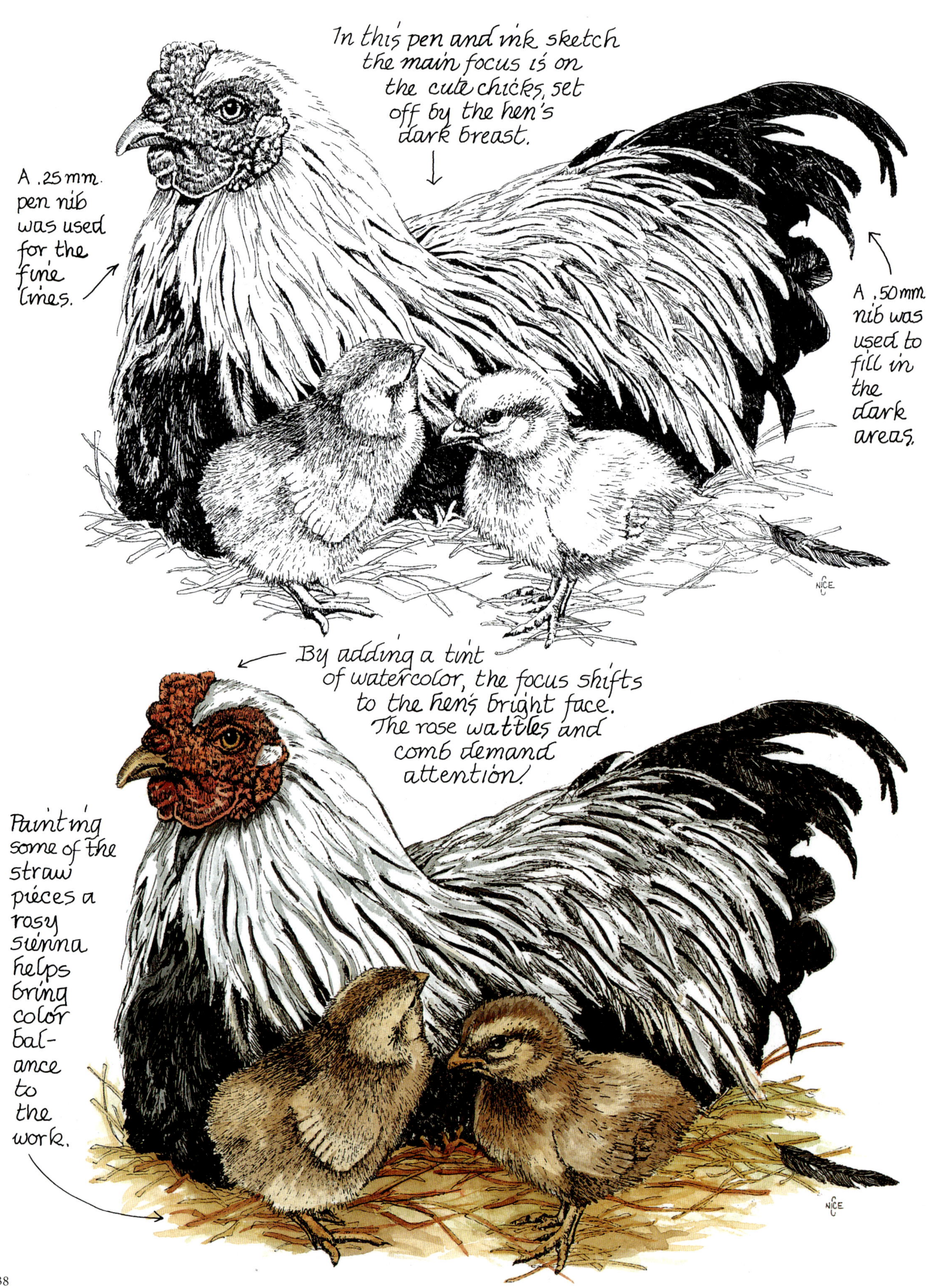
In this pen and ink sketch the main focus is on the cute chicks, set off by the hen's dark breast.
A .25 mm. pen nib was used for the fine lines.
A .50 mm nib was used to fill in the dark areas.
By adding a tint of watercolor, the focus shifts to the hen's bright face. The rose wattles and comb demand attention.
Painting some of the straw pieces a rosy sienna helps bring color balance to the work.

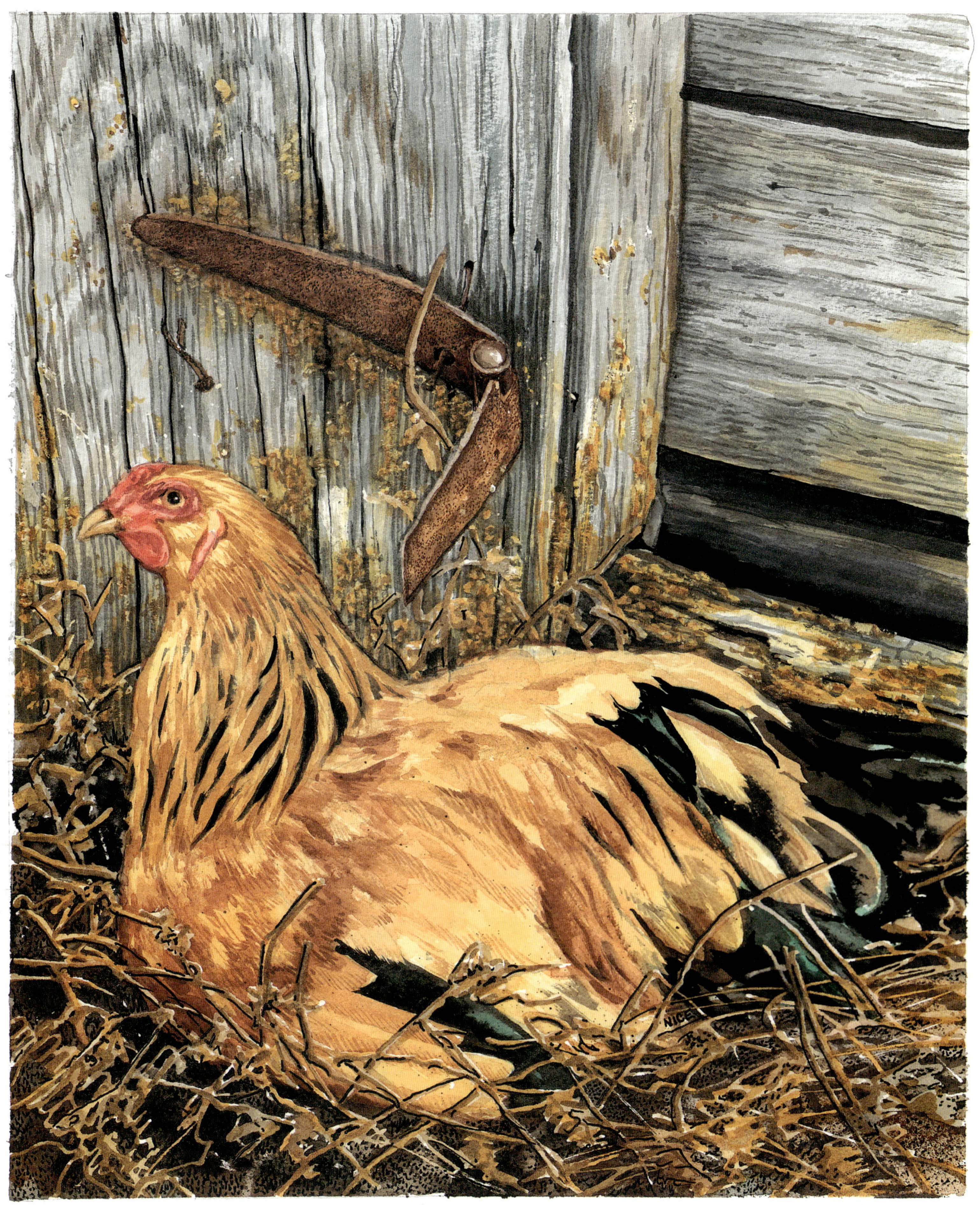

BROODING BY THE OLD BARN 8" x 10" (20.5cm x 25.5cm) This bantam hen on her nest is painted in watercolor and enhanced with pen work. The busy texture of the foreground and barn accentuates the softness of the chicken.

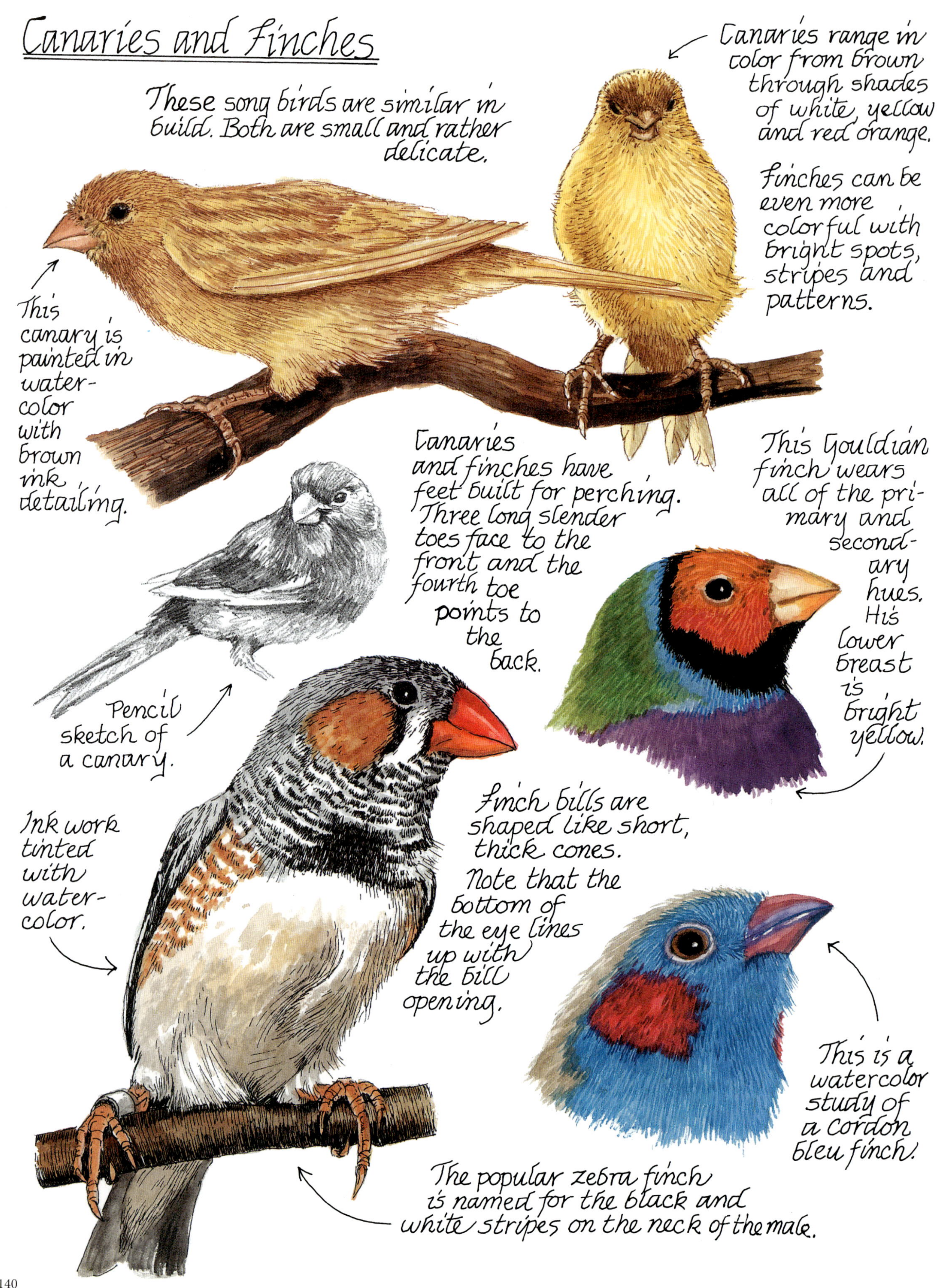
Canaries and Finches
These song birds are similar in build. Both are small and rather delicate.
Canaries range in color from brown through shades of white, yellow and red orange.
Finches can be even more colorful with bright spots, stripes and patterns.
This canary is painted in watercolor with brown ink detailing.
Canaries and finches have feet built for perching. Three long slender toes face to the front and the fourth toe points to the back.
This Gouldian finch wears all of the primary and secondary hues. His lower breast is bright yellow.
Pencil sketch of a canary.
Finch bills are shaped like short, thick cones.
Note that the bottom of the eye lines up with the bill opening.
Ink work tinted with watercolor.
This is a watercolor study of a cordon bleu finch.
The popular zebra finch is named for the black and white stripes on the neck of the male.

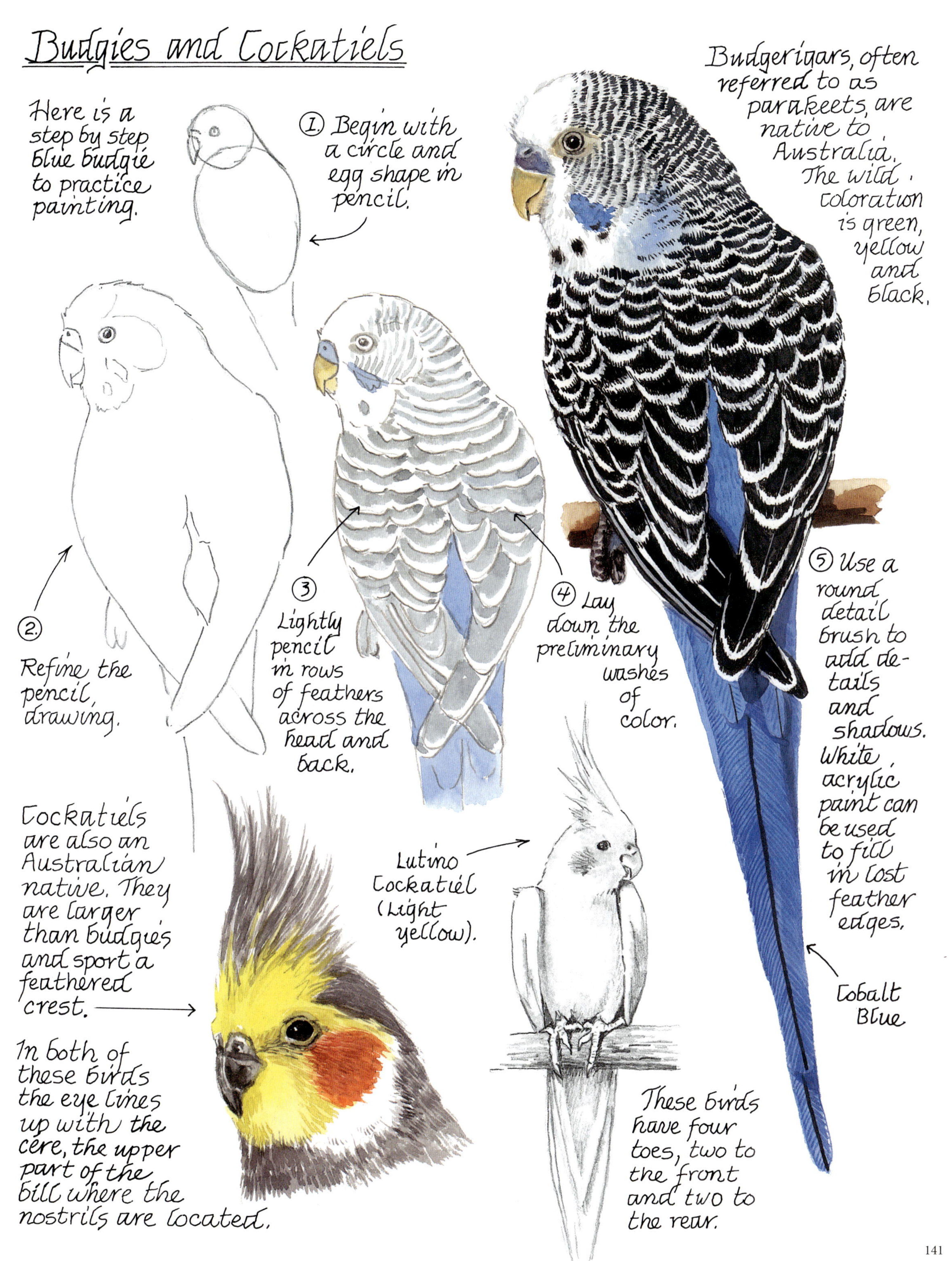
Budgies and Cockatiels
Here is a step by step blue budgie to practice painting.
① Begin with a circle and egg shape in pencil.
Budgerigars, often referred to as parakeets, are native to Australia. The wild coloration is green, yellow and black.
② Refine the pencil drawing.
③ Lightly pencil in rows of feathers across the head and back.
④ Lay down the preliminary washes of color.
⑤ Use a round detail brush to add details and shadows. White acrylic paint can be used to fill in lost feather edges.
Cockatiels are also an Australian native. They are larger than budgies and sport a feathered crest.
Lutino Cockatiel (Light yellow).
Cobalt Blue
In both of these birds the eye lines up with the cere, the upper part of the bill where the nostrils are located.
These birds have four toes, two to the front and two to the rear.

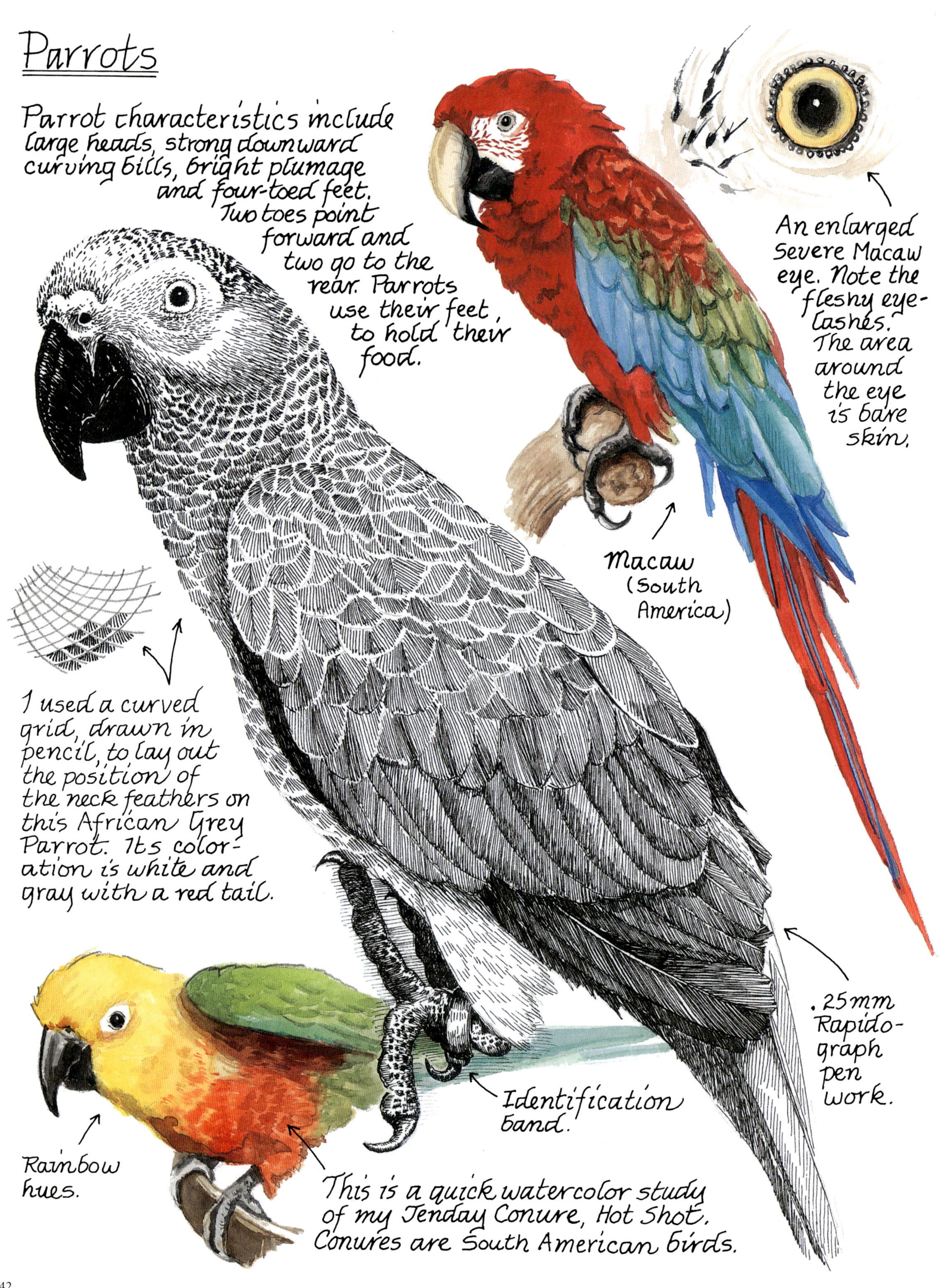
Parrots
Parrot characteristics include large heads, strong downward curving bills, bright plumage and four-toed feet. Two toes point forward and two go to the rear. Parrots use their feet to hold their food.
An enlarged Severe Macaw eye. Note the fleshy eyelashes. The area around the eye is bare skin.
Macaw (South America)
I used a curved grid, drawn in pencil, to lay out the position of the neck feathers on this African Grey Parrot. Its coloration is white and gray with a red tail.
.25mm Rapidograph pen work.
Identification band.
Rainbow hues.
This is a quick watercolor study of my Jenday Conure, Hot Shot. Conures are South American birds.

index

the best in PAINTING INSTRUCTION IS FROM *North Light Books*

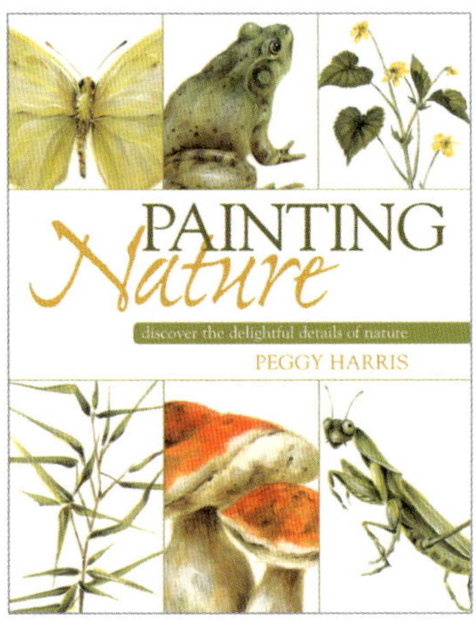

Discover the delightful details of nature in this stunning new book by internationally acclaimed artist and teacher, Peggy Harris. From a perfectly posed butterfly to a delicately tinted leaf to tiny eggs in a bird's nest, natural details enhance any painting's appeal. With tips, more than 50 step-by-step painting demonstrations, fascinating facts and her own beautiful artwork, Peggy teaches you to observe nature accurately and let your knowledge give life and credibility to your painting, no matter what your artistic style.
ISBN-13: 978-1-58180-715-8;
ISBN-10: 1-58180-715-5;
paperback, 128 pages, #33382

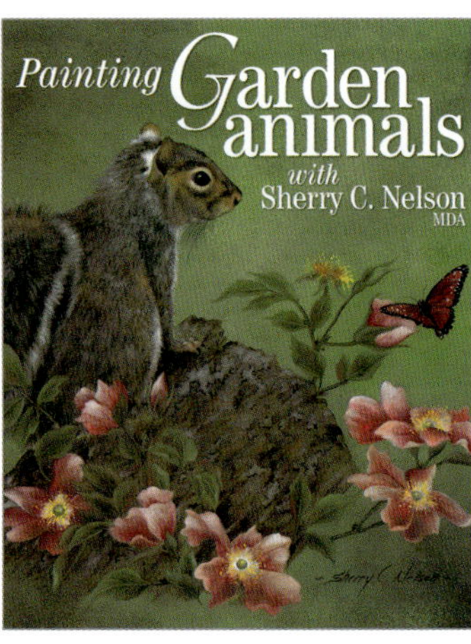

Sherry C. Nelson shows you how to bring life and personality to a variety of adorable garden animals and your favorite household pets, including kittens, puppies, fawns, rabbits, chipmunks, squirrels and more. Through clear, step-by-step demonstrations and full-color reference photos, you'll learn how to paint realistic features, such as eyes filled with awareness and fur that begs to be stroked. These ten projects depicting animals in heartwarming interactive poses will send you straight to your paints and brushes!
ISBN-13: 978-1-58180-427-0;
ISBN-10: 1-58189-427-X;
paperback, 144 pages, #32591

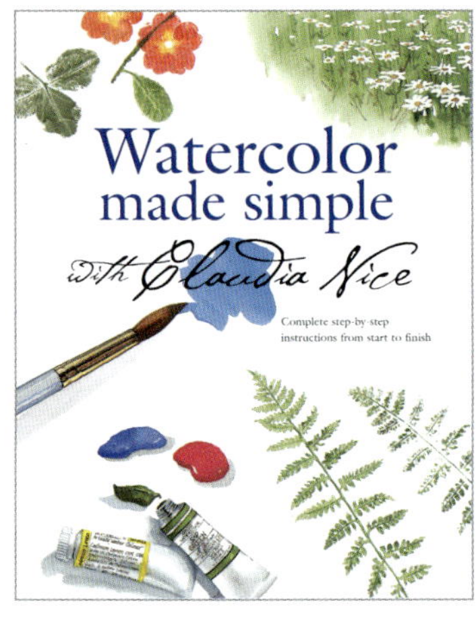

Watercolor is a fun, challenging medium that captures the magic of light and color. In this colorful and easy-to-follow book, world-renowned artist and teacher Claudia Nice helps you get started in watercolor today! With detailed step-by-step artwork, you'll see how to create a variety of special effects, how to blend colors on your palette, and how to create beautiful soft washes with paint and water. You'll learn how to paint everything from flowers to glass to ocean waves, from trees to leaves to weathered wood. Claudia makes it easy, fun and very rewarding.
ISBN-13: 978-1-58180-251-1;
ISBN-10: 1-58180-251-X;
paperback, 128 pages, #32079

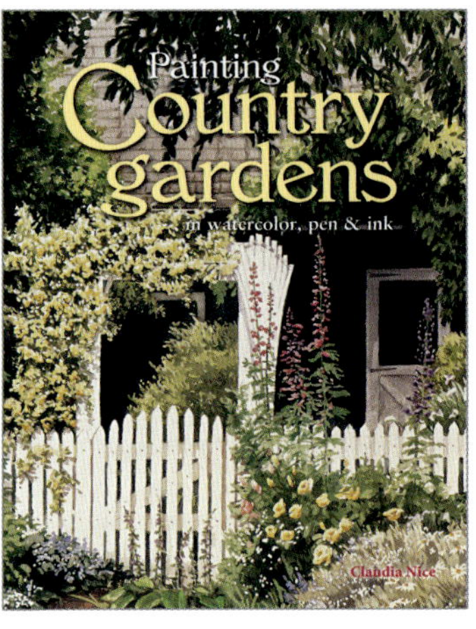

Capture the beauty of the country gardens you love! Best-selling author and artist Claudia Nice shares her advice and experience to help you paint lovely country scenes and gorgeous flowers in no time at all. Step by step you can paint along with Claudia as she shows you how to create colorful blossoms, well-shaped leaves, miniature bouquets, terra cotta flowerpots, birdbaths, picket fences and all the other wonderful things that turn a plain garden into a country garden. You'll even learn how to paint the quintessential hallmark of country gardens—a thatched-roof English cottage!
ISBN-13: 978-1-58180-142-2;
ISBN-10: 1-58180-142-4;
hardcover, 144 pages, #31887

These and other fine North Light Books are available at your local arts & crafts retailer, bookstore, or from online suppliers.